Computers and Education in the 21st Century

Edited by

Manuel Ortega

and

José Bravo

University of Castilla - La Mancha,
Ciudad Real, Spain

KLUWER ACADEMIC PUBLISHERS
DORDRECHT / BOSTON / LONDON

Library of Congress Cataloging-in-Publication Data

ISBN 0-7923-6577-1

Published by Kluwer Academic Publishers,
P.O. Box 17, 3300 AA Dordrecht, The Netherlands.

Sold and distributed in North, Central and South America
by Kluwer Academic Publishers,
101 Philip Drive, Norwell, MA 02061, U.S.A.

In all other countries, sold and distributed
by Kluwer Academic Publishers,
P.O. Box 322, 3300 AH Dordrecht, The Netherlands.

Printed on acid-free paper

Printed in the Netherlands.

Contents

Contents

ConieD'99 Organisation

Programme Committee

Dr. A. Vaquero (U. Complutense)
Dra. M.F. Verdejo (UNED)
Dra. B. Barros (UNED)
Dr. J. Gutierrez (U. P. Vasco/EHU)
Dra. I. Fdez de Castro (U. P. Vasco/EHU)
Dr. A. Fdez-Valmayor (U. Complutense)
Dr. B. Fdez-Manjón (U. Complutense)
Dr. M. Pérez-Cota (U. Vigo)
Dña. A. Rodríguez (U. Vigo)
Dr. J.M. Zamarro (U. Murcia)

Organisation Committee

Dr. M. Ortega (UCLM-CHICO)
Dr. J. Bravo (UCLM-CHICO)
Dr. A. Vázquez (UCLM)
Dr. M. Lacruz (UCLM-CHICO)
D. M.A. Redondo (UCLM-CHICO)
D. C. Bravo (UCLM-CHICO)
D. P. P. Sánchez Villalón (CHICO)
D.J. J. Muñoz (CHICO)

Acknowledgements

The editors would like to acknowledge the Universidad de Castilla – La Mancha, its Rector, the "Escuela Superior de Informática" and the Computer Science Department for the sponsoring of the Congress.

We would also like to thank the "Junta de Comunidades de Castilla- La Mancha" and specially the Major of Puertollano (Ciudad Real) for providing their unconditional support to this event.

Preface

ConieD is the biannual Congress on Computers in Education, organised by the Spanish Association for the Development of Computers in Education (ADIE).

The last Congress, held in Puertollano (Ciudad Real), brought together researchers in different areas, ranging from web applications, educational environments, or Human-Computer Interaction to Artificial Intelligence in Education. The common leitmotiv of the major part of the lectures was the World Wide Web. In particular, the focus was on the real possibilities that this media presents in order to make the access of students to educational resources possible anywhere and anytime. This fact was highlighted in the Conclusions of the Congress following this Preface as the Introduction.

From the full 92 papers presented to the Programme Committee we have selected the best 24 papers that we are presenting in this book. The selection of papers was a very difficult process, taking into account that the papers presented in the Congress (60) were all good enough to appear in this book. Only the restrictions of the extension of this book have limited the number of papers to 24. These papers represent the current high-quality contributions of Spanish research groups in Computers in Education.

Manuel Ortega Cantero
José Bravo Rodríguez
Editors

Introduction

ConieD'99 (1st National Congress on Computers in Education) has brought together a very important group of Spanish and Latin American researchers devoted to studying the application and use of computers in education.

Computer science is evolving fast and steady over the years providing more and more tools for society to use. From the education world we have always seen computer science as a great potential tool. However it has not been until today, and thanks to the new revolution the Internet means, that computer science in education is becoming a reality.

Until now, computer technology has scarcely been understood by professionals if they were not computer specialists. This significantly restricted the use of computers in educational activities and the capacity of computer applications created for educational purposes. These applications have existed from the 1960s; however, their adoption and utilization has been little or unknown.

It is the arrival of the more open, comprehensible new information technologies and mainly the Internet that has made professionals (psychologists, teachers, educators in general, who are necessary in the creation of educational software) participate actively. This has become evident in this Congress where educators, secondary education and university teachers, teachers in different subjects like Physics and Statistics, professionals in computer companies, etc. have shown educational products that in most cases are already being used as a complementary tool in teaching. We want to point out an important event: it is the first time in Spain that such an important and numerous group of professionals has met together to speak long on these topics.

The Internet with all its potential, the publication of documents on the Web, user communication through electronic mail, chats, video-conference, etc. offers us the opportunity to change our educational conventions. Up to now, teaching has been based on an interventionist method (Conductism) where teachers planned their teaching and students participated passively in the process. The reason for this was not the lack of alternatives, but the existing infrastructure in educational contexts. The facilities of the Internet make it possible and accessible to integrate the methods of Constructivist teaching, in which students are an active part in learning. They construct their knowledge themselves exploring and learning in freedom, sharing experiences with other students, etc. Learning is not limited to a place, to a point in time or to an infrastructure. Students, thanks to the direct disposition of the existing materials on the Internet, will study in the contexts and with the schedules that best adapt to their necessities. Tools such as electronic mail and discussion forums make it possible to monitor students from the distance and share opinions and knownoledge with other students and teachers. In addition, the resource that the Internet offers of publishing didactic materials and computer tools (for example, for the simulation of a physical phenomenon) offer the educational community the possibility of sharing, contrasting and exploiting their knowledge at a maximum. Students are the main receivers, not bound by the educational context any more in which due to space-time circumstances they have to be trained.

But, does this imply that the role of the teacher will disappear for ever? By no means. It simply implies a change in their role as an educator. It is obvious that the new technologies make this new form of learning simple. However, knowledge, for the definition of the Internet itself, appears disorganised and in many cases it is difficult to search. In this case teachers will be in charge of filtering the information for their students and they will have to decide which tools are appropriate and what specific topics should be learnt and looked into. The teacher as an expert in the subject will still decide what concepts are important and what the educational objectives are to get, all this regardless of the fact that the student is responsible of their own learning.

Obviously this new form of teaching-learning makes a change of mentality and in the infrastructure in our schools and universities necessary. It is necessary that experts propose syllabuses in the new technologies for all the teachers. Teachers should be trained to create high-quality educational materials which they can leave available for future students.

This Congress has shown that educational computer science is going to be a reality in our lives. In the immediate future many of the products that researchers have presented will be available on the Internet, and definitely in our education centers.

PLENARY LECTURES

PART I

Computers in Education: the Near Future

Manuel Ortega Cantero
Grupo CHICO. Universidad de Castilla – La Mancha
Paseo de la Universidad 4. 13071. Ciudad Real (Spain).
E-mail: mortega@uclm.es

Key words: Collaboration, ubiquitous computing, simulations, The Internet, Discovery learning.

Abstract: This paper presents the basic ideas that learning systems are based on, according to the current ideas on how the teaching-learning process is carried out. The use of the Internet as a means to publish educational materials, together with simulation environments using learning by discovery and with collaborative tools, makes learning improve meaningfully. But in this process of integration of the new information technologies and communications into the classroom three factors we are also considering in this paper are vital: the role of teachers, the roles of the software and the hardware necessary to get the preestablished goals.

1. INTRODUCTION.

There has been a widespread use of computers everywhere over the last few years, together with a reduction in prices and an increase in capacity and versatility. We cannot say the same about their use in educational environments where the introduction of computers, although gradual, does not reach the necessary usage levels to produce the great quality leap that their use can allow.

Although the computer was used for educational purposes from the very beginning, the fact is that the necessities as to their capacity for calculation processes and, above all, graphical presentation of the computer-based

M. Ortega and J. Bravo (eds.), Computers and Education in the 21st Century, 3–16.
© *2000 Kluwer Academic Publishers. Printed in the Netherlands.*

teaching-learning systems have caused the practical application of Computer Science to Education not to reach the general public until, in fact, the 1980s.

The Internet phenomenon have meant a boom in the production of systems that can already be of an interactive type, although some of the achievements from more than 30 years of research have sometimes been forgotten.

This paper intends to show the implications of three vitally important agents in the future development of Educational Computer Science: teachers, who are to subscribe to the approach of the new era based on knowledge; software and hardware, which should both come up to the expectations that these technologies have aroused in our Society.

In this sense, the CHICO team (Computer-Human Interaction and Collaboration) intend to create web-based interactive systems that will allow the use of distance learning systems.

Moreover these learning environments should allow the student to discover the Laws governing the domain to study by means of simulation. The collaboration between learning partners attempting to solve complex problems is, also, vital. In this paper we want to explain these parameters precisely. In addition to these systems we also offer the possibility that the student can plan their solution by means of intermediate languages that allow the solution of the proposed problems in a structured way, ranging from a quite abstract solution to a more concrete one.

As we will see, the three factors to keep in mind, teachers, software and hardware, will be crucial in order to satisfy the necessities of the educational environments that we try to develop. These factors will be the focus in the following sections. The paper ends up with some conclusions on Computer Science and Education.

2.   TEACHERS.

To start our journey on the role of teachers in this revolution in which we are involved we are to remember the content of the Experts Commission when in November 1997 they published the results of a study carried out on the impact of the use of computers in the classroom. The results of this commission were the following [1]:
–   The computer science laboratories are not the right place for computers. We must put them in classrooms.
–   Students with difficulties are accostumed to making use of the computer better than the more gifted ones.
–   Many teachers have not received any kind of training on how to use computers in class yet.

 – School systems should plan the application of the computer thoroughly.
 – The computer is a tool, not a subject. The knowledge of the computer should become integrated in the lessons on the subjects.
 – Students improve when they have each their computer.
 – School use demands the latest brand new machines available, not second hand.
 – The computer does not harm traditional teachings.
 – The Internet and the electronic mail stimulate the students because they notice that they have audience.
 – Students are really fascinated with computers.

The conclusions of the American Commission of Experts could have been predicted by any professional in Education or in Computer Science lacking prejudices on the use of the computer in the classroom. All the students should be provided with the best personal computers and in this context we can see experiences on the Microsoft Website such as "Anytime, Anywhere Learning Initiative" with portable computers in K-12 levels in the United States [2]. All the teachers should receive appropriate training on the new technologies. The computer should become integrated traversely in all the disciplines, not only in "Computer Science" classes. And finally, the Internet and computers are the great opportunity in order to succeed in introducing the students in effective learning without their rejection.

In contrast with these results there is a devastating fact obtained by the Department of Education of the United States: 84% of American teachers consider indispensable only a type of information technology, the photocopier [3].

All this makes us think that the main actor of the change that will take place in the use of the Information Technologies and Telecommunications is certainly the teacher, and the first factor to keep in mind in the process of introducing these technologies is teacher training.

Our idea, not always shared by all the professionals in Education or in Computer Science, on which is the best way to develop learning is the use of the constructivist approach. Constructivists believe that knowledge is not transmitted but rather it is built. Learners, exploring their world and finding phenomena that they cannot understand, familiarize with the problem and find a solution valid for them [4]. Despite this definition, not all the problems to deal with are the suitable ones for a constructivist learning. According to Fishman [5] only the environments where the specification and use of authentic and complex activities are necessary really require this approach. On the other hand it is necessary that the students previously encounter subproblems of smaller complexity before they can approach the most abstract ones [6]. It is precisely this approach the one that has been followed in the diverse learning environments that the CHICO team has carried out on Physics [7], Statistics [8,9] or Domotics [10,11,12].

As a paradigmatic example of an institution devoted to constructivist learning we should point out the 2B1 initiative. This institution tries to communicate groups of schools in primary and secondary education having constructivist learning in common. Among the last generation tools we will point out the construction of projects in robotics by the youngest with Lego - Logo. In this case by means of the pieces of a well-known constructional toy for children and the use of the Logo programming language the learners can build complex projects that promote the development of all types of abilities.

To be able to carry out the complex projects that constructivist learning requires, we frequently need factual databases for the students to consult at any moment. In fact, what we want constructivist learners to do is to know how to relate the concepts and the facts that they can observe in order to find global theories to explain them. Today, the Internet provides with great part of that database of evidences interconnected with links in the way that Vannevar Bush [14] designed his *memex* machine.

Another theory which is currently coming into force is collaborative learning. According to Vygotsky [15] "*In a collaborative scenario, students exchange their ideas to coordinate in the attainment of some shared objectives. When dilemmas arise at work, the combination of their activity with communication is what leads to learning*". In order to be able to negotiate communication, diverse computer tools have appeared facilitating cooperation among students in learning environments. These will be treated in the section of this paper devoted to software.

From this it follows that the effort teachers need to make in order to develop a constructivist and collaborative learning is so important that it cannot be carried out individually, without help of the public institutions. Undoubtedly, teacher training is of vital importance in order not to fail in the attempt to use computers and communications in the classroom.

In the following sections we are going to see how, in the author's view, software as well as hardware can help in our purpose of improving learning.

3.   SOFTWARE.

In this section we are going to present the basic qualities that software should have if we want to guarantee the success of the learning environments to develop. According to a great number of authors [16] computer systems supporting learning should be goal-oriented and aimed at the realisation of complex projects. In these cases the aid of simulation and the "Learner-Centered Design" entail a step beyond in human-computer

interaction systems. These systems advance toward a new paradigm starting from the current perspective called "User-Centered Design" and they take into consideration such aspects as the following ones [16]:
- *The user's or the learner's evolution*, so that a software can also evolve in its forms of presentation and use, as the user's knowledge advances.
- *Diversity,* to adapt to the different types of students.
- *Attempt to involve or to commit the learner,* or how to motivate the student in the learning process. The objective is that solving real problems they would feel as if they were in an addictive videogame and their own desire to continue playing makes them learn more, makes them discover.

To be able to implement the pattern of constructivist learning by means of software, the idea of "goal-based scenarios" [17,18] has been proposed. With this approach the student is provided, in the system itself, with the context, the motivation and the necessary material to build specific projects. The problems are carefully selected, receiving tutorial help from the teacher or teachers at the very moment when the questions arise, if possible. The students are encouraged to collaborate in solving problems and the system gets richer with new proposals from both teachers and students.

The necessary elements to implement these systems are very varied, ranging from the use of the Internet to the use of technologies that come from other fields like databases, artificial intelligence, and hypermedia. These are techniques that foster the following facilities:
- Communication facilities and facilities of access to the work environment in any moment.
- Learning oriented to teams that collaborate in a certain project.
- Direct communication with a personal "mentor" for each student. It is in charge of evaluating their learning.
- Access at any time to the distributed base of knowledge.
- Adaptive Knowledge Bases, depending on the student and of the stage in which the project is.
- Knowledge Bases expandable by teachers and students.

We cannot be exhaustive in the description of experiences, but we will try to reflect some of the most interesting ones according to our view on how learning should be managed in distance education environments.

In our opinion, learning with computers is nowadays based on the conjunction of a series of parameters that help the learners to reach the knowledge that they need in a more efficient way. These parameters are: Collaboration, Learning via projects and goal-based Learning, use of simulation as a tool to improve the proposed solution, and problem solution from the simplest to complex projects with help to the student, being more important in the beginning and with progressive reduction as it advances in the learning process, using what we can call "scaffolding". Each solved problem should also serve as the basis for the solution of new more complex problems.

The first approach to the problem we consider necessary is that of collaboration between students and teachers in the solution of complex cases. This necessity becomes more patent when learning is carried out at distance. The student of a distance education course is usually alone, hardly ever meeting his/her partners, who he/she can only see in exams or in some few face-to-face sessions. This innate isolation of students in distance education systems is solved in certain way intercommunicating each other via e-mail so that they can collaborate to solve problems.

But it would be much more interesting if there were some kind of structuring of the course contents, maybe with a *listserv* supporting indexing of themes centered on topics and marking the time when they were dealt with, this way having something similar to the "Frequently Asked Questions" section in a server of net communities.

In this line of new colaborative tools we can mention the project "Collaborative Visualization" CoVis and its "Collaborative Notebook" [19]. By means of a hypermedia database students can structure their knowledge and hypothesis here in "Notebooks", dealing with complex topics such as weather forecast or ecology.

Also CSILE (Computer-supported Intentional Learning Environments) [4,20] participates of this philosophy of building a hypermedia database, in which communities of students express their point of view, create links to other students' webpages and structure their knowledge. When a certain topic is mature, a note status changes to "candidate for publication" and it becomes part of the collective knowledge of the topic in question.

CaMILE (Collaborative and Multimedia Interactive Learning Environments) [4,21] supports asynchronous collaboration to interrelate students of different engineering careers. For this, it uses web with a discussion forum. For the synchronous interaction the students have McBagel (Multiple Case-Based Approach to Generative Environments for Learning). Their main conclusion is that these problems can be solved by means of collaboration, an extensive library of solved cases, computer modelling and simulation of physical phenomena.

KIE [22] intends K-12 students to carry out small scientific works and at the end, the publication of their results on the web succeed in getting the students to integrate their conclusions together with others' in a collaborative environment.

The main objectives sought with this tool are the following ones:
–   To develop software to foster the use of computer networks in the
    classroom.

– To work with scientists and researchers to encourage the development of scientific materials on the Web for students from Primary Education to Secondary Education.
– To develop effective tools for the Internet used as educational technology.

We will comment the tools integrating this system in short. In KIE there is a palette of tools that allows the student to move over the different software components of the system and that offers help to approach the project that is proposed. The Notebook allows the students to work in group with their projects and documents as well as to collaboratively edit on the Web. The Networked Evidence Database is a collection of data created by the students or already in the system, indexed by author, key words, etc. Mildred is a complete help system with four different categories.

KIE is completed with SenseMaker, a tool for the generation of ideas and factual explanations, and with SpeakEasy that facilitates collaboration by means of the group edition of pages with images, texts and sound.

Inside this type of collaborative tools to structure a domain on the basis of the students dialogues, we should point out the work of the group of the UNED in Spain [23]. In this web-based system, a group of doctorate students work in shared spaces carrying out bibliographical synthesis, discussing, reasoning and jointly deciding the structure and the content of the documents to write.

Finally the CHICO team is also developing a collaborative tool to help in the design of domotic environments. It can be consulted in this book and follows the outline of providing environments to solve complex problems with a series of structured help for the solution of these problems.

This line of goal-based solution of complex problems is underlying in all the cases described previously and also in the example "Broadcast news."

In "Broadcast news" [18], the students should develop the contents of a TV news program, having all the necessary elements to edit video and text. The system provides the following elements on the screen:
– A brief history of the events with references to available videotape fragments.
– A list of available material (texts and videotapes) related.
– A list of questions on history. On each question there are videotapes with answers given by experts in the subject.
– A collection of references in hypermedia format that the students can browse.
– A group of control buttons dedicated to make the editorial of the program.

Also some Multimedia tutoring systems such as "Cardiac Tutor" [24] follow this trend. In this system simulations, animations, sound and video make students feel as if it were a game, while they learn resuscitation techniques for heart patients. In this case, since the system requires certain design of strategies, simulation and some planning by the student make the learners acquire the necessary abilities to apply when the receiver of their resuscitation strategies is a real patient.

Following this line of the use of simulation as part of the design there are also the approaches proposed by Eden et al. [4,25]. These authors claim that the strictly construccionist approach can cause confusion to the learners at the last stages, mainly when they face design tasks. Therefore, it is necessary to apply a certain degree of instruction represented previously in the adoption of goals as already referred. These environments are close to such a well-known simulation game as "SimCity", ranging from traffic simulators, to adventure games of the type "Where in the web is Carmen San Diego™?", through the activities of object design based on "HyperGami" polyhedrons.

Related to this we can find the learning by discovery systems [26], devoted to create applications for the students to discover by themselves the laws governing the proposed experiments.

There is an aspect left to comment as to software development. It is the one related with the systems needed to create hypertext systems. In fact some of the collaborative systems we have mentioned are aimed to create hipertext by linking different pieces of information among learners using collaborative environments. CoVis, CSILE and other environments develop this concept from the student's perspective. But sometimes it is necessary to create hypertexts to develop the necessary contents in an authoring environment. Here, the collaborative environments present againt the biggest advantages.

In this line we will comment the SEPIA system [27]. This is the acronym of "Structured Elicitation and Processing of Devices for Authoring" and its purpose is to offer the authoring environment with synchronous and asynchronous support for the production of hypermedia documents for a distributed group of authors. The system allows diverse activities such as the planning of the actions to carry out, the acquisition of the contents and its structuring and the preparation of the final document.

The development of SEPIA is based on a cognitive model on the authorship activity and it uses a design approach of user- and task-oriented systems. According to the principles of cognitive theories it provides local and global coherence to hypertext designs carried out by means of a process that helps the author to avoid the incongruities in hypertext that can cause the well-known problem of "lost in hyperspace" to the hypernavigator.

In the authorship activity, according to these authors, there are three types of the involved processes deriving into three different models and finally to the three parts of the SEPIA system. The first process is the cognitive process that produce a cognitive model of authorship. This is represented in SEPIA by means of the Activity spaces. The second type of process is the one that has to do with the products to obtain. It uses a document model that is materialized in SEPIA in a construction kit. The last type is the social process that involves a social model of cooperation. It is shown in the system by means of the different "cooperation modes".

SEPIA uses the "Activity Spaces" divided in four specific components to each task that are devoted to give support to the main actions composing the author's environment. These are:
– Planning.
– Representation and structuring of the contents and basic materials.
– Development and representation of the structures of the arguments needed in the presentation, and
– Rhetorical organisation and formulation of the hyperdocument final version for a specific audience.

In asynchronous mode, the system guarantees the control of changes and the notification of the changes to users by means of the CHS (Cooperative Hypermedia Server) and an object-oriented SGBD that stores the persistent objects and the hypermedia object recovery mechanisms.

In synchronous mode, the system provides a shared environment of the type "What you see is what I see" (WYSIWIS). By means of a drawing tool of the type of a shared board (WSCRAWL) the authors can see and edit the content of the nodes.

SEPIA has been used in several projects such as MuSE, HyperStorM, POLIWORK, VORTEL and DOLPHIN. All of them can be consulted in high detail in the server of the Institute of Investigation GMD-IPSI, in Darmstadt (Germany). DOLPHIN is a collaborative tool that, in a very clear way, represents the underlying ideology of all these applications. It is available in the mentioned server for Unix and Windows platforms.

Another example of these systems is CHIPS. To the different utilities of the SEPIA-based systems it adds the management of personal roles, so that each co-author can have different participation according to the role that he intends to carry out every time.

Summing up, we can say that the environments supporting the computer-based teaching-learning process require the use of different techniques such as the content structuring of the simplest problems to the most complex ones, the use of large evidence databases that are used in a learning by discovery environment, the assumption of a model of constructivist learning based on goal search on complex problems and the use of the collaboration among learners or between these and mentors to achieve the best results for the proposed problems.

4.   HARDWARE.

Finally, it is to define how, in the author's opinion, hardware should evolve in order to be used efficiently in teaching–learning environments. Many of the considerations that follow are also valid for other fields using computers since these improvements in the physical devices can be obviously used in all the realisations of Computer Science, but we believe that sensitivity is greater in the applications than involve the interaction taking place when an user is to learn.

In this section we will sometimes introduce tools that cannot be considered related only to hardware, but rather they are a conjunction of programs and devices that lead to a kind of more appropriate interaction. We will mean this when speaking of Virtual Reality, Augmented Reality and, of course, Ubiquitous Computing.

The author's reflection on how the interaction between the learner and the system should be carried out derives from the idea that the Graphic User Interface (GUI), although it is an improvement regarding the interaction style based on command interpreters, it is not the appropriate means for teaching. Even the use of the metaphor of the desk so much used in the current systems is poor. At least we should be able to represent a three dimensional world similar to the one we live in.

It is for this reason that concepts such as Virtual Reality have surged are already begining to be used in the teaching–learning environments, although with the constraints that imply the use of a technology that has such high price that at present most teaching centers cannot afford [28]. However it is evident that it will have an important influence in future educational realms.

Augmented Reality is related with this concept. Augmented Reality is a style of interaction that tries to reduce the interactions with the computer using the information of the environment as an implicit entry.

With this style, the user will be able to interact with the real world with a capacity increased by the synthetic information of the computer. The user's situation is automatically recognised using a very wide range of recognition methods. The focus of the user's attention is not the computer in this case but the real world. The function of the computer will be to assist and to improve the interactions between human beings and the real world. Many recognition methods such as time, position and recognition of objects can be used with the computer's vision. We can also make the real world more comprehensible for the computer by, for example, placing bar codes in objects. As examples of "Augmented Reality" we can mention Metadesk, Ambient room ,Transboard [29] and Kidsroom [30].

In this last example, Kidsroom, the children can participate in children's stories in a room where animations are projected on the walls or on the floor.

By means of sensors, the system can detect the position of the children and other data that allow much richer interaction. For this reason, in the author's opinion, these environments have more future than those that make use of complex devices such as the devices connected to the head (HMD) so often used in Virtual Reality.

To finish we have left the most important innovation source that hardware can produce in the classroom. It is what has come to be known as Ubiquitous Computing.

As Mark Weiser says [31] "The most profound technologies are those that disappear." The overlapping in everyday life of most of the machines used makes them to appear inadvertent. At least it is so until they cause problems. Unfortunately computers are not currently among the tools that are inadvertent. That is just because it is not easy to control them.

In the already widely known article by Weiser and in some later references [32] we can see the philosophy of the intended change to make the computer omnipresent in our life.

If small computers of affordable price were around us in our life helping us in the tasks that we carry out such as the switches that allow us to turn on the lights, these computers would come to help us with their work being unintrusive for us.

The solution, therefore, is to have wireless nets of computers that would pass the information among them and would serve as an interaction mechanism, in turn with users. Ubiquitous computers should be of three types, "Tabs", "pads" and "boards."

Tabs are small machines of a few centimeters long looking like labels but different from these they are active. Pads of the size of a LCD screen are used in the same wayas we use a sheet of paper, a book or a magazine. Finally, boards have the habitual size of these in a class and they serve as a blackboard or as notice board.

Let us imagine the use of these computers in the classroom. The students are identified by a mark with their essential data, what they write on their pad and their position inside the classroom in that moment. Let us imagine that the teacher on the (active)board has displayed a problem to be solved and each student is proposing his/her solution in his/her pad.

In a collaborative way, as the pads emit information via radio waves, we can reach a solution accepted by the majority. The student that has proposed the solution comes closer to the active board to explain his/her reasoning and as he/she comes closer to his/her tab he/she sends the pertinent information to the active board. This changes the previous contents for those stored in the pad or in the tab in that moment. In fact the most important information should be stored in the tab so that the pad either mine or that of another person will present the solution that I have designed.

In the Xerox Research Center in Palo Alto these computers were designed [33] and in a later article Weiser [32] asserts that it is in the university campus where his idea of the Ubiquitous Computing can have more acceptance.

We believe that the University indeed can receive a definitive impulse but it is not necessary to minimize these tools in secondary education itself where learning by discovery environments, goal-based and collaborative, such as those that we have described find its best allies in these tools. In fact, Soloway [34] proposes a series of applications for the handheld type Palm Pilot or Windows CE (Pocket PC in the new terminology) that cover some of the experiences that we have designed. They are a new boost in our way to foster learning by discovery in the classroom. We are to add peripheral components that can be used to enter data for the handheld PCs. Later these data can be managed by the machine itself and collaborative applications can be easily realisable by means of infrared devices, although in fact an evolution is expected towards radio waves.

The dream of the Ubiquitous Computer is about to happen with these tools. Calculation capacities, devices that can be wireless interconnected. As some authors suggest [34] if we add the possibility to use handheld PCs as remote controls for group boards we already have practically the system described by Weiser in the year 1991, that is to say, "The computers for the XXI century."

5.   CONCLUSIONS

Throughout this paper we want to explain our view on how the classroom should be in this century that begins for an effective learning.

Three factors are important in this revolution: teachers, software and hardware.

Teachers are the actors of the process and they have to subscribe to the constructivism principles assimilating the new information technologies and communications as an essential tool in their work.

Software should be oriented in several directions. On the one hand in order to foster knowledge acquisition in a constructivist way, software should be developed aiming at real and complex projects with problem "scaffolding" and the use of the so-called "Artificial Intelligence" techniques in order to guide the students without overwhelming them. On the other hand we must focus the solution of those problems in a collaborative way. For the generation of the necessary contents so that the student can find the correct solutions we should provide the teacher or the engineer that generates the contents with tools of collaborative authorship.

As for the hardware, this author bets for the Ubiquitous Computing as the paradigm of the machines that will facilitate the software environments that we advocate. Only the reduction in the price of these machines will enable us to end up into making the dream of truly interactive systems real in order to solve the problems in the classroom. If we add the most complex systems of Virtual and Augmented Reality the hardware panorama will be complete. The CHICO team (http://chico.inf-cr.uclm.es) at the Universidad de Castilla–La Mancha (Spain) has followed this trend and some of the results of their research can be consulted in the following bibliography.

REFERENCES

1. Gates, W., "Business @ the Speed of Thought", Chapter 22, 1999.
2. http://www.microsoft.com/Education/
3. Negroponte, N., "Being Digital", Chapter 18, Alfred A. Knopf, Inc, 1999.
4. Jonassen, D.H., Peck, K.L., Wilson B.G., "Learning with technology. A constructivist Perspective", Chapter 1, Prentice Hall Inc., 1999.
5. Fishman, B.J., Honebein, P.C., Duffy, T.M. Constructivism and the design of learning environments: Context and authentic activities for learning. NATO Advanced Workshop on the design of Constructivism Learning, 1991.
6. Duffy, T., Jonassen, D., Constructivism and the Technology of instruction, Lawrence Erlbaum Associates, Hillsdale, New Jersey, 1992.
7. Ruiz, F., Prieto, M., Ortega, M., Bravo, J., "Cooperative Distance Learning with an Integrated System for Computer Assisted Laboratory" in "Computer aided learning and instruction in Science and Engineering", Springer Verlag, Vol 1108, 220-227 (1996).
8. Ortega, M. Muñoz, J.J., Bravo, C., Bravo, J., Redondo, M.A., "Scaffolding and Planning Techniques in Distance Education: A case study in Statistics", ONLINE EDUCA BERLIN. Fourth Conference on Technology Supported Learning, International WHERE + HOW, 164-168 (1998).
9. M. A. Redondo, C. Bravo, J. Bravo, M. Ortega, "Planificación, Simulación y Colaboración en Educación a Distancia", "Ciencia al Día Internacional", II-3 (1999). http://www.ciencia.cl/CienciaAlDia/volumen2/numero3/articulos/articulo3.html.
10. Bravo, J., Ortega, M., Verdejo. M.F., "Planning in Distance Simulation Environments", "Communications and Networking in Education: Learning in a Networked Society", Painopaikka Yliopistopaino, 46-54, (1999).
11. Bravo, C., Redondo, M.A., Ortega, M., Bravo, J., "A Simulation Distributed Cooperative Environment for the Domotic Design", Proceedings of 4th International Workshop on Computer Supported Cooperative Work in Design, 3-6 (1999).
12. Bravo, C., Redondo, M.A., Bravo, J., **Ortega**, M., "DOMOSIM-COL: A Simulation Collaborative Environment for the Learning of Domotic Design", Inroads - SIGCSE (ACM), accepted for publication. (2000).
13. http:/www.2b1.org
14. Bush, V., "As we may think", Atlantic monthly, July 1945.
15. Vygotsky, L.S., (1978), "Mind in society: The development of higher psychological processes", Cambridge MA: Harvard University Press.

16. Soloway, E., Pryor, A., The next generation in Human-Computer Interaction, Comm. of the ACM, 39 (4), 16 (April-1996).
17. Schank, R., Cleary, C., Engines for Education, Lawrence Erlbaum Associates, Hillsdale, New Jersey. (1994). URL : http://www.ils.nwu.edu/~e_for_e
18. Schank, R., Kass, A., A Goal-Based Scenario for Higher School Students, Comm. of the ACM, 39 (4), 28 (April-1996).
19. Edelson D., Pea R., Gomez L.M., The Collaboratory Notebook. Communications of the ACM, 39 (4), 32 (April 1996).
20. Scardamalia M., Bereiter C., Student Communities for the advancement of Knowledge. Communications of the ACM, 39(4), (April 1996).
21. Guzdial M., Kolodner J., Hmelo C., Narayanan H., Carlson D., Rappin N., Hubscher R., Turns J., Newstetter W., Computer Support for Learning through Complex Problem Solving. Communications of the ACM, 39 (4), (April 1996).
22. Linn, M.C. Key to the Information Highway. Communications of the ACM, 39(4), (April 1996).
23. Barros B., Rodriguez Artacho M., Verdejo M.F., Towards a model of Collaborative Support for Distance Learners to Perform Join Tasks in "The Virtual Campus". Proceedings of the 3.3&3.6 IFIP Working Conference. Madrid, Chapman & Hall,
24. Woolf, B. P., Intelligent Multimedia Systems, Comm. of the ACM, 39 (4), 28 (April-1996).
25. Eden, H., Eisenberg, M., Fischer, G., Repenning, A., Making learning a part of life. Communications of the ACM, 39 (4), 40 (April 1996).
26. Wouter Van Joolingen & Ton de Jong (1996) "Supporting the authoring process for simulation-based discovery learning". Proceedings of the Euroaied. Lisboa - Portugal.
27. Streitz, N.A., Haake, J., Hannemann, J, Lemke, A., Schuler, W., Schütt, H. y Thüring, M., SEPIA: A cooperative Hypermedia Authoring Environment. Eds. Lucarella, D., Nanard, J., Nanard, M. Y Paolini, P. Actas de ACM Conference on Hypertext (ECHT'92). Noviembre 1992. Milán (Italia), ACM (Nueva York), 11-22 (1992)

Natural Language Processing in Educational Computer Science

Antonio Vaquero Sánchez
Universidad Complutense de Madrid
e-mail: vaquero@ucm.es

Key words: Natural Language Processing, Human-Computer InterfaceLexical Database

Abstract: This is a presentation of the historical development of human-computer interfaces in educational computer science, which makes it necessary for Natural Language Processing to understand and interpret the learner's interventions. It is also an analysis of Lexical Databases and their application in education.

1.   INTRODUCTION

Nowadays most textual information handled by computer systems, in general as well as in educational applications, is managed in English.

It is due to the attention that has been set upon the processing of the English language. This has resulted in the creation of a great variety of programs for linguistic processing (syntactic analysers, disambiguators, etc.) in order to achieve text comprehension and to perform diverse operations on documents. The applications of this kind of programs, regardless of whether they are connected to the Internet or not, directly or indirectly related to education, are numerous and of great importance.

The situation is changing towards solutions that also involve other languages different from English. The spread of the Information Technologies and Communications must allow users to express themselves in their own language, regardless of what they request from the system, which may involve information management in other languages.

17

M. Ortega and J. Bravo (eds.), Computers and Education in the 21st Century, 17–20.

In this lecture we will first study the historical development of human-computer interfaces in educational computer science, which makes it necessary for Natural Language Processing to understand and interpret the learner's interventions. Finally, we will analyse Lexical Databases and their application in education.

2.   HUMAN-COMPUTER INTERFACES IN EDUCATIONAL COMPUTER SCIENCE

Human-computer interfaces are acquiring more and more importance. This is due mainly to two factors:

a) Available computer resources are increasingly more powerful, which makes it possible to assist users in their own environment, and with the problems implied in their requests; and

b) Computers must cover the linguistic distance between the machine and users, adapting to their natural form of communication.

The beginning of Educational Computer Science was characterized by rigid interfaces, in accordance with the times. However, it was sufficient for the educational software (Programmed Instruction) available at that time, based on conductive methods.

Gradually other more flexible interfaces emerged, in accordance with the cognitive theories closer to Constructivism.

3.   INTERFACES IN NATURAL LANGUAGE.

There are discrepancies in the interpretation of what interface means in Natural Language. We can hear about the concept of language inhabitation. A used language is inhabitable if it is comfortable for the user in four domains: the conceptual domain (what), the functional domain (how), the syntactic domain and the lexical domain.

1. the conceptual domain of the computer system is a subset, whether big or small, of the conceptual domain involved in Natural Language.

2. concepts can be expressed in many ways. The system is prepared to understand some of them, according to the built-in functions, but not others.

3. The syntax of the language the system understands is limited.

4. The system also has lexical limitations, more or less important.

To use a system by means of an interface in Natural Language the user should be aware of the capabilities of the system as much as he/she should know the language to exploit that potentiality.

4.   NATURAL LANGUAGE PROCESSING.

Computer systems were applied to process Natural Language from the end of the 1950s. It began with very arduous problems, such as language translation. These objectives were soon abandoned, although they were later taken on.

In the last decade intense work is being undertaken in the representation and management of linguistic knowledge, from different perspectives and with very diverse applications.

NLP systems are wide to certain degree, depending on the extension of the covered domain. Their effectiveness is usually inversely proportional to this extension. However, there are systems that try to cover the complete domain of the language. That happens with Leical Databases (LDB).

5.   LEXICAL DATABASES

A Lexical Database is much more than an electronic dictionary. However it contains all the information in an electronic dictionary and, also, LDBs are usually built starting from electronic dictionaries.

An LDB is a knowledge database on the lexicon, with the meaning, the word classes, the relationships among the words, their morphology, their use, etc.; that is to say, the whole linguistic knowledge of a language.

The most characteristic LDB in the last decade is, without doubt, WordNet[1], on the English language, naturally. LDBs have also been built in other languages, such as Japanese.

Typically in a LDB the words are divided in word classes. For example, in WordNet there are 4 classes: noun, verb, adverb and adjective. The lexical relationships are also represented (synonymy, hiponymy, meronymy, antonymy), syntactic relationships, etc. The resulting structure is quite complex.

There are also multilingual LDBs [2], although among these we should distinguish the multi-monolingual ones, such as the EuroWordNet project for EC languages and the EDR project for English and Japanese, and the truly multilingual ones. The difference lies in the fact that the latter have the conceptual knowledge separated in its own specific level (ontology), different from the linguistic knowledge, although this is synchronized with the conceptual knowledge.

An example of a truly multilingual LDB is MikroKosmos [3]. The lexical and linguistic knowledge depends on the specific language. On the one hand, there is the ontology and, on the other, for each language that the system can manage (English, Spanish, Russian, Turk, Chinese,...) the corresponding lexico-linguistic knowledge base is built. MikroKosmos is a continuously developing system, but it already allows important and useful applications, such as translating newspaper articles about economy from Spanish into English.

6.   LDB APPLICATION

Monolingual LDBs are applied to operations traditionally catalogued in text classification and, in general, to text comprehension in the language for which the database is made.

The most habitual classifying operations are: retrieval, routing, filtering, grouping, segmentation and categorization.

Text comprehension is the most ambitious objective in Natural Language Processing. It is necessary to carry out more complex operations than those of mere classification, such as automatic creation of summaries, answering to questions in Natural Language, etc.

Beside the applications of monolingual LDBs for each language managed by the multilingual system, these, naturally, can be applied to solve problems in which more than one language are involved.

Two applications are crucial for the human-computer dialogue:
1. Language Translation and
2. Cross Language Information Retrieval.

With multi-monolingual LDBs, crossed operations can also be made between different languages, such as translation, e.g., EDR. However, in those cases, it is much more appropriate and more effective to apply LDBs based on ontologies.

REFERENCES

1. Miller,G."WORDNET:An Online Lexical Data-base"Int. J.of Lexicography,3(4)1991.
2. Vaquero, A.; Sáenz, F.; Barco, A. "Multilingual Electronic Dictionaries for Cross-Language Information Retrieval". ISAS'99. Vol. II, pp 523-530. Int. Inst. of Informatics and Systemics-IEEE Computer Society.
3. http://crl.nmsu.edu/Research /Projects/Mikro

Educational Web Sites: Some Issues for Evaluation

M.Felisa Verdejo

Universidad Nacional de Educación a Distancia.
Ciudad Universitaria s/n, 28040 Madrid, Spain.
e-mail: ,felisa@ieec.uned.es

Key words: metadata for educational web sites, pedagogical evaluation

Abstract: This presentation addresses the need to describe educational web sites
              explicitly in order to offer precise information to potential users/search engines
              that are looking for resources to fulfill a particular educational need. It
              introduces EUN DC, a model currently being proposed, and discusses other
              proposals for evaluating the design and content of a site, a topic closely related
              to quality control for Web based education.

1.   INTRODUCTION

There is a wide range of web sites specifically related to education. Web sites cover different purposes: many of them just contain information; others also include communication facilities; some are dedicated to teachers, providing guidelines, best practice cases and educational software; while others are courseware or software repositories for students. You can also find a diversity of sites devoted to local, national or international learners' communities, as well as several virtual spaces for the organisation and deployment of educational activities in the framework of institutional networks involving schools, universities, companies and a variety of social partners.

M. Ortega and J. Bravo (eds.), Computers and Education in the 21st Century, 21–33.

Since web technology began to be used extensively, a clear need has emerged for making all these rapidly growing resources really available to potential users. A pre-requisite is to know about their existence. Searching tools provide better results if sites include an explicit description, informative enough to decide whether or not what the site offers is related to a specific educational purpose. But, a more important aspect for learning purposes, is to be aware of the content quality, beyond superficial multimedia aspects, and whether or not this issue has been explicitly taken into account in the design of a particular site.

In this paper we will concentrate on the criteria to describe, from an educational perspective, the content of a web site.

Some of them aim at identifying relevant information; others are useful for evaluation purposes. The lack of standards for learning technologies has been recognised as a bottleneck for the development of educational resources. Reusability and interoperability are seen as two of the main objectives for learning technology standardization. There are international initiatives currently working on these issues and proposals are emerging concerning metadata and structuring for learning content.

Section 3 deals with meta-information issues (i.e. what kind of descriptors of an educational web site are being proposed), in order to offer precise information to potential users/search engines that are looking for resources to fulfill a particular educational need.

Section 4 focuses on criteria for evaluating the design and content of a site, a topic closely related to quality control for web based education.

The next section outlines some background ideas about learning and teaching activities and how technologies come into play to support these processes.

2.   THE ROLE OF TECHNOLOGY IN LEARNING AND TEACHING

Each time a new information technology appears there is a strong push to consider it as a fundamental change for education. Usually there is an agreement on the new features offered by a particular technology, but a divergence in how they are perceived as a key change for learning purposes. Positions depend on the theoretical approach one considers most appropriate for supporting learners, and whether the new technology provides better ways to achieve the required processes.

When time passes, and some practice on the use of the technology becomes available, then it will be possible to carry out an analysis with a broader perspective. Learning goals will be identified and it will be feasible to study, through practice, how these have been better achieved, mediated, facilitated or supported by a particular kind of technology. Sometimes it is argued that the technology has not been understood or applied to its full potential, nevertheless it is also an occasion to reflect on principles and theoretical frameworks in order to check their value for building teaching and learning environments.

This is now the case with the Web. Despite its potential, many educational sites are designed as information or content providers, offering limited opportunities for the learner's action and interaction. However, learning conceived as knowledge construction involves a variety of rich processing where information is selected, analysed, interpreted, articulated, applied, and evaluated. Web technologies allow the designing of a variety of structured activities with a learning purpose, to be carried out individually and in collaboration, a potential to be exploited beyond the most frequent use of mere content delivery.

Models for education have evolved from a knowledge delivery perspective, where the teacher must transmit a body of established knowledge to the student, to a knowledge construction perspective where the role of the teacher is to facilitate the student's processes in order to construct their own perspective. In this approach, dialogue (an interplay between learner and teacher, but also between peers) appears to be a fundamental mediating tool for interactive learning [5]. Based on conversational theory, Laurillard has analysed dialogue properties allowing learning and has pointed out the following features:
– Discursive
      Students and teachers exchange their views on conceptualizations and actions.
– Interactive
      Students, acting to achieve objectives, receive meaningful feedback.
– Adaptative
      Teachers focus next topics or activities depending on the relation between their understanding and the students descriptions or actions.

• Reflective
      Teachers support the process by which student's link feedback on their actions to reflect upon their learning
      Her proposal is to describe technologies for educational purposes in terms of these categories, in order to understand how they can be better exploited and combined for learning purposes. For instance, simulation tools are considered interactive because they give intrinsic feedback on students actions, but not discursive because they do not provide opportunities for teacher or students to describe their conceptions.

This idea of combining multiple media and tools to support the large number of facets of a learning process is now being implemented through computer networking. Recent developments in Internet based software provide a framework to integrate all these technologies in a way quite transparent to the user. Furthermore, it offers individuals, groups or institutions the possibility of sharing resources, goals and activities, widening the learning space not only to other schools, but also to the professional sphere as well as to the growing international virtual communities. This is a completely new opportunity to expand the boundaries of existing educational systems.

The possibility of implementing a wide range of learning projects requires and at the same time encourages the sharing and reuse of digital resources in different contexts and for different purposes. For this reason, making the resource accessible on the Internet is a first step, but a more important one is the task of ensuring that others will be able to find it.

Metadata is structured descriptive information about a resource. Metadata allows making the search on the Internet more efficient and targeted. To have a standarized resource description is an important issue and a number of initiatives have appeared to deal with this topic. Dublin Core (DC) is the most widely accepted candidate. Based on the DC minimal set other extended schemes are proposed to meet the need of describing educational objects.

3.   DESCRIBING EDUCATIONAL WEB SITES

Current educational proposals for standards are based around the existing Web and Internet work on standards.

The Dublin Core[1] Element set is a standard candidate, which has been developed by an international community of librarians, information specialists and scientists from a variety of fields. DC has achieved wide international recognition. It is a sample metadata scheme, which aims at resource discovery on the Internet. DC consists of 15 elements: Title, Creator, Subject, Description, Publisher, Contributor, Date, Type, Format, Identifier, Source, Language, Relation, Coverage and Rights.

---

[1] The Dublin Core: A Simple Content Description Model for Electronic Resources
http://purl.oclc.org/dc/

The EUN Dublin Core Metadata element set is an initiative of the EUN[2] consortium, aiming at facilitating the search for information on European Schools and European educational materials. They are using the results of DC, extending these with new elements and sub-elements to deal with multimedia and commercial requirements. They have considered elements from other metadata initiatives related to education such as the IMS[3] project in the US, and Ariadne[4] and PROMETEUS[5] in Europe. They propose 18 elements (see table 1) and some sub-elements. The set provides a simple manner to describe a variety of resources such as documents, animations, music, chat services, virtual reality, exercises, and tools [1].

Some of the elements are mandatory, others are recommended, and the rest are fully optional. For each element there are two parts, a name and a content. In addition, each element can have three qualifiers: sub-elements, scheme and language. For example the full syntax for Date is as follows:

```
<META NAME "DC.Date"  CONTENT= "(SCHEME=ISO8601) value">
```

DC. indicates that the element is a Dublin Core element, the content includes in this case a scheme(i.e. the date is to be interpreted using ISO8601), so the value for the instance is:

```
<META NAME "DC.Date" CONTENT="(SCHEME=ISO8601)2000-04-08">
```

which is read as 8th April, 2000.

The values for elements not having the scheme qualifier are specified through controlled vocabularies to ensure a consistent use by different persons. Only a few elements admit free text.

For instance DC.Type values are defined by a vocabulary list. These include as top-level terms: dataset, image, interactive resource, physical object, software, sound and text. These are further refined. For example dataset is expanded to: dataset.numeric, dataset.spatial, dataset.spectral,

---

[2] EUN stands for European Schoolnet is a framework for collaboration between European Ministries of Education bringing together national education networks in Europe and around the world. http://www.en.eun.org/front/actual/

[3] IMS Global Learning Consortium, Inc. http://www.imsproject.org/

[4] ARIADNE is a research and technology development (RTD) project pertaining to the "Telematics for Education and Training" sector of the 4th Framework Program for R&D of the European Union. http://ariadne.unil.ch/

[5] PROMETUS partnership initiative – PROmoting Multimedia access to Education and Training in EUropean Society. http://prometeus.org/

dataset.statistical and dataset.structured-text. In the same vein interactive resource is refined into: chat, games, multimedia, VR, askanexpert, and simulation.

Table 1

Element	Obligation	Description
Title	Mandatory	Title of the resource
Creator	Mandatory	Name and address of the personal/corporate creator
Subject	Recommended	Keywords (freely chosen by the creator), indexing terms(from a thesaurus), classification codes,
Description	Mandatory	A textual description of the content
Publisher	Optional	Name and address of the personal or corporate publisher
Contributor	Optional	
Date	Recommended	The date, when the resource was created, issued and last modified
Type	Mandatory	General nature of the content of the resource (text, image, sound, data, software, interactive)
Format	Mandatory	Technical format, technical requirements and the size of the resource
Identifier	Mandatory	Unique identification of the resource
Source	Optional	The (digital, printed or other) source from which the electronic version was derived
Language	Mandatory	The language of the resource and the derivation of a translated version
Relation	Optional	The relation to other resources
Coverage	Optional	Indicates if the resource covers a special place or period
Rights	Recommended	Rights conditions and price
User level	Mandatory	Indication of the intended user group and the level of usage (school grade)
Version	Optional	The version of the resource
Metadata	Recommended	Information on the metadata release. Name of the approver of the resource for the EUN context.

EUN provides a tool for creating metadata descriptions. The use of metadata is being promoted as a requirement for publishing educational material within the European Schoolnet.

There are attempts to propose a more comprehensive classification scheme, for instance Nachmias et al. [6] present a taxonomy according to four main dimensions:

− Basic descriptive information
− Pedagogical and educational considerations to identify relevant learning aspects
− Knowledge attributes to characterize the representational means and structure of the conveyed knowledge

– Communications features, to describe the added value of communication and networking for instructional and learning purposes.

Each dimension is defined in terms of a set of categories. For pedagogical dimension 10 categories are proposed: Instructional configuration, Instructional model, Instructional means, Interaction type, Cognitive process, Locus of control, Feedback, Help functions, Learning resources and evaluation. Each category involves a group of variables. For example, for Instructional configuration the following are proposed: Individualized instruction, classroom collaborative learning and web collaborative learning. For cognitive process: information retrieval, memorizing, data analysis and inference making, problem solving and decision-making, creation and invention.

Taking into account this proposal EUN-DC would cover the first dimension, which is a preliminary characterization of the site. This first dimension is where a common language and a wide consensus in the granularity of descriptors are easier to reach. While the other dimensions would provide an in-depth analysis of pedagogical or content-related features of an educational web site, it raises much more controversial questions, both from a theoretical and a practical perspective. This is certainly a matter for further discussion and research.

4. QUALITY CONTROL: ESTABLISHING CRITERIA FOR EVALUATION

A crucial need closely related to the above issue is how to evaluate web based learning from an educational perspective. This is a quite difficult task due to the diversity and complexity of goals, approaches, audiences and actors involved. Not only a judgment is needed about the quality of content and approaches but also the impact on behaviour and practice. A way to address evaluation is by grouping proposals with similar goals and intended participants in order to develop a range of evaluation designs, identifying criteria appropriate for each of these clusters. Two case examples follow:

Networked technologies have the potential to change educational practices, by providing teachers and students with an expanded scope and quality of content, activities and resources. Educators need opportunities to work together, to carry out projects on similar interests and learn from each other's experiences. Beside Institutional programs, we can see certain initiatives from some teachers, related to their particular specialties, to face this situation. An example comes from an experience in which we were directly involved, the Language Engineering Training Showcase, aimed at showing a variety of examples of how computer and internet technology can be used for education and training in natural language and Speech Processing. The evaluation [2], primarily directed to judge the quality of project materials, was carried out under the responsibility of two SOCRATES/ERASMUS[6] thematic networks, ACO[1]HUM[7] and Speech Communication Sciences. The evaluation criteria, debated and shared by educators related to these areas, are listed in the appendix.

Focusing on higher education, Britain and Liber [3] have studied a number of current systems, grouped within the label of virtual learning environments (VLE). These systems offer a potential to allow a resource-based and student–centered model. Courses can be defined as collaborative activities, discussions, and joint assignments. Participants or tutors contribute resources as the course develops. Traditional roles using VLE would also change: students can be more actively involved in structuring their learning, and teachers would act more as trainers or facilitators. They would need to learn and develop abilities such as structure group memberships and roles to support productive collaboration, in order to monitor and provide feedback, and to assess the progress of students as individuals and as team members. There are currently a number of VLE systems offering a range of technologies such as conferencing software, e-mail, on-line resources, search engines and multimedia databases, videoconferencing, shared whiteboards and interactive simulations, all in a customized and integrated way. The functionality provided by a prototypical VLE comprises: a noticeboard, a course outline, e-mail, conferencing tools, class lists and student homepages, assignments, assessments, synchronous collaboration tools, multimedia resources, a file upload area, a calendar, search tools, and bookmarking and navigation models. Most of the reviews and reporting of these systems up to now describe and compare their technical features, but there is not much analysis about how the features are integrated to facilitate learning and how well they can fulfill educational requirements; in particular, how they can support constructivist and conversational approaches to learning as an alternative to a more traditional delivery approach.

In their study, Britain and Liver have explored Laurillard's model to evaluate VLEs from a pedagogical perspective. They have used the

---

[6] SOCRATES/ERASMUS are European community action programmes in the field of Education http://europa.eu.int/comm/education/socrates.html

[7] ACO*HUM is A SOCRATES thematic network project aimed at developing an international dimension for investigating the educational impact of new technologies in humanities disciplines. http://helmer.hit.uib.no/AcoHum/

principles of the conversational model (discursive, adaptive, interactive, and reflective) to characterize the features offered by these systems.

Following the model, they establish what means are provided by a particular system for structuring and carrying out conversations and actions. For example, looking at discursive tools, how well a VLE leverages e-mail technology to support the conversation as an integral part of learning. This issue is addressed by questions such as: is conversation accessible directly from the learning topic within the course structure or does the user have to move out of the course work to continue the conversation? Does the tool allow learning goals to be specified and recorded on the basis of the conversation?

Their analysis concludes that the adapted model shows the crucial distinctions between systems, but fails to capture the functionality associated with managing a group of learners (i.e. how the systems help a tutor to manage the complexities of teaching a resource based course with a large number of students). So they propose a number of additional organisational criteria: resource negotiation, coordination, monitoring adaptability, self-organisation and individualization are mentioned as crucial. All these issues can be affected by the facilities and flexibilities a particular system could offer, and then should also be taken into account for the choice of a VLE.

Judgments grounded in research suggest criteria for comparing systems. These criteria, elaborated from theoretical perspectives, must be confronted with the needs of potential users. In this sense the agenda of theorists does not always fit completely with the users' concerns. Crawley [4] discusses the case for a study on CSCL where a survey revealed that 49% of the criteria proposed by users were not considered among the theorist's criteria.

A better matching between theoretical frameworks and applicable methodologies is needed to deploy new learning environments in order to understand the educational qualities of networking technologies.

REFERENCES

1. G. Berger, M.Kluck, CH.Linderorth, S.Lundberg (1999). The EUN Data Handbook and Publications Guidelines. http://www.educat.hu-berlin.de/Kluck/datahandbook.htm
2. William J Black, Andy Way, Koenraad de Smedt (1999).ELSNET LE Training Showcase. ELSNET LE Training Showcase, NLP projects: Evaluation Report. http://fasting.hf.uib.no/elsnet-showcase/evalreport.html
3. Britain, S. , Liber, O. , (1999) A framework for pedagogical evaluation of virtual learning environments. http://www.jtap.ac.uk/reports/htm/jtap-041.html
4. Crawley, R.M. (1999) "Evaluating CSCL- Theorists'&Users'Perspectives" . http://www.bton.ac.uk/cscl/jtap/paper1.htm

5. Laurillard, D. (1993) *Rethinking University Teaching, a framework for the effective use of educational technology*. London and N.York: Routledge
6. Nachmias R., Mioduser D., Oren A., Lahav O. (1999) "Taxonomy of Educational Websites – a Tool for supporting research, development and implemention of Web-Based Learning". *I.J. of Educational Telecommunications*. 15, (3)

APPENDIX

Evaluation criteria were first proposed by the Speech Communication Sciences group and were revised by the ACO[1]HUM group in July 1999. Below is the list of final criteria which were applied in the evaluation report

Goals and Objectives

- How should this item be characterized as an aid to learning?
  E.g. distance/self-study learning package, package of exercises in support of conventional course, animation/simulation/analysis tool for a specific task/phenomenon in the field?

- Are the goals and objectives clearly stated?
  A goal is a general description of the intended outcome; an objective is an operational description of details in the intended outcome.

- Does achieving objectives realise the goals?
  Goals are achieved by proper objectives.

- Can the individual components of the tutorial, taken together, be said to satisfy the overall goals?

- Are the target audience and their pre-requisite knowledge clearly stated? Is the means of use of the materials matched to the expected computer literacy of the students?
  As well as the goals, both students and teachers need to know what knowledge and skills are expected in the tutorial. If the tutorial requires specific computer skills, are these reasonable given the target audience, or are means of acquiring those skills provided?

- Does the pilot meet the aims of the project application and does it show proof of concept?

- How complete is the pilot for actual use with student or is further development required?

- Does the pilot make extensive use of the possibilities of the medium and current technology?

Content

- Is the content coherent, consistent and factually correct?
  Do the materials form a logically organised and coherent entity? Are they free from self-contradiction and use technical vocabulary consistently? Is the subject material accurate and up to date?

- Does the content appropriately reflect the stated objectives?
  For each component of the tutorial in turn, the content of the teaching material needs to be relevant to and justified by the objectives of that component.

- Is the content appropriate and reasonable given the intended audience?
  Firstly is the material an appropriate means of obtaining the stated objectives? To answer this it is also necessary to take into account the target audience: is the material reasonable given the expected skills and background knowledge? It may also be necessary to assess its reasonableness with regard to the amount of time the tutorial takes or the necessary additional resources it exploits.

Teaching and Learning

- Is the tutorial a cost-effective means of achieving the stated learning goals?
  Does the tutorial deal with a subject matter that can be taught effectively using the teaching and learning methods employed? It may be necessary to ask a more basic question: is the tutorial constructed in such a way that its cost- effectiveness can be measured at all? In other words, are the knowledge and skills learnt measurable?

- Is the content fully self-instructional?
  The materials need to be sufficiently self-contained, easy to use and easy to understand so that a student can use them without additional help.

- Are there means for students to test their understanding?
  This almost always means that tutorials should have some built-in self-assessment materials. This is one good means of providing interactivity. Clearly these assessments should also be linked to the objectives.

- Does the tutorial create and maintain learner motivation and interest?
  Students studying alone need to be motivated and encouraged.

- Does the tutorial encourage active learning?

Learning by making active choices is generally considered superior to rote or passive memorizing of facts.

- Are there means for students to communicate with a tutor and/or to other students?
  A significant benefit of Internet materials is the provision of many means of computer-mediated communication: e-mail, news, chat, and conferencing.
  Since tutorials can never be complete, and authors of tutorials can never pre-guess all possible questions, means must be available for students to ask for help.

- Are there means for students and teachers to provide feedback to the authors of the tutorial?
  Tutorial development is a continuous process and feedback from users will help create and maintain an interesting and useful resource.

Implementation

Note: the following are only relevant to actual courses, not to tools:

- Is the topology of the material an appropriate way to implement the content and realise the objectives?
  Tutorial materials can be: linear, hierarchical, networked or based on simulation. Linear presentation may be overly restrictive if students can come from a range of backgrounds or if the material is rather large. Expert users may want to skip introductory components. On the other hand, networked material may be hard to explore or use effectively for learning. The current location in the tutorial and the available means of navigation should be clear at every stage.

- Is there a fair balance of time and content between different sections of the tutorial?
  Students' expectations of the length of time required for each section should not be contradicted: this means that sections should be of approximately equal learning time.

- Is there a logical progression between the different sections?
  Do later sections build on and re-inforce earlier sections? Is this logical development obvious to the users?

- Does the design of the tutorial make it easy for re-use by other tutorial authors?
  If a tutorial is separable into independent components, then these may find use as parts of other tutorials. In the future we would like to see courses comprised of component tutorials from many authors. For this to happen, it must be possible to "dip in" to a tutorial.

Note: the following questions are relevant to tools as well as courses.

- Are the computational requirements clearly stated?
  This is a particular issue with the current state of incompatibility between browsers. The use of high fidelity sound or video may mean that the tutorial is not effective over a slow network connection.

- Is the tutorial easily portable to other platforms?
  Tutorials requiring specific computer hardware are more difficult to re-use than those based on widely available non-proprietary technology.

- Is the design and presentation of content suitable for translation to other languages?
  An issue here is the embedding of specific languages in graphics or simulations. It is assumed that basic text will always have to be translated by hand.

- Ease of authoring, extensibility, interfaces with other systems and courses?

- Robustness?

- Effective/efficient architecture or buildup?

Availability

Free or low cost
Need licence
Need account
Documentation available
Support tools, examples available

PAPERS

PART II

Building a Virtual Learning Environment Using Agents

Alex Abad Rodon, Enric Mor Pera, Francesc Santanach Delisau
Universitat Oberta de Catalunya, Computing and Multimedia Studies
Av. Tibidabo, 43. 08035 Barcelona. Tel. 93 253 75 02
E-mail: {aabad,emor,fsantanach}@campus.uoc.es

Key words: agent, interactive exercise, ITT, virtual learning environment, Java

Abstract: This work presents the initial results of the ALF (Adaptive Learning
             Framework) project, a development framework to facilitate the auditing,
             management and maintenance of interactive and multimedia didactic materials
             that can be adapted to suit the user's requirements. ALF aims to build software
             components that are reusable in educational environments, providing for: a
             parameterizable system (writing of contents, definition of pedagogical
             strategies and management and subsequent maintenance), a personalized
             display of educational modules (adaptation of contents to the student's needs)
             and the automatic formulation and solution of exercises. The first prototype
             built with ALF is described, which is an interactive exercise for teaching
             mathematics.

1.   INTRODUCTION

The UOC (Universitat Oberta de Catalunya [*Open University of Catalonia*]) is a non-contact university, based on the Virtual Campus concept (an Internet-based communication academic environment) and on the use of didactic multimedia and interactive materials. The methodology used by the UOC implies that all the members of the academic community – students and lecturers – have a PC which is on line with the Virtual Campus.

M. Ortega and J. Bravo (eds.), Computers and Education in the 21st Century, 37–46.
© 2000 *Kluwer Academic Publishers. Printed in the Netherlands.*

The students, from their own homes, and with the help of didactic multimedia materials, go through the learning process guided and stimulated by a *tutor* and his/her *consultants*[1]. Thus, one of the points of interest of the UOC lies in the study and application of new technologies and techniques that make it possible to create didactic materials geared towards mitigating the problems involved in distance learning (student isolation, lack of communication...). For the didactic material to be of interest, it must include functionalities which a printed book does not (and cannot) have.

A great body of knowledge, as well as a series of mechanisms to make it possible to handle this knowledge, must be available in order to create this new type of didactic material. Thus, a distinction should be made between two important facets to consider when designing a virtual learning environment: *the knowledge representation* and *the didactics of the system.*

Some reasons that justify the use of techniques for the knowledge representation to work with on the domain of educational materials are: working with digital didactic materials, enabling the didactic materials interactivity, reusability of different parts of the materials. In this work the knowledge representation is based on the division of the different educational contents prepared by the teacher or lecturer for the process of student teaching/learning into *nodes of information.*

The didactics of the system is aimed at accomplishing an educational effect on the user through so-called *pedagogical activities* [7]. Didactic or pedagogical operations are addressed from a computational perspective. The work presented here aims to grant a greater number of pedagogical responsibilities to the system, placing more decisions dynamically under its control. A strategy could be defined as the mechanism that dictates sequencing in a virtual learning environment, where sequencing does not refer to linearity but rather to a series or episode of actions. The strategy would determine the action the system has to carry out at a given moment, depending on the environment and on what the student does.

The ALF project (Adaptive Learning Framework) is being developed in line with the aspect mentioned previously. It is a development framework to facilitate the auditing, management and maintenance of interactive and multimedia didactic materials that can be adapted to suit the user's requirements. Using Java, ALF aims to build software components that are

---

[1] In the UOC environment, the mission of the tutors is to accompany and guide the students in a personalized fashion from the beginning of their course at the University till the end. The consultants guide the student's learning process in each one of the subjects studied by correcting exercises and tests, and taking care of any queries and questions the student may have as to the content of the subject.

reusable in educational environments, providing for: a parameterizable system (writing of contents, definition of pedagogical strategies and management and subsequent maintenance), a personalized display of educational modules (adaptation of contents to the student's needs) and the automatic formulation and solution of exercises.

2. MODELLING OF A VIRTUAL LEARNING ENVIRONMENT WITH AGENTS

This work proposes the utilization of intelligent agents for the design and building of the components and the architecture of an *Intelligent Tutoring Tool* (ITT) [4]. Agent is taken to mean any entity with the capacity to perceive and act, although formally it may be defined as a system that is located in and forms part of a specific environment, which perceives it and in which it acts continuously with its own planning, with the aim of changing its own perception [2]. This definition of the characteristics of an agent can be related to the properties described above about the pedagogical strategies. If a strategy determines the action the system must carry out according to the environment and what the student does, it seems right to use agents to design and implement these strategies.

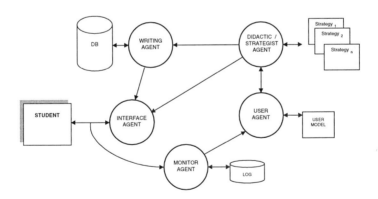

Figure 1

The architecture proposed for the design of ITT with agents [1] can be seen in Figure 1. This type of system proposes the use of five generic designs. Interface agents, writing agents, didactic/strategist agents, user agents and monitor agents. An interface agent manages all the communication of the system with the user or student. A writing agent accesses the database which stores the contents, based on the pedagogical strategy in progress. A didactic/strategist agent generates or selects the didactic operations or the most suitable strategy for the user from a library. A user agent is in charge of generating and maintaining a model for the user. A monitor agent, as its name indicates, monitors what the student does and generates a plot. This plot allows the user agents to update the student profile.

ALF (Adaptive Learning Framework) came into being in order to create a framework that permits the development of ITT and virtual learning environments in general.

3.   ALF: ADAPTIVE LEARNING FRAMEWORK

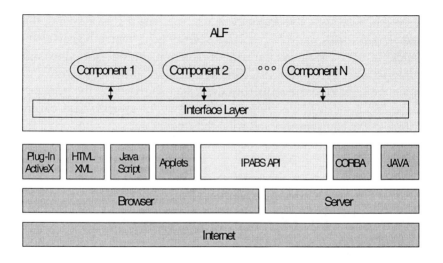

Figure 2.

ALF may be regarded as an ensemble of autonomous and reusable components -agents- which work on a client/server platform. This framework makes it possible to create specialised agents or components in educational tasks as well as the integration of new agents or systems into existing infrastructures. This facilitates the integration of applications, the subsequent maintenance and the easy inclusion of educational elements with intelligent capacities. Figure 2 gives an idea of its architecture in layers. The first level features the use of the Internet, WWW browsers and server programs. The second level includes the technological resources that use the different components of ALF. At this level, particular mention should be made of Visual IPABS [3], a visual environment for building agents. The third level comprises the components or agents that make up this *framework*. The design and building of these educational components entails the use of techniques common to Artificial Intelligence.

Agents for the processes of control and event generation, information display, interaction with the user, etc., were used. At this moment in time, ALF uses the following typology of agents:

- *Monitors*: are agents for detecting the interaction of the user with the system.
- *Task*: agents that perform a specific task, generally a response to an event. Examples of such designs are:
- *Speaker* agent: can read (aloud) any text in web format.
- *Writing* agent: displays the information required.
- *Didactic agents:* they guide the learning of the student according to the didactic operations (pedagogical and navigation strategies...) defined by the lecturer.
- *Wizards*: they help students and lecturers. They can generate reports, recommendations, etc.

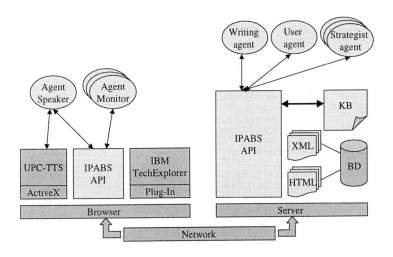

Figure 3.

Figure 3 shows the location of these agents, comprising a virtual learning environment.

ALF proposes a specific solution for the *representation of knowledge* for virtual learning environments and the use of navigation and learning strategies, generally known as *didactic operations*.

The representation of knowledge in ALF is based on the semantic networks. The knowledge engineer must give a network structure to the contents or didactic materials written by the lecturer, and each node of the semantic network will be an information core and each connection between them will be a conceptual or semantic relationship between contents.

It is therefore necessary to find a standard that supports this definition. In view of the major boom in mark-up languages nowadays on the Internet and in computing in general, XML (Extensible Mark-up Language) [6] was chosen, a standard proposed by W3C for the representation of metadata. Within this standard, RDF (Resource Description Framework) [5] is also used, which makes it possible to express properties on resources, thereby obtaining a semantic network.

Having seen the domain of knowledge we are going to work on, and having studied the different alternatives mentioned to carry out the didactic operations, a strategy is taken to be a robot. Statuses, transitions and conditions for changing from one status to another via each transition are consequently defined. Particularly, each status represents a possible configuration of the material to be learnt (e.g. a student sees some concepts instead of others depending on his or her status). Each event detected by the system (data input, navigation, clicking...) or a set of them may be the condition for a change of statuses through a transition.

Transitions take place as a result of an event. A common technique used to distinguish between the transitions produced by different events is colouring them. Transitions may mean the execution of a series of actions, and in this case the actions may be indicated as labels of the transition.

3.1   Interactive exercise using ALF: implementation considerations

A prototype interactive exercise implemented in Java and using ALF was developed. This exercise is integrated within the didactic materials of Discreet Mathematics of Technical Engineering in Computing of the UOC. It is the *Problem of Mismatches*. This prototype has made it possible to make an initial approach to some of the properties and functionalities pursued by the didactic materials:

– *Use of hypertext*: the exercise is a hypertext document. This means it can be integrated in the didactic materials used by the UOC.
– *Mathematical notation*: the graphic formats normally used to represent mathematical formulae have been replaced by a *plug-in* (TechExplorer-IBM) which enables the definition of the formulae in Latex or MathML. This will make it possible to interpret and evaluate formulae

automatically (in real time). This *plug*-in must be installed for the interactive exercise to work properly.

- *TTS (text to speech)*: the incorporation of a speech treatment system developed by the Speech Processing Group of the Universitat Politécnica de Catalunya has made it possible to add the functionality of having a text read by the system when it is selected. The interaction between the TTS system and the browser was implemented by an ActiveX control and JavaScript. These technologies impose the use of Internet Explorer 4 (or higher) as Web browser. In the future this interaction is expected to be offered through Java to facilitate the portability of the system and extend it to any navigator and/or platform.
- *Formulae reading*: this is a system for the translation of mathematical formulae written in Latex to text, thereby enabling the use of the aforementioned TTS system to read the TechExplorer formulae.
- *Bookmark*: this functionality is applied to all didactic material, providing the possibility of marking pages of interest as bookmarks. An icon located at the top of the material allows us to access the bookmark in question at any time. Since it is impossible to use the browser's bookmark property (as the latter only saves the page in progress and not the whole frame structure the interactive book is comprised of), this functionality had to be created. This is a Java *applet* that sends information to the server as to the structure of *frames* to be saved or reloaded.
- *Dynamic exercise building*: a server (*servlet*) which builds the hypertext document that forms the exercise was used to implement this functionality. This server also makes it possible to save the configuration of the problem at all times and to retrieve it in subsequent accesses.
- *Printable version*: the student can print out the steps he or she has followed to solve the exercise at any time (these steps correspond to the content of the page being worked upon). Furthermore, the student has an icon that allows him/her to view a developed version of the exercise.
- *Personalization of the didactic material:* the student can personalize each one of the pages of the material by marking and adding any notes to the parts of the text he or she wishes. These annotations can be shared via e-mail to add greater interactivity and cooperation between students and lecturers, and are integrated automatically in the target material. *Scripts* (text selection), *applets* (note editing) and a server *servlet* program (storage) were used to implement this utility.
- *Knowledge representation*: the representation of the knowledge used for the Problem of Mismatches comprises the following elements: context, formalism, simulation and questions. In turn, each question contains the following elements: solution, data input and simulation.

    – *Strategies*: the robot that represents the strategy designed for the Problem
       of Mismatches is shown in Figure 4.

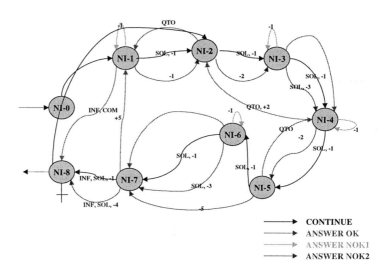

Figure 4.

This strategy allows for four possible events: *"Continue"*, *"Ok"*, *"Nok1"*,
"Nok2". *"Continue"* means pressing the continue button, *"Ok"* that the
answer was right and the *"Nok n"* that the answer was wrong for the n-th
time. *"INF"* means that the student evaluation report can be generated. This
will consist of a mark (A, B, C or D) and detailed information of the steps
followed to solve the exercise. *"SOL"* indicates that the solution icon should
be shown. The numbers in the transitions indicate the value with which the
mark that appears in the student evaluation report should be modified.
The strategy has the following rules of operation which should be
emphasized:
    – When the student gets the right solution, the *"Ok"* chain is followed
       until a non-solved status is reached.
    – When the student gets the wrong answer (*"Nok2"*) and the target
       status has already been solved, the *"Ok"* chain is followed from this
       status until a non-solved status is reached..
    – the solution to a problem is shown when the next status is the current
       one.
    – In a final status stage, the solution is shown if a wrong answer is given
       (*"Nok2"*). Statuses 3 and 6 are final status stages.
  – *Interactive simulation*: this is a Java *applet* which makes it possible for
    the student to understand and practise the problem. This *applet* is
    parameterizable, which means it can be run with the initialization

required in each case. This *applet* was designed specifically for the Problem of Mismatches. Other exercises will require different *applets*.
– *Monitor agents*: there are three types of Monitor Agents.
  – *Monitor agent of a data input*: a Java *applet* that generates an event to the system indicating that the user has input data.
  – *Monitor agent of the selection box*: a Java *applet* that generates an event to the system indicating which selection box was chosen.
  – *Monitor agent of a button*: a Java *applet* that generates an event to the system indicating that the button has been pressed.
– *Didactic agent*: It manages strategies. This agent is located in the server part and is implemented in Java.
– *Writing agent*: it generates the display required for the exercise at all times. For this purpose the RDF files that configure the exercise are used, as well as the indications provided by the Strategist Agent. This agent is located in the server part and is implemented in Java.
– *Student agent*: compiles all the information from the system, and processes it according to the indications of the strategy and drafts a report for the student. This agent is located in the server part and is implemented in Java.

4.   CONCLUSIONS AND FUTURE WORK

The use of agents is the natural way of building ITTs. The combination of different ITTs may lead to the building of a general ITS, and the use of agents solves the possible problems of integration and communication between them.

This work has presented the development of an exercise prototype applied to a virtual learning environment. Intelligent agents are used to manage the student's personal evolution via an ensemble of information nodes. This makes it possible to adapt the presentation of the pages of the book and obtain personal reports. Furthermore, facilities have been brought in for the personalization of materials and for reading mathematical formulae.

The making of this prototype has brought to light the need for author tools to facilitate the labelling of texts and the definition of evolution strategies through contents.

REFERENCES

1. Abad, A.; Mor, E.; Santanach, F.; (1999) *ALF. Building an ITT with Autonomous Agents.* Catedra IBM-LaCaixa, 1999. Universitat Oberta de Catalunya
2. Franklin S., Graesser A., (1995) *Is it an Agent, or just a program?: A taxonomy for autonomous agents.* 1996. http://www.msci.members.edu/~franklin
3. Mor, E. et al; (1999) *Visual-IPABS: Un Framework para la Construcción Visual de Agentes.* Presented at the VIII Conference of the Spanish Association for Artificial Intelligence, Murcia 1999
4. Patel, A.; Kinshuk; (1997) *Intelligent Tutoring Tools on the Internet, Extending the Scope of Distance Education. International Conference on Distance Education,* ICDE 97, State College, PA, USA, June 1997
5. REC-rdf-syntax (1999) Oral Lassila, Ralph R.Swick, *Resource Description Framework (RDF) Model and Syntax Specification W3C Recommendation 22 February 1999,* World Widew Web Consortium http://www.w3.org/TR/1999/REC-rdf-syntax-19990222
6. REC-xml (1998) Tim Bray, Jean Paoli, C.M.Speberg-McQueen, *Extensible Mark-up Language (XML) 1.0 W3C Recommendation 10-Feb-98,* World Widew Web Consortium http://www.w3.org/TR/1998/REC-xml-19980210.html
7. Wenger, E.; (1987) *Artificial Intelligence and Tutoring Systems.* Morgan Kaufmann Publishers, 1987

Integration of Simulation and Multimedia in Automatically Generated Internet Courses

Manuel Alfonseca, Juan de Lara
Dept. Ingeniería Informática, Universidad Autónoma de Madrid
Campus de Cantoblanco, 28049 Madrid
E-Mail: {Manuel.Alfonseca, Juan.Lara}@ii.uam.es

Key words: Continuous simulation, Internet, Multimedia, Automatic generation of courses, Java

Abstract: This paper describes the automatic generation of simulation-based Internet courses by means of an object-oriented continuous simulation language (OOCSMP), and a compiler for this language (C-OOL). Several multimedia extensions added to the language are also described. These extensions provide the student with a better understanding of the simulated models. The paper finally describes a course developed using the multimedia extensions.

1.   INTRODUCTION

Systems simulation [15] is one of the older branches of Computer Science: it was already advanced in the sixties and reached maturation in the seventies. Continuous simulation has been programmed traditionally either in special purpose languages, or in general purpose programming environments. According to their syntax, there are three main classes of continuous simulation languages: block languages [1], mathematically-oriented languages (such as *CSMP* [11]) and graph languages [13, 14].

Internet is becoming an important educational tool. New courses appear every day [10,18], ranging from a simple translation of classroom notes, to more advanced materials including sophisticated elements, such as simulations, animated graphics, etc. In particular, the Java language [17] has made the courses more interactive, faster in execution and easily

M. Ortega and J. Bravo (eds.), Computers and Education in the 21st Century, 47–54.
© 2000 *Kluwer Academic Publishers. Printed in the Netherlands.*

transportable. The obvious interest in the field has created a need of appropriate tools to help in course elaboration, which should provide all the facilities offered by the Internet-based education [8,16].

The integration of simulation tools with multimedia elements makes it possible to express in a richer way the knowledge we are trying to provide, and gives the student a better comprehension of the problem, as explanations by means of video, images, texts, etc. are not statically included in an *HTML* page, but are dynamically synchronized with the simulation.

In this paper we describe the multimedia extensions added to our continuous simulation language, together with a course on Ecology that incorporates these elements.

2.   THE OOCSMP LANGUAGE

We have designed the OOCSMP language [2-4] as an object-oriented extension of the CSMP language. It is a true extension, meaning that CSMP programs are correctly compiled and executed with our C-OOL compiler. The object-oriented extensions added to the language make it possible to build very compact object-oriented models when the system to be simulated consists of a number of similar interacting components.

The OOCSMP language has been used to build several courses in the web: a course on Newton's gravitation and the solar system, a course on Ecology [5], a basic course on Electronics [6], and a course describing the capacities of the language to solve partial differential equations [9]. All of them are accessible from the following address:

www.ii.uam.es/~jlara/investigacion

3.   THE C-OOL COMPILER

C-OOL (a Compiler for the OOCSMP Language) is a compiler we have built to translate the *OOCSMP* language into C++ or Java. Its structure and the way it works are shown in Figure 1:

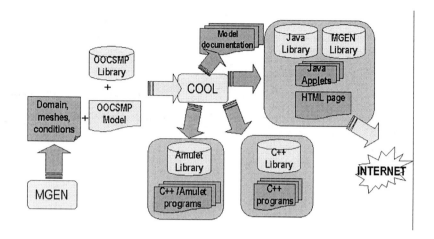

Figure 1: Outline of the use of the C-OOL compiler

Both the compiler and the Java libraries used at execution time have been extended to support the four multimedia primitives described in the following section.

4. MULTIMEDIA EXTENSIONS TO THE *OOCSMP* LANGUAGE

We have added several multimedia extensions (images, video, audio and text) to the output formats associated to the *OOCSMP* language. They are described as follows:

– Image panel: A panel or window is displayed where several images may be shown subsequently. Each image appears when a certain condition is true. A condition may be any *OOCSMP* logic expression, using the logic operators <, >, <=, >=, ‖ (logic OR), && (logic AND), which have been added to the language. The *OOCSMP* syntax of an image panel declaration is:

```
IMAGEPANEL [position]
    (, START( <OOCSMPexpression>), "file")+
    [, DEFAULT , "file" ]
```

Where `position` is one of the nine positions in the main panel (*N, S, E, W, NE, NW, SE, SW*) or *WINDOW*, which is shown in a separate window. The image in "file" appears in the indicated position when condition <OOCSMPexpresion> becomes true during the simulation. As many image-condition pairs as desired may be specified. If the DEFAULT clause is given, the associated file is shown when none of the other conditions holds. Several image panels may be created. Image formats accepted are gif and jpeg.

- Video panel (VIDEOPANEL): The same syntax as the previous, but videos are shown instead of images. Java Media Framework v2.0 [12] is used to show the video. Formats accepted are mov and avi.
- Audio (AUDIO): Similar syntax as the two previous, although in this case there is no associated graphic object, thus a position must not be specified. Java Media Framework v2.0 is also used here. This element accepts audio files in wav format.
- Text panel (TEXTPANEL): The same syntax as IMAGEPANEL.

5.   A COURSE ON ECOLOGY WITH MULTIMEDIA ELEMENTS

Our course on Ecology [5] has been modified to incorporate the multimedia extensions, which have been specially useful in the pages where one species invades the ecosystem. Using them, it is possible to provide the student with detailed explanations of what is happening at the appropriate moments.

We shall add multimedia elements to the ecosystem model which displays a predator, a herbivore and a primary producer in a total equilibrium which is broken by the invasion of a new predator. This model is explained in detail at [14].

When the predator invasion takes place, predator and herbivore populations get smaller (there is more competition and more predators) while the population of primary producers increases until a new state of oscillating equilibrium is reached.

We will use the multimedia elements to underline three phases in the simulation:

1. From the beginning until the predator invasion (static equilibrium).
2. From the predator invasion until the oscillating equilibrium.
3. After the oscillating equilibrium has been reached.

We have to provide conditions to identify the three phases:

1. The first phase is defined by the condition TIME>=0 and TIME<50, because the new predator invades the ecosystem at TIME=50. The associated multimedia panels should thus include the condition:

```
START ( (TIME >=0)&&(TIME<50) )
```

2. The second phase happens when TIME > 50 and while the derivative of the predators and herbivore populations are negative (all three populations are getting smaller). Thus, the condition would be:

```
START(  (TIME>=50)&& (Lion.XP<0)
     && (Cheetah.XP<0)&& (Gnu.XP<0))
```

3. Oscillating equilibrium is reached when none of the two previous conditions holds, i.e. we can use the DEFAULT clause.

Now we should prepare the multimedia elements to be used by our model. In our case, we shall add a text panel and an image panel.

Listing 1 shows the *OOCSMP* model. Figure 2 shows the state of the simulation before the predator invasion, and figure 3 displays the situation after the predator invasion, but before the ecosystem reaches oscillating equilibrium.

The model used in previous versions is the same, except for the declaration of the two new panels. As the figures show, the resultant applet is divided into 4 areas:

- On the upper left (North), a panel showing the populations of the four species in the ecosystem in the form of a bidimensional plot.
- On the bottom left (Centre), a panel showing the percentage of the four populations in the form of an iconic graphic.
- On the bottom right (East), a multimedia panel showing the trophic chains in the different phases.
- On the upper right (Northeast), a text explaining what is happening in the different phases.

This applet, together with the other pages in the course on Ecology, can be found at the following Internet address:

http://www.ii.uam.es/~jlara/investigacion/ecomm/africa1.html

```
TITLE Three species , invasion of predator
INCLUDE  "Species.csm"
¹ Actual species
Species Cheetah("Cheet", "http://www.ii.uam.es/~jlara/wcat.gif",
                4,-.028,.0014,.0,50)
Species Lion    ("Lion",  "http://www.ii.uam.es/~jlara/lion.gif",
                2,-.02, .001)
Species Gnu     ("Gnu","http://www.ii.uam.es/~jlara/bovin.gif",
                20,-.02,.0001,.016666666)
Species LGrass ("LGrass","http://www.ii.uam.es/~jlara/leafs.gif",
                400, .01, 0, .0005)
Species Ecosystem := Cheetah, Lion, Gnu, LGrass
    Ecosystem.STEP()
    Cheetah.ACTION(Gnu,        1, 1)
    Lion.ACTION    (Gnu,        1, 1)
    Gnu.ACTION     (Lion,   - .6, 0)
    Gnu.ACTION     (Cheetah,- .4, 1)
    Gnu.ACTION     (LGrass,    1, 1)
    LGrass.ACTION (Gnu,     - 1, 1)
¹ Timer and show data
```

```
TIMER delta:=0.01,FINTIM:=900,PRdelta:=.5,PLdelta:=5
PLOT           [N], Cheetah.X, Lion.X, Gnu.X, LGrass.X, TIME
ICONICPLOT     [C], Cheetah.X, Lion.X, Gnu.X, LGrass.X
TEXTPANEL      [E],    START((TIME>=0)&&TIME<50), "inicio.txt",
                       START((TIME>=50)&&(Lion.XP<0)&&(Cheetah.XP<0)&&(
                       Gnu.XP<0)), "inv.txt",
                       DEFAULT,"equilib.txt"
IMAGEPANEL     [NE],   START((TIME>=0)&&TIME<50), "inicio.gif",
                       START((TIME>=50)&&(Lion.XP<0)&&(Cheetah.XP<0)&&(
                       Gnu.XP<0)), "inv.gif",
                       DEFAULT,"equilib.gif"
METHOD ADAMS
```

Listing 1: A model of an ecosystem invaded by a new predator

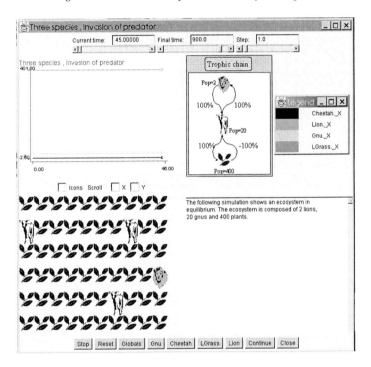

Figure 2: State of the simulation while the first condition holds

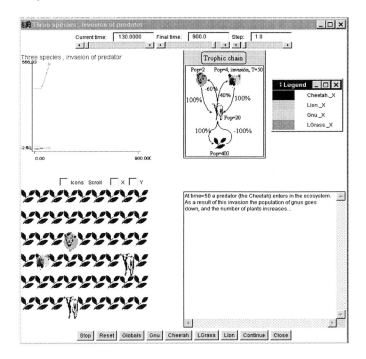

Figure 3: State of the simulation while the second condition holds

6.   CONCLUSIONS AND FUTURE WORK

The inclusion of multimedia elements in our language enhances student comprehension of the simulated model. The mechanisms that synchronize the multimedia elements with the simulation (the clauses START and DEFAULT) make it possible to display each element in the appropriate moment, thus holding the student attention better than a static presentation in *HTML* pages separated from the simulation.

The cost of adding multimedia elements to a course generated with *OOCSMP* is very small. One has just to identify the appropriate conditions associated to each of them, and prepare the images, video, texts, etc., the remainder of the model is not changed.

It is also unnecessary to modify by hand the *HTML* pages generated by the compiler, as those elements previously included in those pages can now be introduced as dynamic multimedia elements inside the simulation applet.

In the future, more multimedia elements will be added to the language, such as HTML panels and animation. The student activities may also be monitored either through a database or with special task control mechanisms [10]. The system will also be enhanced with a graphic environment to build

OOCSMP models, to plan the course pages, and to synchronize the multimedia elements. With this environment, *OOCSMP* and *C-OOL* would become full-fledged author tools.

We are starting to work with distributed objects, using *RMI. C-OOL* will generate distributed code for several machines. In this way, the performance of some simulations will be substantially improved.

REFERENCES

1. Alfonseca, M. 1974. *"SIAL/71, a Continuous Simulation Compiler"*, in "Advances in Cybernetics and Systems", Ed. J. Rose, Gordon & Breach, London, Vol. 3, 1319-1340.
2. Alfonseca, M., Pulido, E., de Lara, J., Orosco, R.. 1997. *"OOCSMP: An Object-Oriented Simulation Language"*, Proc. 9th European Simulation Symposium ESS'97, pp. 44-48.
3. Alfonseca, M.,de Lara, J., Pulido, E. 1998. "Semiautomatic Generation of Educational Courses in the Internet by Means of an Object-Oriented Continuous Simulation Language", Proc. 12th European Simulation Multiconference ESM'98, pp. 547-551, 1998.
4. Alfonseca, M., Carro, R., de Lara, J., Pulido, E.. 1998. "Education in Ecology at the Internet with an Object-Oriented Simulation Language", Proc. Eurosim'98 Simulation Congress, Fed. European Simulation Societies, ed. K.Juslin, pp. 118-123, 1998.
5. Alfonseca, M., de Lara, E., Pulido, E. 1998. "Educational simulation of complex ecosystems in the World-Wide Web", Proceedings ESS'98, Nottingham, pp. 248-252.
6. Alfonseca, M., de Lara, J. 2000. "Automatic generation of a web course on electronics with associated documentation", to appear in EUROMEDIA'00
7. Alfonseca, M., García, F., de Lara, J., Moriyón, R., "Generación automática de entornos de simulación con interfaces inteligentes", ADIE n° 12, Octubre-Diciembre 1998.
8. Aviation Industry CBT Committee Computer Managed Instruction. 1977. *Computer Managed Instruction Guidelines and Recommendations*, AGR 006, Version 1.1, AICC. http://www.aicc.org/agr006.htm.
9. de Lara, J., Alfonseca, M. 1999. "Simulating Partial Differential Equations in the World-Wide-Web". EUROMEDIA'99. Munich, pp 45-52 .
10. GNA The Globewide Network Academy. 1997. http://www.gnacademy.org.
11. IBM Corp. 1972. *"Continuous System Modelling Program III (CSMP III) and Graphic Feature (CSMP III Graphic Feature) General Information Manual"*, IBM Canada, Ontario, GH19-7000, 1972.
12. Java Media Framework v2.0, at: http://java.sun.com/products/java-media/jmf/2,0
13. Karnopp, D. 1990, *"Bond Graph Models for Electrochemical Energy Storage: Electrical, Chemical and Thermal Effects"*, Journal of the Franklin Institute, Vol 324, pp. 983-992.
14. Legasto A.A. Jr., Forrester, J.W., Lyneis, J.M. editors, *"Systems Dynamics"*, North Holland, 1980.
15. Monsef, Y. 1997. *"Modelling and Simulation of Complex Systems"*, SCS Int., Erlangen.
16. Schutte. 1997. *Virtual Teaching in Higher Education: The New Intellectual Superhighway or Just Another Traffic Jam?*. In Internet at: http://www.csum.edu/sociology/virexp.htm
17. Sun Corp., at http://java.sun.com
18. Thomson Publishing. 1997. *Internet Distance Education with Visual C++*. http://www.thomson.com/microsoft/visual-c/teacher.html

A Visual Simulation Environment for MIPS Based on VHDL

J.M. Álvarez Llorente,[1] N. Pavón Pulido,[1] J.Ballesteros Rubio,[2]
[1] *Departamento de Ingeniería Electrónica. Universidad de Huelva, Escuela Politécnica Superior; Carretera Huelva-La Rábida, 21071, Palos de la Frontera (Huelva).*
Phone: 959 530 580 ext. 2321 & 2339
E-mail: {llorente,npavon}@uhu.es
[2] *Departamento de Informática. Universidad de Extremadura, Escuela Politécnica;*
Ctra. de Trujillo s/n, 10071, Cáceres. Phone.: 927 257 189
E-mail: julioba@unex.es

Key words: VHDL, Hardware simulation, Graphics, Multimedia and Hypermedia in education, Evaluation of educational environments.

Abstract: An application to perform a visual simulation of a machine based on MIPS is presented in this paper. The advantage of this system in relation to conventional simulators is that the simulation engine is the result of a real simulation under a VHDL development environment, so that hardware description can be modified and simulated in several ways to test and study its performance. So, it is possible to join the versatility of a commercial VHDL development tool with the simple handling of a graphic environment. In addition, an assembler language has been defined to write simple applications in order to test the simulated computer.

1.   INTRODUCTION

Nowadays, a MIPS machine, described in [4] is the most frequently referred system in computer architecture teaching. There are many simulators showing how MIPS works, and it is very easy to find complete VHDL MIPS descriptions on the Internet. Our system uses a machine based on the MIPS segmented version with hazard control and a subset of reduced format instructions.

M. Ortega and J. Bravo (eds.), Computers and Education in the 21st Century, 55–63.
© 2000 *Kluwer Academic Publishers. Printed in the Netherlands.*

The VHDL simulation of a MIPS machine helps to learn the real construction of a CPU. However, many existing tools designed to work with VHDL produce, as a result of simulation, a very abstract and long time-state sequence, that the students who begin to know how a pipelined CPU works can hardly interpret.

Our simulation system wants to offer a graphic interface to make it easier to interpret the numeric results obtained using a conventional VHDL tool, concretely, the *VSIM simulator* distributed by *Model Technology Inc.*, version 1.2.

Because of limitations of the compiler version used *[Mod91]*, a simplification from the structure of MIPS machine has been performed, reducing the number of instructions and the memory capacity. The result is described below.

The simulation process of this new system begins with the construction of the VHDL machine description [1], where it is possible to make modifications to check out its operation (for example, changing a behaviour description for a structural one). This description is compiled with the Model Technology environment [3].

The next step is creating a program to test the designed CPU. An assembler language is defined for this purpose. This assembler language allows us to make simple programs using the instruction repertory, labels, variables, etc. An editor for the source code, and an assembler program to translate the source code into a representation accepted by the VHDL description through a file, have been designed.

Later, from the graphic environment, the VSIM simulator is called. This simulator is used to show the state of the interesting signals, programming the desired time resolution, and performing a simulation, long enough to get a complete running of the program.

Finally, it is necessary to analyse the results file, trying to identify the operations in each segmentation stage, the state and control signals, etc., through a group of binary and decimal numbers taken from the VHDL simulator. But this is very tedious and difficult. So, it is very useful to have a translation graphic environment: the graphic analyser. This tool enables us to repeat the simulation, showing the results in a graphic scheme where all blocks and signals in the machine are represented. The activation of the control lines is represented with different colours and the data lines show its contents with a label. There are options to advance and go back in the running process, and perform an auto-animated running process. Thus, it is very easy to study how a program running is performed through the different segmentation stages.

2.　　GOALS

The proposed goals for this system are mainly the following:

a) To provide a simple and intuitive graphic environment that shows the machine state and allows us to advance and go back in the simulation running process.

b) To provide a programming language to test the performance of the machine with different programs in an easy and quick way.

c) To use a real VHDL environment to describe the computer. Thus, it is possible to study this language with a real example, taking advantages of a graphic simulation and a suitable compiler.

d) To perform a simulation at an electric digital signal level. Since initial simulation from the VHDL environment can be configured in order to show different groups of machine signals, it is possible to attempt to isolate CPU components, as well as to study it in a global way. It is also possible to do both operations in the simulation itself, showing or hiding signals for the simulation at different moments.

e) To get an adaptable tool with regard to other VHDL simulators.

3.　　METHODOLOGY

As we have remarked above, three fundamental components have been designed to compose the application. The core of the simulator is the implementation of the behaviour of a reduced VHDL version of the MIPS machine that performs a real simulation in a file with information about times and states. The application takes this file to show the results in a visual way. Besides, the application allows us to create simple programs using an assembler language, to compile and translate them to a MIPS machine code. Thus, the student can quickly familiarize with a pipeline operation. The simulator can show the data and instructions memory contents. The list of machine code instructions obtained from the compilation process forms the program loaded in the instruction memory. MIPS will run these instructions during simulation from the VHDL environment. At this stage, the file with the simulation data is generated. Later, the application translates this simulation file to make it possible to graphically see how different components in the machine change their state as time goes by, and to understand how information flows through segmentation stages.

Each component of the simulator is described below, in detail.

3.1 Reduced MIPS VHDL description

A 5-stage segmented RISC architecture is used as a pipeline. Each stage is separated from the next one by a segmentation register: IF Stage (Instruction Fetch), IF/ID Register, ID Stage (Instruction Decode), ID/EX Register, EX Stage (Execution), EX/MEM Register, MEM Stage (Write in Memory), MEM/WB Register, WB Stage (Write Back).

There is a register bank which consists of eight 16-bit registers, called R0 to R7. Instruction memory design uses 2 words in memory (16 bits) for each instruction. The suitable instruction memory size is 128 two-byte words: a 256×8 words RAM. For data memory, also a 256×8 RAM has been used. Thus, the memory can be completely addressed by the address field of the instruction format. Two instruction formats are given: register-register instructions (used in ALU operations), and memory instructions (load, store and jump operations).

Register-register instructions use three 3-bit register addressing fields, two as source operand (*RS*, *RT*) and one as destination operand (*RD*). Besides, there is an operation field (*CO*) identifying the instruction format (*value 00* for register-register instructions), and an extended operation field (*COX*) identifying the specific register-register operation (*Figure 1-A*). There are five instructions: *ADD*, *SUB*, *AND*, *OR* and *SLT*, whose meaning is resumed below in *Table 1*.

Instructions with memory addressing have got a single operation field (*CO*), two register fields (*RS, RD*), and an 8-bit address field (*Figure 1-B*). The following instructions are available: *LW*, *SW* and *BEQ* (see *Table 1* below).

A)	CO		RS			RT			RD			COX				
	0	1	2	3	4	5	6	7	8	9	10	11	12	13	14	15
B)	CO		RS			RT			ADDRESS							

Figure 1. Instruction format: A-register-register, B-memory

Segmented CPUs have a higher efficiency, but two kinds of hazards are generated because of data dependency between consecutive instructions and jumping control. The first kind of hazards is solved by stalling the pipeline flow until the hazards disappear, and the second one is solved by assuming that the jump is not made.

Thus, the resulting block scheme is shown in *Figure 2*. All the blocks have been described in VHDL at the behaviour level. This description can be softly modified, as it is by testing different implementations of the elements defined at the behaviour level (for example to prove a structural definition).

The possible alterations are limited because the changes made cannot be shown in the graphic simulator without modifying and recompiling all the system (it has been developed in Borland Delphi 4 language [2]).

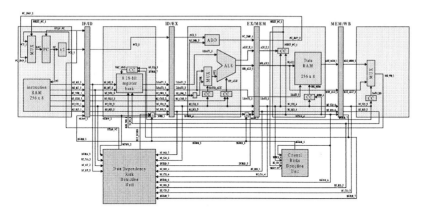

Figure 2. Pipeline block scheme

3.2   Assembler language description

In order to allow the programming of the machine, a simple assembler language has been designed. An assembler program is made with a sequence of lines, where each line can be one of the following possibilities:
–   A blank line, which is ignored.
–   A comment. This kind of line begins with two dashes (*"--"*) and fills the rest of line.
–   The definition of a variable (*DB* or *DW*, the identifier, and an optional default value).
–   The definition of a label (the label name followed by a colon).
–   An assembler instruction.

The system is not *case-sensitive* and all the instructions and directives are considered reserved words: *ADD, SUB, AND, OR, SLT, LW, SW, BEQ, DB, DW*. A valid name for a label or a variable can be any combination of characters made with letters, numbers and underscores, different from any reserved word, any other variable or label.

The set of valid instructions for the assembler is shown in *Table 1*.

Table 1. Set of assembler instructions

Instruction	Means	Assembler format	Performed operation
ADD	Addition	ADD R1 R2 R3	R1 ← R2 + R3
SUB	Subtraction	SUB R1 R2 R3	R1 ← R2 – R3
AND	Logic AND	AND R1 R2 R3	R1 ← R2 ∧ R3

Instruction	Means	Assembler format	Performed operation
OR	Logic OR	OR R1 R2 R3	R1 ← R2 ∨ R3
SLT	Set if Less Than	SLT R1 R2 R3	If (R2<R3) R1←1 else R1←0
LW	Load Word	LW R1 VAR [R2]	R1 ← Memory [VAR + R2]
		LW R1 [R2]	R1 ← Memory [R2]
SOFTWARE	Store Word	SW R1 VAR [R2]	Memory [VAR + R2] ← R1
		SW R1 [R2]	Memory [R2] ← R1
BEQ	Branch if Equal	BEQ R1 R2 VAR	If (R1=R2) PC = VAR

The eight registers of the machine are addressed by the instructions that use this type of addressing with codes *R0* to *R7*. Memory addressing is made through the use of variables. Variable definitions can be made at any place of the assembler program, using reserved words (*DB*, *DW*) to specify the variable size. Variable definitions optionally accept an initial value. Label definitions involve the declaration of destination points to perform jumps with the conditional branch instruction (*BEQ*).

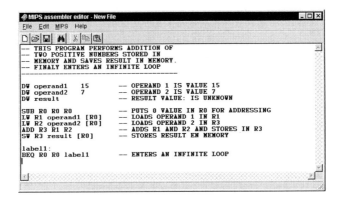

Figure 3. Assembler editor window showing a program to perform a simple addition

Programming is very easy as the system includes an editor with the most popular options in Windows applications (cut, paste, find, etc.). The Editor is the main window of the system and it provides access to the rest of the options through menu bars, tool bars and hot keys. *Figure 3* shows the Editor with an example of a simple program that performs the addition of two numbers.

3.3   Simulation graphic interface description

The graphic analyser allows a visual study of the behaviour of the machine when a certain group of instructions is presented. After writing the program using the assembler language, the following sequence of steps to analyse the behaviour must be taken:

1. Assemble the program.
2. Simulate assembled program with VSIM (VHDL simulator from Model Technology [3]). Here, we can decide if all signals must be simulated or not, how long the program is to run, etc.
3. Finish VSIM and graphically analyse the simulation.

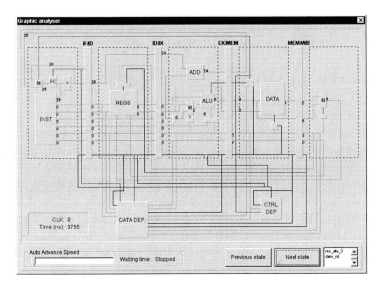

Figure 4. Graphic simulation window

When the assembled program has been simulated with VSIM, the result of this process can be repeated under our graphic analyser (*Figure 4*). Our tool allows advancing and going back in simulation time. The machine state is shown by different line tones and labels in the lines that represent the pipeline scheme:

– Binary control lines are shown in dark lines when they are enabled (logic 1), in darker lines when disabled (logic 0), or in softer lines if the state is unknown (if such signal has not been traced for the VSIM simulation).
– Data lines show their states by a label with their decimal value, or a symbol "?" when their value is unknown (if such data line has not been traced for the VSIM simulation).

Besides manually advancing and going back through time, the file can be simulated by *automatic advance* with a given speed (this is, the time spent between two changes of state). The bottom-right corner of the simulation screen contains a window with information about the names of the signals displayed at the moment.

VSIM simulation data are stored in a text file (*listfile*) that contains a list of signals and states. This file is interpreted by the graphic interface to show the machine states, and can be saved for later use. So it is possible to analyse stored files that contain information about previous real simulations made with VSIM.

VHDL description takes, as data to fill the simulated computer memory, two files, *ram_mips.dt1* and *ram_mips.dt2*, corresponding to the last successful compilation of a assembled program. These files can be consulted in the environment.

4.   CONCLUSIONS

In conclusion, our simulation system gives a lot of advantages and reaches all the proposed goals at the beginning of this paper. Visual environment allows us to understand how a pipeline works. It is possible to probe the behaviour of the system with different programs in a very quick and simple way because the system gives an assembler language to perform this task.

Besides, the fact of using a real VDHL environment to make a computer description extends the possibilities of the system, as it is a powerful tool to study and understand this language through the simulation and design of real machines. Using the graphic simulator, the results obtained from a real VHDL simulation are easily interpreted. This kind of graphical simulation environments is a frequently demanded tool for its use in computer architecture teaching.

However, it could be desirable that the simulation was not restricted to a short subset of the original MIPS machine. This limitation exists because the version of the VHDL development tool used for the system construction does not allow us to work with a large amount of information.

5.   FUTURE WORK

As limitations of the system are known, future work is centred on solving them, following three guidelines:
– Adapting the system to a modern VHDL environment that allows more possibilities for simulations and more complexity in the description of a segmented unit.
– Extending the machine to the original size with a wider instruction repertory, as much for the VHDL description as for assembler language.

– Generating an environment to define graphics extensions to the computer architecture without recompiling the system, in order to get the modifications made on the VHDL code accurately reflected on the graphic simulator.

REFERENCES

1. Ashenden P.J., (1996). *The Designers Guide to VHDL*, Morgan Kaufmann Publisher.
2. Díaz, P., Plaza, A., García, F.J., Álvarez, J.M., Pavón, N. (1999). Manual Avanzado de Delphi 4. Anaya Multimedia.
3. Model Technology Inc. (1991). *V-System PC, User's Manual.*
4. Patterson, D.A., Hennessy J.L. (1995). *Organización y Diseño de Computadores.* McGraw Hill.

An Authoring Environment for the SimulNet Educational Platform

L. Anido, M. Llamas, M.J. Fernández, J.C. Burguillo, C. Brandin, J. Santos and M. Caeiro

Área de Ingeniería Telemática. Depto. Tecnologías de las Comunicaciones
ETSI Telecomunicación, Universidad de Vigo
Campus Universitario s/n, E-36200 Vigo, SPAIN Ph: +34 986 812174, Fax: +986 812116
e-mail: lanido@ait.uvigo.es

Key words: Authoring Tools, courseware, labware, CBT, ODL.

Abstract: This paper presents a Web-based authoring tool to develop courses for the World Wide Web. This tool is included as one of the facilities of the SimulNet educational environment. SimulNet, originally conceived as a platform for virtual teaching laboratories, has enhanced their functionality to cover the whole learning process, from theoretical lectures to practical training through experimental work. In this paper we focus on the SimulNet courseware capabilities. First, we present a brief survey of current available authoring tools on the Web. Then, we present the main functionality of the SimulNet authoring environment, including the editor tool and the authoring tool for quizzes and learning paths structures.

1.   INTRODUCTION

Nowadays, the advances in the field of Information Technologies (IT) and Communication Networks along with an increasing bandwidth, allow us to access a huge amount of multimedia information. Distance Learning environments benefit from this and are continually adding new facilities in their courseware (animation, simulation, real time audio and video, 3-D

M. Ortega and J. Bravo (eds.), Computers and Education in the 21st Century, 65–78.
© 2000 *Kluwer Academic Publishers. Printed in the Netherlands.*

virtual reality, etc.) to improve their educational capabilities. One of the main challenging tasks for those organisations using ODL technology is how to build and organise all these materials.

The development of courseware becomes a real challenge for those instructors who want to take advantage of IT for their teaching but have little or no experience with hypermedia structuring. Even if they are familiar with word processors and other basic computer tools, they are not prone to learn new advanced development tools, just because they need their time to focus on teaching instead of developing teaching material.

Authoring tools appear as an attempt to overcome this problem. According to Sara McNeil [1]: "Authoring is the term which is applied to those computing languages and programs that allow users to develop and publish courses". This paper focuses on authoring tools for Internet-based courseware. We will show a tool whose aim is to facilitate the task of those instructors who want to develop their own Web-based courses but who are unfamiliar with computers and IT. This tool is embedded in the SimulNet educational environment [2] which was originally conceived as a platform to deliver labware and which, thanks to the incorporated authoring tools, allows the delivery of courseware as well.

The rest of this paper is organised as follows: the next section presents several currently available authoring tools on the web. Section 3 shows the main functionality of the SimulNet authoring system. Finally, some conclusions are presented.

2.   COURSEWARE AUTHORING TOOLS

Courseware is much more than several hypermedia documents linked with each other. Educational systems on the Web need to provide a pedagogical environment where students feel as if they were in a virtual classroom, whatever teaching pedagogical methodology is followed, assisted by their instructors as well. HTML editors and converters do not provide such educational framework and therefore, several course authoring tools have come out in the last years. What follows is a summary of some of them:

2.1   ToolBook

The set of tools, ToolBook II, developed by Asymetric [3], is one of the most widely used to develop Internet-based and CD-based courseware. They provide the following modules to develop courseware:
– *Assistant*. It provides a drag and drop graphical interface to develop interactive learning tools in a quick and easy way.

- *Instructor*. It allows the development of advanced courses, combining libraries of pre-programmed objects and page layouts, to provide an environment as powerful as a programming language can provide.
- *CBT Systems Edition*. It is oriented towards the development of training-based courseware.
- *Synergy*. It is used to facilitate exporting and the process of contents development.
- *CMS Plus 6.0 (Course Management System)*. It manages LAN-based courses and allows them to be exported to an Internet-based environment. This part of the system is the one which is responsible for course delivery, user management, students tracking, etc.

2.2 Web Course in a box

Its development was started by the Virginia Commonwealth University [4], USA, and now its commercial development is supported by madDuck Technologies [5]. It has a colourful, attractive interface with an announcement symbol that pops up when there is an important announcement, class information, a scheduling component, learning links and online help. It has an e-mail component, both synchronous and asynchronous discussion forums, a whiteboard, team grouping and it allows file sharing. It also has assessment components that allow instructors to both create and administer a variety of assessment items and to perform the students tracking. It has a student sign-in and sign-out section to help the instructor monitor the students' involvement, and a student portfolio and a profile section as well.

This program has a tutor section where students can ask and receive feedback on questions, problems and assignments. It also records information in archives for later use, if needed. The whiteboard has a variety of features built into it, such as ready-made graphing, formulas and the like. To assist in training on using the system, there is a presentation with streaming audio and PowerPoint-like slides. It presents a lot of useful information and discusses the features of the program.

The Learning Link feature is a section with links to instructor-noted important data. These could be links to several Web sites, or links to certain items in the syllabus. The Web Course in a Box also has five different templates from which instructors can select in order to create their lessons: full screen without a border; half screen; list with and list without graphics. It allows extremely easy Web-based instruction creation, custom icon selection and easy font substitution.

2.3   TopClass

Top Class [6] was created by WBT Systems. Its functionality can be easily classified according to the different Top Class modules:

– *Top Class Creator*. It simplifies the creation of the course, the edition of contents, the creation of several types of questions (there are more than 20 different types of questions available). Furthermore, this module permits different points of view about the same topic, different ways to explain the same concept. Thus, if the system detects that a student does not understand a given concept it offers an alternative explanation instead of repeating the previous explanation.
– *Top Class Converter*. It converts Microsoft Office documents, HTML and RTF to Top Class format. Thus, external documents can be easily included in Top Class courses.
– *Top Class Assistant*. This module allows the edition of Top Class documents using commercial tools by Microsoft such as PowerPoint or Word. In this way, apart from being tools familiar to most users, TopClass allows an easy integration of multimedia such as video and animations when using these commercial tools.
– *Top Class Analyser*. This module is responsible for monitoring the use of the system. From the data generated by the students' traces it reports about the most frequently used features and the level of efficiency of the learning process.

In addition to this, WBT systems provides a three-day course for those who are interested in learning how to use this system. The first day is devoted to introducing the user to the Top Class basic functionality and course structure. How to develop learning contents using available commercial tools, like those by Microsoft, is taught on the second day. Finally, on the last day users learn concepts related to security and administrative tasks.

2.4   Learning Space

Learning Space [7], developed by Lotus, is targeted both at academic institutions and industries. Apart from assisting instructors in the creation of the educational contents, it allows real-time lectures to be stored for later supervision. The system is divided in different modules:

– *The Media Centre* allows instructors to develop the course contents.
– *The Assessment Manager* allows instructors to monitor the students' progress. It also allows the edition of tests, questionnaires and exams which are delivered to the Scheduler to be included in the students' agendas.

- *The Scheduler* provides every facility required to supply students with a schedule to know what the objectives of every module are, when they have to finish them and which questionnaires, tests and exams must be fulfilled.
- *The Course Room* permits the creation and management of different working groups.
- *The Learning Space Central.* It allows the administrations of the course on the whole.
- *The Data Bean Learning Service* provides virtual lectures via teleconference including real-time graphics, audio and video according to the ITU standard H.323. In this way it provides compatibility with collaborative tools like NetMeeting by Microsoft.

2.5   WebCT

WebCT [8] was developed at the University of British Columbia. It is designed to create Web-based courses through the Internet without any knowledge about the underlying technology.

The WebCT server is based on a standard WWW server with some added functionality to develop learning contents. Designers of WebCT courses are allowed to use any of the following features:
- WebCT provides designers with the possibility to establish the structure for this particular course, linear or tree structure. The students' traces will be stored and the learning session can be resumed at any time.
- Glossary. Any word or concept can be included in the WebCT glossary with additional comments from instructors.
- External references in any page related to the existing learning contents.
- Index Generation. Those words selected by the course designer will appear in the course index automatically.
- Quizzes. Instructors are allowed to include multiple-choice tests in the course. They are responsible for providing the correct answer as well as the amount of time the student will be given to complete the test.

The course designer is also responsible for including different communication tools in the course. Some tools available are e-mail, chat and forums. Students may also be allowed to include private notes in the course pages.

Developers only need to know how to use a WWW browser. It provides automatic creation of every compulsory feature in a Web-based course. Its importance is accepted among the international scientific community.

These systems are only an example of what we can find in the field of Web-based education authoring tools. From this concise survey we want to point out the importance of importing external documents to new courses as well as the creation of electronic question papers and monitoring facilities. These features have been borne in mind and are included in our authoring tool.

3.   THE SIMULNET COURSEWARE AUTHORING ENVIRONMENT

3.1   A brief overview of SimulNet

SimulNet is a distributed, remote access Computer Based Training system. Unlike other teleteaching systems whose aim is to achieve a virtual classroom, SimulNet provides a virtual laboratory to put theoretical knowledge into practice. The use of SimulNet as a platform for the delivery of labware was its primarily purpose in its first phases. This is achieved by delivering software (Java applets) through the Internet which can be run on any computer. These distributed applications are simulators of those tools which can be found in a conventional laboratory. The system also provides an on-line communication channel between students and teachers to follow the students' traces in their interaction with the simulator and to assist students. These features allow us to achieve a real collaborative atmosphere overcoming the drawbacks caused by the geographical separation between teachers and students and increasing the advantages of telelearning and teleteaching.

We should not forget the first phases in the learning process: the theoretical lectures. In order to carry out the full learning process we need to provide our students with a suitable tool to follow Web-based courses. In addition to this, instructors should be supplied with the corresponding Web-based authoring tool to develop these courses. We include both tools in our system as two new business applets which can be used by teachers to develop courses, and by students to follow them. In order to improve the interactivity between the course engine and the students, we implemented a forward navigation mechanism that downloads, in the background, the document the student is likely to request next. Therefore, the network use is reduced during the course navigation process.

3.2   The SimulNet Courseware Tool

The SimulNet courseware tool provides two different course access modes: free access (everyone is allowed to access the course contents) and restricted access (the user must be properly identified using a pair username/password). The instructor who develops the course is responsible for defining its access mode. Students' performance in those courses whose access mode is defined as restricted can be tracked by the SimulNet courseware. Furthermore, for this type of courses it is possible to define access restrictions between different parts and, thus, to design predefined learning paths. On the contrary, if the course access mode is defined as free, users would access the course contents with no limitation.

Once a student selects one of the courses he/she is allowed to access to, he/she is shown the main page of the course and the course index where the whole course structure is displayed. Course contents are organised in a tree-like structure. This structure remains on the left side of the window (see figure 1). Therefore, the students are continually shown a perspective of the whole course and where they are at that particular moment. This structure also provides all the information needed to know which parts of the course can be accessed and which cannot. Those parts of the tree which contain additional parts (i.e. the tree branches) can be expanded to show their contents (i.e. tree leaves or more tree branches); see figure 1.

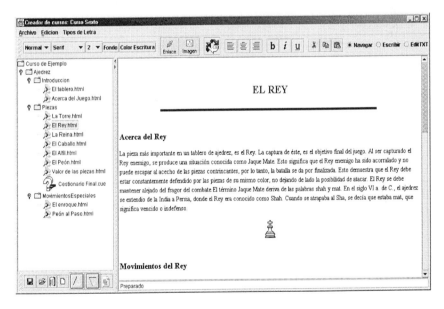

Figure 1. The SimulNet Courses Tool

Those parts which can be accessed by a particular student depend on the concrete access definition among the different parts of the course. This access philosophy is defined by the instructor who created the course. Accessibility is graphically shown in the index (left part of figure 1):

- Those pages which can be accessed will be marked with the sign:

- The ones which cannot be accessed yet will be marked with:

- Those pages already visited will be marked with the sign:

- Quizzes will be marked with the sign:

- The current page title is displayed with a different background colour:

El Rey.html

There are three different restriction modes to access the contents of those restricted access courses:

– *Suggested learning path.* There exists a recommended learning path to follow. Nevertheless, students are allowed to access the whole course contents with no limitation and in the order they consider the best. The situation from figure 1 can be considered as an example of this mode.

– *Compulsory learning path.* Students have to follow a predefined learning path which would have been designed by the instructor who developed the course. Once a page is accessed it could be accessed again later. However, in order to be able to access a new page, it is necessary to access all those pages which have been listed before in the compulsory learning path and successfully complete every quiz found in the path. Figure 2 shows an example of this situation:

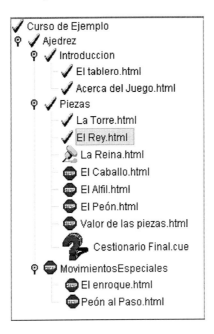

Figure 2. Compulsory learning path

— *Section-based compulsory learning path.* In some way it is in the middle of the two previous learning paths. The restrictions are not defined on a page basis but on a section basis. Before being allowed to access the next section, students need to visit every page of the current section and successfully complete the quizzes that may have been included. Figure 3 shows an example of this mode.

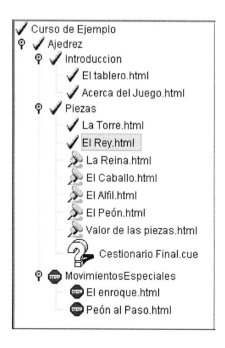

Figure 3. Section-based compulsory learning path

3.3   The SimulNet Authoring Tool

The system manager and those instructors with the appropriate permission can develop their own Web-based courses using the SimulNet authoring tool. They only need to know how to use a Web-browser. This was our main goal in the design phase: to keep the use of the tool as easy as possible with no further knowledge of computers needed. From the client point of view there is no need to install additional software as the SimulNet authoring tool will be sent client-side in the form of a Java applet to be run on any Java-enabled browser.

Thanks to the tree-like structure our system is based on, instructors are able to define courses with a high level of flexibility. Instructors are provided with a tool to define the particular structure for their courses defining as many contents containers and course pages and quizzes as desired.

In addition to course contents and structure, instructors can define the course access as free or restricted. In the latter, they are also able to choose between the three different restriction modes: advised learning path, compulsory learning path and section-based compulsory learning path.

Instructors can add, modify or delete contents pages from any course structure they are responsible for. For every page, they have to define: title, access restrictions for this page and the page contents themselves. The contents authoring tool is designed as a simple WYSIWYG ("What you see is what you get") editor; see figure 4. Instructors will edit the page contents in the way that they will be displayed to students. The edition component includes the common features for this type of tools: Cut, copy and paste text and other contents, font size and type, colour for the main text and links, image managing, links to different parts of the page or to external resources, etc.

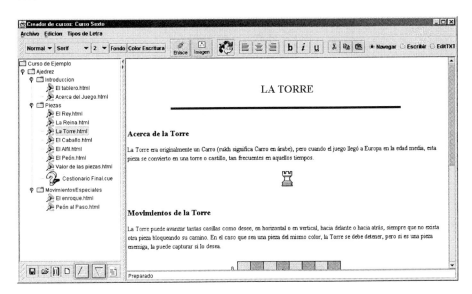

Figure 4. Contents Authoring Tool

There exists a special authoring tool for quizzes, see figure 5. This tool enables the inclusion of different type of quizzes in any course section or module. Quizzes are automatically checked by the courseware at the students' side. Once the student finishes the whole quiz or the time determined for its completion expires, the system collects the entered answers and checks for its correctness, showing the results to the student immediately. In addition, the student profile is updated to reflect the mark obtained in the quiz. Thus, instructors will be able to follow the students' performance and the system will allow the student to access any course section or page which this question was a prerequisite for.

Figure 5. Quizzes authoring tool

We have defined three different types of questions; see figure 6:

1. One-choice questions. In this type of questions there is only one correct answer among the whole set of possibilities offered by the instructor. Every time the question is shown to a student the correct answer and the particular set of wrong options, which are to be shown, are selected from a pool in a random basis.

2. Multiple-choice question. There are several options, from those shown to the student, that can be considered correct. For every question, the instructor defines a set of correct answers, a set of incorrect answers, and the ratio right/wrong answers to be shown to the students. The system will randomly select from both pools the number of the answer according to the previously defined ratio.

3. Short-answer question. Students are requested to introduce a short answer to a given question. The system will parse their answer to check whether it is correct or not according to a set of possible answers given by the instructor.

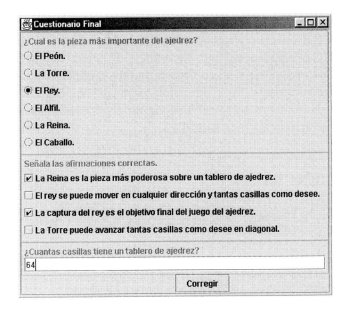

Figure 6. The three different types of questions

The instructor responsible for a given course is able to follow the students' performance through their traces and quizzes marks. Every student's traces are stored at server side in order to be delivered to those instructors who may request them (and are allowed to access them). As an additional feature we also provide the possibility to transfer all the contents of a particular course to CD-ROM in order to be followed in a standalone way. Collaborative learning is provided through the SimulNet communication facilities [2].

4. CONCLUSIONS

We have presented an authoring environment to facilitate the task of those who want to develop educational contents available on the Web. Its use is easy enough for those who are unfamiliar with the Internet and computers. We also include a course viewer to follow these courses using any conventional Internet browser since there is no need to install additional client-side software.

The educational framework for the presented courseware and authoring tool is provided by the SimulNet educational environment, which provides every functionality necessary to allow collaborative learning and students' tracking. SimulNet was originally conceived as a simulation-based teaching laboratory platform. A course viewer and authoring tool was develop as simply other simulators and thus, we have enhanced the SimulNet capabilities also covering Web-based theoretical lectures.

We are concerned about the importance of course authoring tools for those who are unfamiliar with computers and the Internet. We are constantly collecting requirements from our "non-technical" colleagues in order to improve our tool. Instructors need to concentrate on educational content, not on how to implement them technically.

REFERENCES

1. Sara McNeil, "A Practitioner-Validated List of Competencies Needed for Courseware Authoring", Proc. of ED-MEDIA and ED-TELECOM ' 96, Boston, Mass, USA, June, 1996.
2. M. Llamas, L. Anido and M.J. Fernández, "Student Participation and First Results from SimulNet, a Distance Access Training Laboratory," Proc. of Teleteaching'98. XV IFIP World Computer Congress, vol 2, Vienna (Austria) and Budapest (Hungary), August, 31st to September, 4th, 1998, pps 615-626.
3. Asymetric page at: http://www.asymetric.com
4. Virginia Commonwealth University page at: http://www.vcu.edu
5. Madduck page at: http://www.madduck.com
6. Top Class homepage. http://www.wbtsystems.com/soluctions/products.html
7. Learning Space homepage. http://www.lotus.com/products/learningspace.nsf/
8. WebCT homepage. http://homebrew1.cs.ubc.ca/webct

BabelWin: An environment for learning and monitoring reading and writing skills.

Laura Aranda[1]; Santiago Torres[2]; Mónica Trella[1]; Ricardo Conejo[1]
[1]*Departamento de Lenguajes y Ciencias de la Computación*
[2]*Departamento de Psicología*
Universidad de Málaga
E-mail:[1] {aranda,trella}@iaia.lcc.uma.es,[2] monreal@uma.es

Key words: Interactive learning environment. Computer Assisted Instruction.

Abstract: In this paper we describe the structure and behaviour of an interactive learning environment for reading and writing exercises. This environment lets the teachers configure and personalize the exercises from a set of templates. It also lets them analyse the pupils' results and delivers reports, substantially improving tracking the learning process. To develop this environment, the cognitive processes that form part of reading and writing skills have been taken into account, as well as other aspects such as easy user interfaces, graphical presentation, and visual reinforcement.

1.   INTRODUCTION

Computers have been widely used in tutorial environments. The development of Computer Assisted Instruction (CAI) programs is a complex task because it requires the contribution of different expert knowledge from the fields of science of education, psychology, computer science and engineering, and from the domain of knowledge that is being taught. Within the computer and engineering science domain, several techniques and systems have been developed in areas such as Artificial Intelligence, Multimedia, Hypermedia, and Communications which have been applied to CAI.

M. Ortega and J. Bravo (eds.), Computers and Education in the 21st Century, 79–91.

Within the Artificial Intelligence approach, CAI systems have been transformed into Intelligent Computer Assisted Instruction (ICAI) systems. Several proposals have been made since this branch emerged at the end of the 1970s. Over time, different systems have been constructed based upon different techniques, from the simple IF-THEN rules that guided instruction in GUIDON [4] to the current Intelligence Tutorial Systems (ITS) that deal not only with domain knowledge, but also with a pupil model including his/her knowledge, abilities, and behaviour. These models allow the personalization of instruction and tutorial strategies and the adaptation of the system's behaviour to each pupil in the most suitable way [5].

Regarding the advances in multimedia and hypermedia, we have to mention the hypertext techniques that became very popular with Apple's program Hypercard [2] that lets the user navigate among a linked set of texts by selecting some textual tags. Later on, hypermedia techniques appeared. These combined the advantages of multimedia and hypertext, letting the user navigate among linked pages that include pictures, sound tracks, and videos. These techniques were not initially developed for tutorial purposes, but they were very quickly incorporated into CAI programs. Currently, they are commonly known as Interactive Multimedia and Hypermedia Learning Environments [1]. This branch is also drawing closer to ICAI and ITS programs, including some user model components and allowing new adaptive capabilities [3].

Reading is one of the most powerful cognitive tools because the person must apply all his/her linguistic and encyclopedic knowledge to access new knowledge in an autonomous way. For example, 50% of a postgraduate's passive vocabulary has been acquired through reading. It is also important because it assumes access to the third of the great learnings that a human being must undertake, mobility being the first, and oral expression the second. The acquisition of reading and writing skills is closely linked to the basic architecture of the human cognitive system that includes attention, perception, and memory structures, along with the complex process involved in language and thinking [8].

BabelWin is an interactive learning environment for reading and writing activities that is based upon the expertize of several years of work of professional teachers in the field of reading and writing. Multimedia CAI programs are very useful in the classroom to introduce new learning skills, systematize and reinforce them, etc. They offer the user a great number of stimuli, a high degree of motivation, along with very powerful tools for the pupil's cognitive development.

The use of computers in this field brings an added value to instruction via other classical techniques [9]. From the pupil's point of view the exercises are designed to be used dynamically and interactively. Some of them simply could not be taken using paper and pencil because they require an immediate reaction from the teacher. In all other cases the system brings a set of stimuli and reinforcements that improve learning performance. From the teacher's point of view the system yields complete and detailed information about the performance of each exercise that contributes to a better analysis of the results and their causes, and allows better monitoring of the pupil's progress [10].

2. GENERAL DESCRIPTION OF THE SYSTEM

Figure 1 shows a general view of the system architecture. It has an exercise template catalogue, a database with information about pupils, teachers, and tutorial sessions, and two clearly separate interfaces, one for the teachers and another for the pupils:

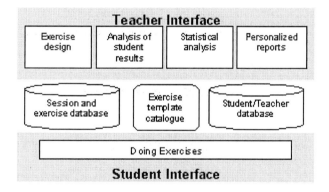

Figure 1. General view of the system

- The teacher module is where the tutorial sessions are generated and where the results of the tests are analysed. This module also allows the teacher to consult the statistics and make personalized reports for each pupil. Using this module a superuser can also manage the teacher and pupil databases.
- The pupil module is used by the pupils to do the exercises. Basically, it is a window where the exercise to be done appears along with some drawings to stimulate the pupil to achieve better performances. It is possible to access an option dialogue box to control and configure the session on the fly, just in case the teacher would like to modify something while the session is going on.

Figure 2 shows an overall view of system use. Each teacher may be in charge of some pupils and he/she can design a set of exercises for each one.

The pupils perform these exercises by themselves, or occasionally with the teacher's supervision. Once they finish, the teacher analyses the results obtained by each of his/her pupils in the last session and evaluates the pupil's skills and where the main problems lie. The system does not evaluate the pupil by itself, but offers a simple statistical module where the teacher can see the result of each of the exercises and a comparison with the results obtained by other pupils that have used the system. By analysing this information and knowing the type and features of the exercises, the teacher can design a new session of personalized exercises for the pupil.

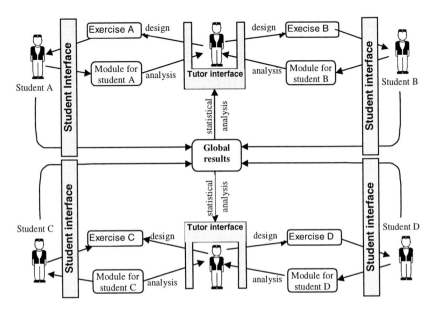

Figure 2. Operation cycle

The system also offers an anonymous function mode, both for the teachers and for the pupils. In this case, the system turns into an autonomous tool that can be used for self-learning, the teacher and pupil are the same person, and of course, there is no supervision of the learning process except for succeeding or failing the exercises. In order not to interfere with the regular sessions, the anonymous pupil's results are not saved to the database, nor is any other information saved regarding execution. To guarantee the privacy of the data the anonymous teacher cannot access the pupil's record, nor the statistics. He/she can only configure and execute his/her sessions.

The following sections give a detailed description of the features of each module.

3. EXERCISE TEMPLATE CATALOGUE

There is a set of 18 templates of different and independent exercises that can contribute to the learning of mechanical and comprehensive reading, to the acquisition of functional spelling, and to the development of fundamental metalinguistic abilities in order to process written information. Among these are phonetic, syllabic, and lexical segmentation, iconic memory, short-term memory, both semantic and episodic, the establishment and mastering of syntactical and semantic linguistic schema, etc.

From a previously written text, BabelWin can generate exercises that range from the typing of a single letter or a sequence of letters to improve keyboard skills, in the same way as classical typewriting learning programmes, to the classification of a large amount of vocabulary in different semantic fields, or the rearrangement of a complex text that involves a test of semantic and episodic memory and the mastering of the language's syntax and semantics.

BabelWin basically deals with the response rate, which is one of the classical parameters applied in the research of basic and complex cognitive processes. The eighteen exercise templates cover the following levels or modules:

1. Alphanumeric sign recognition
2. Recall of dynamically hidden signs
3. Recall of segments (words or strings separated with blank characters)
4. Recall of phrases (groups of words separated by a dot)
5. Recovering vowels
6. Recovering consonants
7. Recovering a totally hidden text, especially designed for dictation
8. Recovering of hidden text segments (with or without guiding hints)
9. Phonemic segmentation
10. Syllabic segmentation
11. Lexical segmentation (word division within a context)
12. Review and replacement of punctuation signs
13. Replacement of difficult orthographic signs in a text (i.e., v and b in Spanish)
14. The same but in lists of words
15. Rearrangement of signs (letters in a word)
16. Rearrangement of words in a line
17. Rearrangement of lines in a text
18. Recombination of items by semantic fields

These exercises are useful to test the more important metalinguistic aspects that mark a proficient reader. They take into account recent research in written and spoken language perception, undertaken in the framework of cognitive psychology for information processing. Some of the metalinguistic tasks that can be developed and/or improved by using BabelWin are the following:

a) *Word segmentation*: It is still not well known how the brain processes continuous spoken information in order to extract the different words that make up a valid sentence in a language, or in a speech act. The research currently available is not conclusive on this point (see [11], for a review). It is known that this learning takes place very early, that it takes place earlier than phonemic segmentation, and may even be prior to syllabic or phonological group segmentation. BabelWin contributes to the development of this process both in normal people and those with perceptual impairment (e.g., pupils with hearing deficiencies).

b) *Phonological segmentation*: This is the last metalinguistic process developed and is not achieved without explicit learning. Illiterate people and some types of dyslexic people never undergo this process [7]. In alphabetic languages like Spanish, a very useful program is one that generates exercises in order to strengthen the correspondence between the phoneme and the grapheme.

c) *Rearrangement of words*: The flexibility of language to combine words while maintaining the sense of sentences says a lot about personal cognitive styles. Its use contributes to the development of creativity and intelligence. The rearrangement of words which is so common in spoken language is a strong argument in favour of independence in word perception.

d) *Rearrangement of prepositions*: This process has a strong relation with the semantic development of language. BabelWin includes exercises to rearrange a sentence or a simple tale where it is necessary to deal with several hypotheses to reorganise the text. It is not surprising that these types of exercises are much more difficult than the rearrangement of words in a sentence, because they force the pupil to make inferences. Fundamentally, what marks a good reader is linguistic awareness, his/her world view, the processes of categorization, and even his/her beliefs, attitudes, and values.

Besides training the complex linguistic processes described above, each of the exercises is associated with the following basic psycholinguistic processes that take place during reading. Table 1 shows these associations:

Tabla 2. Babelwin exercises and psycholinguistic processes that take place during reading

Processes	1	2	3	4	5	6	7	8	9	10	11	12	13	14	15	16	17	18
Visual Field	√	√	√															√
Iconic memory		√	√	√	√	√	√									√		√
Eye fixation	√	√																√
Short-term memory	√	√																
Visual analysis				√	√	√	√	√				√		√				
Letter recognition														√	√			
Word recognition								√						√		√		
Word order (syntax)															√	√	√	
Temporal sequences															√	√	√	
Causal sequences															√	√	√	
Functional words												√	√	√				
Cloze	√	√	√	√	√		√					√	√	√	√			√
Semantics											√	√	√		√	√	√	
Phonetic segmentation	√		√		√							√	√	√				
Word segmentation								√	√	√	√		√	√		√		
Sentence segmentation									√	√	√	√			√	√	√	

For instance in exercise number 7, which is the *"Recovering of hidden text"*, the psycholinguistic processes that take place are: *"Iconic memory"*, *"Short-term memory"*, and *"Visual analysis"*.

The results obtained by the pupil in each exercise are collected by the system's statistic module according to these psycholinguistic processes. These results are analyzed by the teacher who determines the causes of the pupil's success or failure and designs the next session which includes the most suitable exercises.

4. TEACHER MODEL

The teacher and pupil session data are managed from this part of the application and the statistical and reports are created.

Exercise configuration and session management is done in an easy and intuitive way, offering several options that facilitate the educator's task. Exercises can be done singly or grouped together in a session. Also, there are two alternatives to configure a session: selecting the exercises directly or using classification by area of knowledge offered by the system: Basic Processes, Segmentation, Spelling, Morphosyntax, or Semantics.

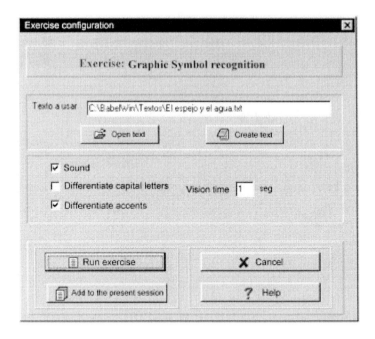

Figure 3. Exercise configuration

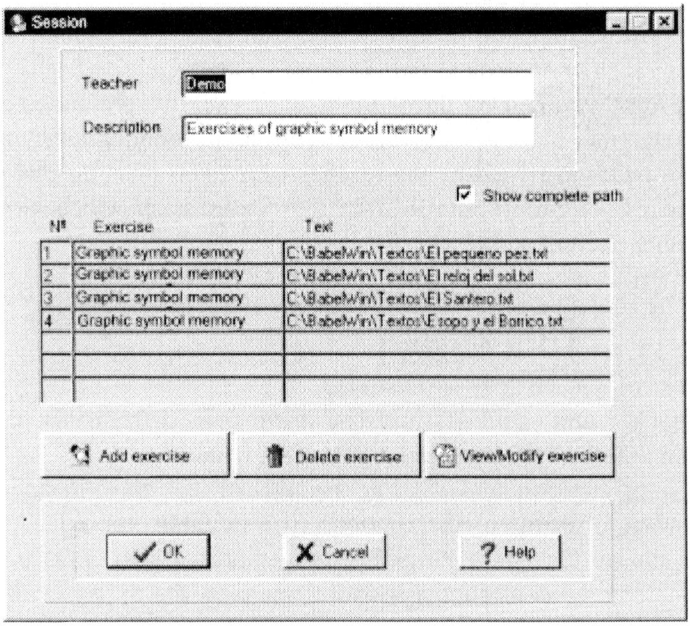

Figure 4. Session configuration

When we talk about exercises we are referring to their complete configuration. This includes two essential data: the type of exercise and the text to work on. Furthermore, the run time environment can be configured to adapt it to the pupil. In order to do this, some options can be chosen:
– The time left for the original text to be on the screen can be specified,
– Whether there will be sounds or not,
– Whether the system will differentiate upper or lower case,
– Whether the system will allow accented vowels or not (in Spanish),
– Etc.

A simple example of an exercise configuration on *Graphic Symbol recognition* can be observed in Figure 3, and a complete session is shown in Figure 4.[1]

The system stores the information about pupils, teachers, and sessions. Teacher and pupil data are introduced by filling forms that allow easy navigation through the existing cards. Each teacher can only access his/her pupils' data to avoid possible interference between teachers. Session data are introduced automatically during run time and are used to make statistics and reports.

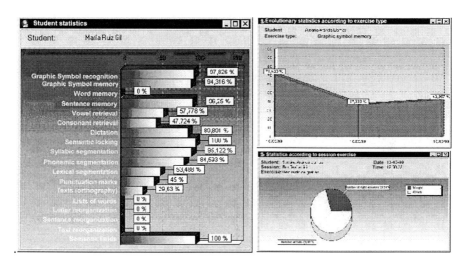

Figure 5. Examples of Statistics

---

[1] All texts, results, and graphical dialogues of the system were originally in Spanish. They have been manually translated in this paper to improve its comprehension.

BabelWin offers the possibility of generating statistics with graphics in different forms (bars, pie or evolution) with the requested information (Figure 5). This information can be very useful to manage pupil evolution and to establish new exercises. Four types of statistics exist, with different criteria: by type of exercise, by exercise session, by pupil, and by the way a given type of exercise develops.

In the same way, reports can be generated with the "Quick Reports" tool, that allows saving to files, printing, formatting the documents, etc. Two sorts of reports can be generated: ones about a pupil, or ones about every exercise type for each pupil. Figure 6 shows an example report of the latter.

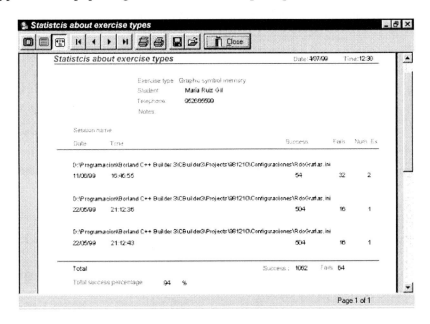

Figure 6. Report example

5.   PUPIL MODULE

The screen in this module is similar to the one in the Teacher Module except for some elements that can distract the pupil and that have been eliminated to avoid loss of concentration on the exercise. A new element that does not appear in the Teacher Module has been added: *the reinforcements*. These elements help to stimulate the pupil to get good results. In any case, if it is considered that the reinforcements might distract the pupil and are not useful they can be hidden. Three main reinforcements exist:

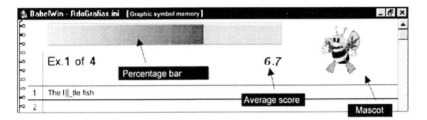

Figure 7. Reinforcement

- The bar which indicates the success percentage. This is a horizontal bar where the green band grows or shrinks depending on the success percentage that the pupil has at each moment.
- The average mark value. This mark is evaluated depending on the pupil's number of right and wrong answers.
- The mascot "Babelia". This is the most visually attractive element. It is in motion while an exercise is being done. Babelia's expression changes depending on whether the results are good or bad.

Different useful options can be accessed using the mouse right button during a session. The *Control Bar* is shown in Figure 8. It includes the most frequently used functions: session navigation, show the correct text (hints), go to a specific exercise, etc.

Figure 8. Control bar

Several work environments exist depending on the exercise type. Each time one is finished information about the session name, pupil, date and finish time, and number of right and wrong answers is stored in the database. Figure 9 shows some examples.

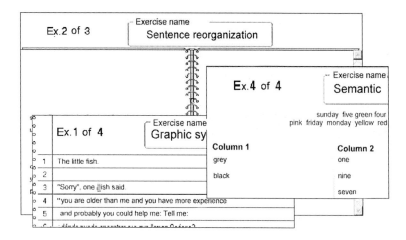

Figure 9. Example of working environment

After finishing an exercise a screen appears with the results obtained by the pupil and a brief message about the development of his/her work. Also, a musical theme plays according to the mark obtained.

6.   CONCLUSIONS.

BabelWin is a multimedia environment for doing reading and writing exercises and tracking them, with a solid educational base. Aspects such as ease of handling, presentation, and audio and visual reinforcement have been taken into account and carefully developed. Educator and computer expert criteria have been unified to obtain better results.

One of the future lines of development of this work could be adapting the system to children with motor deficiencies (using push-buttons with panning techniques) and sensorial deficiencies (blind and deaf, among others).

As yet, the possible advantages of the software for learning foreign languages have not been analysed. English, for example, is a language in which spelling barely transparent and that necessitates visual recognition as a step prior to its correct articulation. This implies paying greater attention to the written word which is an aspect that could be facilitated via this program's teaching exercises. Research could be carried out to confirm this hypothesis with the tool in its current state of development.

Another line of work which remains open is the development of an intelligent agent that substitutes or complements the work of the teacher in the system. This would transform the system into an Intelligent Tutoring system, thus strengthening its features as a self-learning environment. The current system has all the elements needed to build a pupil model based on basic cognitive processes. Using this information the system could make a diagnostic of the results obtained in each session and automatically configure new exercise sessions using these conclusions and the a priori information about the pertinence of the tests. But before systematizing the teacher's task it is necessary to acquire experience in the use of the program and calibrate the degree of participation of each of the basic cognitive processes in the tests. These experiments should be carried out with groups of pupils that are learning to read and with groups of pupils with experience in reading. The results would give valuable hints regarding improving the program for optimizing the processes of teaching reading and writing.

REFERENCES:

1. Educational Multimedia and Hypermedia, *Proceedings of Ed-Media 94, the World Conference on Educational Multimedia and Hypermedia,* Vancouver (Canada). Association for the advancement of Computing in Education (Charlottesville, Virginia). (1994)
2. *HyperCard User's Guide.* Apple Computer Inc. Cupertino, California (1987)
3. Brusilovsky, P.: Method and techniques of Adaptive Hypermedia. In Brusilovsky, Kobsa, Vassileva (eds.) *Adaptive Hypertext and Hypermedia.* Kluwer Academic Publishers. Dordrecht, Netherlands (1998) 1-44.
4. Clancey, W.J. Knowledge-based tutoring: the GUIDON program. The MIT Press. Cambrige (1987).
5. Goodyear, P. Teaching Knowledge and Intelligent Tutoring. Ablex Publishing Corporation. Norwood, New Jersey (1990)
6. Harley, (1997) Psychology of language: from data to theory. Psychology Press Publishers, Taylor & Francis group, UK, Hove
7. Morais, Bertelson & Alegría, (1986) Literacy training and speech segmentation. *Cognition, 24,* 45-64.
8. Torres, S. & Ortega, J.L.(1993) BABEL (Batería para Aprendizaje Básico de Estimulación Lectora). Implicaciones cognitivas de un programa informático para entrenamiento en el proceso lector.
9. Torres, S. & Rodríguez, J.M. (1990), Fundamentos teóricos y documentación sobre Babel para MS-DOS.
10. Torres, S., Rodríguez, J.M., Moreno, J. & Conejo, R. (1997), BABEL (versión para Windows). Batería para aprendizajes básicos de estimulación lectora. En Actas de EDUTEC'97.
11. Vega & Cuetos, (1999). Psicolingüística del español. Madrid: Trotta (1999).

An Internet Distance-Learning Operating Model

Jesús G. Boticario, Elena Gaudioso[1]
Departamento de Inteligencia Artificial, Universidad Nacional de Educación a Distancia
Avenida Senda del Rey, 9, 28040 Madrid. Tel. 91 398 71 97
[1] *PhD grant from UNED*
E-mail: {jgb, elena}@dia.uned.es

Key words: Virtual University, Active and personalized distance learning, Interactive learning-apprentice systems.

Abstract: Distance learning is characterized by the systematic use of technical means and resources. Learning in this kind of teaching is conditioned by isolated study and a variety of information needs. In order to exploit the Internet to satisfy some of these needs, this work presents the main aspects of a higher education distance-learning operating model in this medium supported by the use of a Web interactive system that aims to match different user/student requirements (information, contact, administration).

1. INTRODUCTION

Given the difficulties encountered in distance learning (DL), new educational models should be tested in students' interests. Furthermore, any theory about learning stresses the quality of the existing communication between lecturer and student as it is a decisive factor in the process. Therefore, since the very nature of this kind of teaching will ultimately impose it, DL must take advantage of the media which, like the Internet network, particularly enrich the sources of information and the quality of communication with students.

The intensive use of telematic media available on the Internet can considerably enhance higher education distance learning, teaching and research, and speed up teaching administration and administrative

93

procedures, as the experience of numerous educational centres illustrates: Open University, http://www.open.ac.uk; University of Wisconsin-Extension, http://www.uwex.edu; Penn State University, http://www.cde.psu.edu; Oberta de Cataluña, http://www.oc.es. Firstly, a clear improvement is observed thanks to the incorporation of services which, like notice boards or news, mailing lists and electronic mail, file servers and Web pages, significantly increase direct communication possibilities in different formats among all the protagonists, irrespective of geographical or time factors. Hence, communications are no longer essentially radial (lecturer-students, lecturer-tutor-students, etc.), with the restrictions of the students/lecturer ratio. It is obvious that one of the most valuable sources of information for any student is the possibility of contacting other fellow students and being able to access complementary sources of information quickly. Secondly, telematic media speed up enrolment, grading and the management of academic records. Thus, from the beginning of the course, the actual number of students enrolled is known, the lecturers can consult their student record and the distributed grading processes are much faster.

Bearing in mind these considerations, a specific model is proposed that meets the needs of the *Universidad Nacional de Educación a Distancia (UNED)*. This university is characterized by a variety of students (professionals with family ties, handicapped people, teachers requiring further training, young people who have finished vocational training courses or secondary education). Another characteristic of the university is its dispersion of existing sources of information (news, mailing lists, different kinds of pages: institutional, subjects, most frequently asked questions, lecturers, exercises, distance-assessment tests...). The model proposed, which we have called PERSONAL-DE, is based on the specific organisation of telematic services (Boticario, 1997a), teaching material adapted to the medium (Boticario, 1997b) and the construction of an interactive system that assists and acts as a guide for users as they access the services offered on the Web. The specific information and communication needs of each student are thereby satisfied (Boticario and Gaudioso, 1999).

The interactive system of assisted teaching that is being used for the personalization of learning subject exercises at the Computer Science School (CSS) and the third year courses at UNED's Artificial Intelligence Department, will be especially advantageous when this medium becomes widely used as the main way of contact between the different agents participating in the process (Head Office lecturers, tutor-lecturers and students).

2.   MODEL OBJECTIVES

The primary teaching objective of the DL model proposed is to focus teaching on the student's performance. The aim is thus to foment the student's autonomy using the basic Internet services (*news*, mailing lists, electronic mail, file servers, Web pages). The precise courses of action are as follows:
- To motivate students' learning.
- To lighten the administrative load.
- To offer a wider range of alternative teaching organisation techniques to foment student autonomy.
- To present the material following the guidelines that encourage *significant and active learning*.
- To increase the flow of information between all the agents participating in the process.
- To focus the student's attention to the most relevant personalized information at each stage of the process, without having to complete complicated forms to discover their needs.

This proposal is based on a set of basic and different points: a psycho-pedagogical teaching-learning model, specific teaching organisation in the Internet, didactic material suitable for this medium, basic accessibility criteria, Web page design utility and efficiency, and an interactive *learning-apprentice* system capable of adjusting to the user's needs as the system is used. The main aspects of all these elements are described below.

3.   THE TEACHING-LEARNING PSYCHO-PEDAGOGICAL MODEL

Current teaching-learning models try to satisfy a set of basic needs that tend to encourage *significant and active learning*, where the main protagonist is the student. For the PERSONAL-DE model we have not assessed different teaching strategies but have merely followed the prevailing tendency. The model is based on the *natural learning model* proposed in different contexts (as a thought causal model by Pozo, 1987 and an architecture for constructing interactive learning systems by Schank, [12]).

The natural learning method that we have adopted is basically the same as Roger Schank's, it is based on the principle that once a question has been formulated about a theme in which we are interested, then we will be prepared to learn the response. In other words, people cannot only learn from responses given to them. The aim is therefore to suggest attractive objectives —or rather useful ones— and let the generated questions contrast with the subject contents instead of introducing these contents out of context. Figure 1 shows the three basic actions of this method:

a) Raising interesting objectives.
b) Generating questions that respond to established goals.
c) Processing responses to the questions raised.

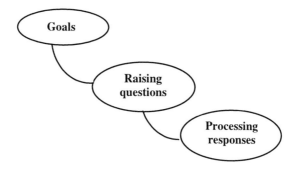

Figure 1. Natural learning model

4.   TEACHING ORGANISATION ON THE INTERNET

In every teaching-learning model first its *structure* is perceived. This consists of *agents* that participate in the process and the *media* used, which in turn are subdivided into communication channels, tools and techniques for the elaboration of the material, the assessment and revision of the model. The interactions between these models are determined by the searched *functionality*. Both components, functionality and structure, are interdependent, they cannot establish objectives without taking into the account the agents and/or without considering the media available for attaining them.

Starting from the characteristic needs of the functionality required in the prevailing distance-learning methodology at UNED, telematic services are specifically assigned for the different protagonists participating in the process: Head Office lecturers, tutor-lecturers and students (see Figure 1). This university has approximately 1,200 lecturers and over 150,000 students, so trying to satisfy the extra attention of its students is really complicated. Our proposal tries to satisfy the information and communication needs of each of the protagonists so that the flow of information between them is very

Although the description of the services proposed for the students and tutor-lecturers and the Head Office lecturers have already been described (Boticario, 1997a), by way of illustration the usefulness of some of these options is given below:

- *Exercises forum*: it includes information on the contents and organisation of the exercises, the distribution of the necessary material (trying to offer different options for its development and additional existing documentation on the Net), other related services like FAQ's (*Frequently asked questions*) in the *exercises forum* (for this we propose the use of tools like MhonArc, http://www.oac.uci.edu/indiv/ehood/mhonarc.html, which generate FAQ pages from folders with mail messages), etc. There should also be an initial period for sending proposals to form distance-exercise groups in the subjects that need it.

- *First solutions forum*: in order to make students aware of the prior conceptual structure of a topic that they are beginning to study (following the recommendations of Novak and Gowin, 1984, who tried to clarify the so-called *psychological structure* of the subject to facilitate learning), we propose using this service organised by topics. Students can consult the questions and answers given by other fellow students to the topic's introductory exercises prepared by the teaching team and updated according to the student's indications. Those students interested, without consulting the rest of the material available, can leave their own solutions. These solutions can provide other students with an initial approach to the topic and will reveal the limited prior knowledge of the problem in question.

- *Subject mailing list*: this medium provides the lecturers with direct access to all the students of a particular subject. A list should be created at the Head Office and another at each Associated Centre, since the problems, speakers and contents are different in both instances. For this we recommend the instructions on the effective use of electronic mail (http://www.webfoot.com/advice/email.top.html?Yahoo).

- *Self-assessment exercises forum*: with this utility the students can gather sets of problems labelled by topics and by sections of the syllabus. Each exercise identifies the difficulty of the problem so that students can classify their selection. Each of these problems has the solutions given by the other students. A mechanism establishes that first the students send a file with their solution to a problem before they gain access to the solutions to the problem.

For the teaching organisation to be effective, as well as the proposed services, a large accessible database should be used for administrative management. This database should contain all kinds of documents, forms and data used for administrative purposes at UNED, and it should also have an automatic service for accrediting receipt of documents and supports for their elaboration thereby guaranteeing security. Many of the aforementioned services would require establishing limited access spaces for the groups involved.

5.   ELABORATION OF THE DIDACTIC MATERIAL

Before detailing the main characteristics of the new didactic material —some of which have already been described (Boticario, 1997b), the proposed measures for effectively developing this kind of material are given. Firstly, *technical support groups* should be created to guarantee the management and maintenance of available services (Web, forums/newsgroups, and mailing lists...) and to maintain information pages on the Web in different formats, with the tools available and following good use norms. Similarly, *teams for developing electronic teaching material* need to be formed consisting of the teaching team of lecturers and the team for the medium technical support. *Mailing lists* should be created to facilitate communication between the members of the development team. Finally, these actions can be accompanied with *periodical teacher training courses* and *newsgroups* and *documentation pages* on these topics.

As regards the teaching material itself, the options are as follows:
- *Programmed class*: (or telematic class) based on an interactive text showing the contents of a topic according to the student's responses and preferences (see the section below on the interactive system). The main advantages of this material are: the possibility of going back over a line of argument, visualizing the student's reasoning structure (expecting that an erroneous path occurs), choosing formats that clarify abstract concepts, responding to questions according to the context and having all the desirable time available. These kinds of classes complement or substitute (depending on the personal conditions of the student) the physically attended tutored classes.
- *Personalized videoconference*: it is a teaching class where the lecturer in charge of the subject (Head Office), from his/her own personal computer (the cost of the equipment necessary is now in fact affordable), gets in contact with the students of one or several associated centres (it is a service currently available for all those lecturers interested).
- *Exercises class*: it is proposed that the *exercises forum* described above and the pages with the corresponding documentation should be used, wherever possible, with freely distributed, user-friendly (there is a great deal of educational software available on the Net) and executable portable computing material in different platforms (Windows, Linux).

- *Hypermedia material*: apart from leaving the material as printed text, most of which matches the linearity imposed in the exposition of its contents, other alternatives must be encouraged in the creation of hypermedia material. *Multiple paths*: starting from the material available (inside and outside the subject Web site) alternative paths can be established, formed by different link chains between the pages, which are aimed at satisfying the student's alternative interests (e.g., a student who is only interested in finding references to the practical applications of the subject contents. *Guided Tour*: a previously structured tour on some of the syllabus contents (e.g., *intelligent agents* available on the Web). *Personalized tour*: personalization in the development of a topic via the free choice of alternative active elements and the answer to different questions.

Since electronic material has a completely different functionality to that of printed material, its elaboration requires a set of norms described in the following section.

6. ACCESSIBILITY, DESIGN UTILITY AND EFFICIENCY

Different studies stress that Web users are impatient and do not want to waste time waiting for pages to be loaded with excessive and unnecessary images. There are various aspects related to this statement: users do not read large amounts of text on the Web, they move quickly over it, they are not tolerant with unfinished sentences or paragraphs, they do not accept errors because of incompatibility in the versions of the products used, they are reluctant to load additional software to gain access to some contents, and they do not want to scour page after page. A list of the ten main errors (Nielsen, 1999) to avoid has been specified for *usability* (a term used to refer to the effective and efficient design of a web resource).

Other analyses on the *usability* of specific resources (the quality of the study done by Carl Arglia in 1998 on electronic commerce) draw the following conclusions: quite a lot of confusion is produced in users when they have to go deeper than 7 ± 2 levels into the hierarchical structure of the pages given; users are eager to receive relevant information on the domain, they do not want to waste time trying to find what they are looking for and they are reluctant to repeat complicated access paths to reach the information that they want (the problems that sometimes occur when *noting down* the address of a page as a *bookmark* when the frames are incorrectly used); trust is important, users lose it when they find pages that are not updated or services no longer in use.

All this considered, in order to improve PERSONAL-DE *usability*, the design proposed has as its starting point a first page in *portal* form (http://sss-mag.com/portals.html contains some of the best Internet *portals*) that includes a large part of the most relevant information for students on: subjects in which they are enrolled (any kind of updating related to these subjects), activities in which they participate on the net (newsgroup messages that may be of interest, updated shared work folders ...), new services available (searchers, indexes, glossaries...), new interesting links, extracurricular activities. That is, any new or updated information envisaged as being of interest, clearly structured and hierarchized around the most significant elements. Obviously, with this approach the initial page should be dynamic and contain variable information in the successive access sessions (see the following section). Basically, the aim is to access the relevant information with the least possible number of accesses and at the same time maintain a clear and explicit guide of the navigation done. In short, our objective is to have a clear and simple design that bases its utility on the services offered to satisfy the user's information and communication needs, and on the efficient access to these services as well.

7.   INTERACTIVE DISTANCE-LEARNING SYSTEM

As well as the telematic model described, an interactive assisted distance-learning system is being constructed that matches the user's needs on the Internet so that they can gain efficient access to the most relevant information and use the communication channels of their choice (a first operating version of this system has already been described by Boticario and Gaudioso, 1999). The objective of this system is *to guide* the user to access those elements of interest on the Web, without conditioning their actions, since they are always free to accept the system's advice or not.

The architecture of the system is based on our earlier experience in the personalized management of calendars (Dent *et al.* 1992). The approach coincides with what in machine learning literature is termed *learning-apprentice systems*: personalized assistants that learn from observing the user actions managing the elements in a specific domain.

In particular, personalized access to DL teaching services is done via a Web server that permits interaction with the Assisted Teaching system without the need for any specific software, since students interact with the system via the pages offered by the server. These pages are generated dynamically, concatenating static information with the information that the system detects as being possibly relevant for students. A model is kept of each user (*student model*) that considers the most stable information available: name, electronic identification, personal data, subjects registered in, subjects passed, current projects membership (e.g., if users belong to the *telematic laboratory* or not), and the most volatile information resulting from interaction with the system as time passes: accessed resources, access traces done, contact media chosen (forums and accessed *folders*, mailing lists in which they participate, contact pages consulted...), added web links (students can introduce new active references of their interest on dynamically constructed pages, as illustrated in *Figure 3*).

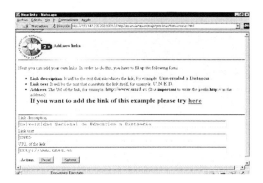

Figure 3. Data collection screen for a new link

As regards experiments done up to now, access has been personalized to the learning subject exercises at the Computer Science School (CSS) and the third year courses at UNED's Artificial Intelligence Department. The system provides advice on: exercises that can be done, pages that should be consulted as the problem statement is studied, web addresses related to the chosen topic, alternative contact and consulting media. The development of the exercises is based on the model proposed by Schank in the ASK system (Schank, [12]), where the contents are presented via a network of concepts (nodes) which must be learnt by students and the arcs represent the transition of a concept to another according to the knowledge that the students are acquiring and their personal interests.

Experience has shown that it is possible to do personalized interaction with users transparently (without the need for any specific software) and efficiently, based on dynamic HTML pages capable of requesting data directly in HTTP protocol.

8. CONCLUSIONS AND FUTURE WORK

This article describes the bases of an Internet distance-learning operating model. The main objectives of the model are: to motivate the student's active significant learning, increase the flow of information and facilitate access to the rest of the protagonists in the teaching system, to assign specific telematic resources for each of the information and communication needs detected, to specify the most appropriate teaching material to the medium and provide rapid, efficient and personalized access to the relevant information.

To take advantage of this model an interactive system has been built on the Web whose main objective is to learn the students' needs from their use of the system and from the recorded data available (academic and personal). This application is being used in the personalization of the learning subjects at the Computer Science School (CSS) and the third year courses at UNED's Artificial Intelligence Department (AID).

The main courses of action in the immediate future are: to extend the application of the interactive system to the rest of the AID subjects and services and the rest of the CSS services when they are operating; to improve the effectiveness of learning via collaborative learning among the different interactive agents that make up the multi-agent architecture that we are using (some of the functionalities assigned to these agents are: study assistance, contacts, administrative management and extracurricular activities), to improve the representation of the system elements using meta-data descriptions of the web page in combination with information filtering techniques and introducing learning methods of ontologies that match the Web structure (Craven *et al.* 1998).

ACKNOWLEDGEMENTS

The authors would like to acknowledge the helpful comments of Anita Haney, arising in the course of her language revision of this article. We also thank the entire Artificial Intelligence Department for providing support for this project.

9.   REFERENCES

1. Carl Arglia. (1998). E-Commerce tools: part II —storefronts. *Corporate Internet*, 4(2), 1-16.
2. Jesús G. Boticario (1997a). Internet y la universidad a distancia. *A Distancia, Otoño*, 64-69. Available: http://www.dia.uned.es/~jgb/publica/index.html#arti [1999, March 5]
3. Jesús G. Boticario (1997b). Material didáctico y servicios para la educación a distancia en Internet. *A Distancia, Otoño*, 70-76. Available:
   http://www.dia.uned.es/~jgb/publica/index.html#arti [1999, March 5]

4. Jesús G. Boticario, Elena Gaudioso (1999). Towards Personalized Distance Learning on the Web. In *Foundations and Tools for Neural Modeling*. J. Mira and J.V. Sánchez-Andrés (Eds.). Springer Verlag, Lecture Notes in Computer Science, 1607, 740-749. Available: http://www.dia.uned.es/~jgb/publica/index.html#arti [1999, June 14].

5. M. Craven, D. DiPasquo, D. Freitag, A. McCallum, T. Mitchell, K. Nigam and S. Slattery (1998). Learning to Extract Symbolic Knowledge from the World Wide Web. In: *Proceeding of theFifteenth National Conference on Artificial Intelligence (AAAI98)*. Available:http://www.cs.cmu.edu/~webkb/ [1999, June 14]

6. L. Dent, J.G. Boticario, J. McDermott, T. Mitchell, D. Zabowski, (1992). A personal learning apprentice. In: *Proceeding of theTenth National Conference on Artificial Intelligence*, 96-103. San Jose, CA. Mit Press.

7. Jakob Nielsen. (1999). "Top Ten Mistakes" Revisited Three Years Later. *Alterbox*. Available: http://www.useit.com/alertbox/990502.html [1999, May 2].

8. J.D. Novak, D.B. Gowin, (1984). *Learning how to learn*. Cambridge, Cambridge University Press.

9. J.I. Pozo (1987) Aprendizaje de la ciencia y pensamiento causal. *Madrid: Aprendizaje Visor*.

10. Roger C. Schank, Chip Cleary (1995). *Engines for education*. Lawrence Erlbaum Associates, Hillsdale, New Jersey, 1995.Carl Arglia. (1998). E-Commerce tools: part II —storefronts. *Corporate Internet*, 4(2), 1-16.

Synchronous Drawing Actions in Environments of Collaborative Learning of Design

C. Bravo, [1]; M.A. Redondo,[1] J. Bravo, [1]; M. Ortega,[1]; M. Lacruz,[2]
[1] Department of Computer Science. Universidad de Castilla - La Mancha (Spain)
E-mail: {cbravo,mredondo,jbravo,mortega}@inf-cr.uclm.es
[2] Department of Pedagogy. Universidad de Castilla - La Mancha (Spain)
E-mail: mlacruz@mag-cr.uclm.es

Key words:

Abstract: In this work we present a collaborative environment used in learning communities to solve design problems applied to the domotics domain. This design consists in the construction of a scenario, which is made through drawing tools oriented to the domain. To implement these tools, the different tasks the students have to develop in the solution of a problem and the collaborative drawing synchronous actions that they perform in every task are studied.

1.   INTRODUCTION

The reference frame in which this work is included is the building of a collaborative learning environment. These kind of environments are characterized by answering these questions:

Who learns? High school students.

What do they learn? The domotic design.

Where do they learn? In class or from home. The learning is done in group and/or at distance.

How do they learn? The student carry out a discovery learning through a design tool based on simulation.

The collaborative aspects that are presented in the synchronous design and in other synchronous and asynchronous learning tasks, are the most

M. Ortega and J. Bravo (eds.), Computers and Education in the 21st Century, 107–118.

related to the study done in the present work. Particularly, the drawing actions performed by the students in their design are the most interesting. The research areas related with this work are CSCL[1] and the CSCW[2].

CSCW systems are categorized according to a space-temporal matrix, using a differentiation between the same (synchronism) and a different moment (asynchronism) and between the same (face-to-face) and different place (distribution). Maher & Rutherford (1997) apply this matrix to the development of product through CAD, as is shown in Table 1.

Table 2. Use of CAD according to place and time.

Place/Moment	Same Moment	Different Moment
Same Place	Single-user CAD	CAD with Data Management
Different Place	Collaborative Design	Distributed CAD

Of course, a domotic design tools is a CAD tool. When a group of students are performing a domotic design, each one from a different place, we say they are performing a collaborative design. It is the aspect studied in the following sections.

2.   COLLABORATIVE DRAWING TOOLS

The groupware designers, or the collaborative work/learning environments designers, who develop collaborative drawing applications know that their work is not easy. On the one hand, there are human factors owned of the group interaction that, if ignored, the usability of the tool could be limited; and on the other, the implementation, which presents important difficulties.

Collaborative design systems handle two kinds of informations: they need information to build the environment (which is more or less virtual), allowing us to bring collaborative work to fruition, and the data of the models built collaboratively. The first kind of information is related to tele-presence and the second one to tele-data. Tele-presence (Egido, 1988) is the way to give to the distributed participants the feeling that they are having a meeting in the same room. Its goal is to transmit both the most explicit and

[1] CSCL: Computer-supported Collaborative Learning.
[2] CSCW: Computer-supported Collaborative Work.

the finest dynamics happened between the participants. It includes corporal language, hand gestures, visual contact, communication signals, the knowledge of who is talking and who is listening, etc. The tele-data (Greenberg & Chang, 1989) allow the participants in a meeting to show or to access physical materials that are not normally accessible to the distributed group. These include notes, documents, drawings and any common surface that allows each person to make notes, draw, save and transmit ideas during the progress of the conference session.

We will focus on tele-data. These provide small groups (from two to five people) a real time access to a shared drawing space through a collaborative multiuser drawing programme.

3.   DOMAIN OF APPLICATION: THE DOMOTICS DESIGN

It is well known that we experiencing a technological advance of great magnitude. It combines a set of techniques: building, regulation systems, computer science, data transmission, electronics, electrical engineering and, above all, the communications between the Internet, intranets or extranets (Ruiz, 1995). This new area is called domotics[3]. Ruiz defines it as the set of elements that, installed, interconnected and automatically controlled at home, release the user of the routine from intervening in everyday actions and, at the same time, providing optimized control on comfort, energetic consumption, security and communications.

We model domotics as a set of operators and a set of management areas to be able to build a learning environment of domotic design. The domotic operators are all the elements that can be manipulated (inserted, related and parametrized) and that will make the function assigned into the built-in automation of the house. The operators are grouped in sensors or receivers, activators and systems. The different management areas of an automated house are the thermal comfort, luminosity, security and energetic control.

4.   A COLLABORATIVE DESIGN ENVIRONMENT

In this section we describe DOMOSIM-TP-COL. This environment is a domotic design system at distance applied to the built-in automation of

---

[3] Domotics: Intelligent Building or House Automation.

housing (domotics). It has been developed so that secondary school students can learn a subject in which computer aided design is the centre of their actuation. This implies the elaboration of a complex project. This learning is collaborative and at distance. The simulation is the basis of all the system and allows the students to contrast their design with the optimal design generated by the system itself.

4.1   Environment Characteristics

The aim is to perform the scenario design. This scenario is a background that schematizes the house structure, and the different domotic operators will be inserted in it. The designed environment will be able to be simulated in order that the student can study the system's behaviour. There is a planner to define an intermediate solution strategy for this design problem.

In this way, the learning that the student carries out is doing by discovery. The student has a set of support tools for distance education: chat, electronic mail, a note board and a diary.

The client/server architecture on TCP/IP nets (the Internet or intranets) is used for the implementation, using Java as language in order that the system can be accessed from the Web, facilitating distance education.

In the study of this environment, we centre on the design tool. This drawing tool (figure 1) has four significant parts:
1. Left: It contains the panel of domotic operators.
2. Central: The drawing whiteboard.
3. Right: It contains the panel of drawing tools.
4. Bottom: The zone for messages.

As a design tool in which collaborative drawing actions are carried out, the different active pointers, which identify to the users, are always visible in all the screens. It allows the simultaneous interaction, although any user cannot do anything. Any action, although it is small or insignificant, is immediatly visible in all the screens.

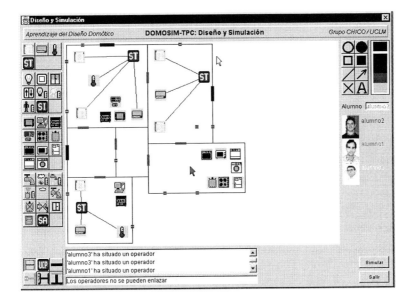

Figure 1. The Drawing Tool (Whiteboard) of the collaborative learning environment

Each user has a pointer with a particular colour associated to his/her name (see the different arrows in Figure 1). The drawing tool is a drawing program which is object-oriented with some characteristics that make it similar to the structured drawing environments. The users can create, move, change the size and delete drawing objects.

4.2   Tasks

In order to solve a problem, once the student has chosen the appropriate background (house plan) according to the chosen problem, he/she must perform the following four tasks [2]:
- Edition: It consists in selecting the elements to place in the background. The operators panel is available for that.
- Parametrization: The different values of the internal variables of each operator or the external variables of the work environment can be altered.
- Link: The elements inserted previously are linked in the background to define the system behaviour in the simulation.
- Simulation: It allows to contrast the designed scenario with the planned actions.

There are two workspaces: individual and group. In the individual space, the students work in isolation and can perform any task. All the actions perform by the students are registered in the database (D.B.M.S.). In this way, the teacher or the students themselves can query this database to build the student trace.

Bravo C. et al. [1] describes how these tasks are performed in a collaborative way. In the **edition** task the students can place the elements (heaters, plugs, lamps, etc.) in an interactive synchronous way. The server engine of DOMONET-TP-COL informs through a textual message to all the students of a session when one of them has placed an element. What is more, the icon that represents the element will appear on the screen of all the students of the group who are carrying out the edition jointly.

The **Parametrization** consists of editing a sequence of numeric parameters (temperatures, times, etc.) in a combined way. In this case, each student has a particular parameter screen and two buttons, one for each parameter; the first one makes it possible to suggest the typed value on the local screen, and the second one to accept or to reject the suggestion other student has just done. The server, like in the edition task, will inform to all the members of the session of the suggestions and decisions through messages.

The **link** task is a highly interactive process consisting of linking the different operators graphically with the pointer of the mouse. For each student there is a pointer that enables him/her to view what the others are doing. The lines that represent the connection between elements are displayed in all the screens too.

The **simulation** produces an outcome that will be displayed on the screens of all the students, so it will be the same for them all. With a button the student will be able to stop the simulation at a local level or to stop it for the whole group.

4.3   Actions

We name actions to the different events (produced by the mouse, the keyboard, etc.) which are carried out by the user while he is designing with the drawing tool. The tasks we study are the Edition and the Link. We do not consider the Parametrization because it is not performed with the drawing tool. Neither do we consider the Simulation because the possible actions are only to start, pause and end the simulation, and these are not relevant because of their simplicity.

The actions that a user can perform are:

– <u>Registering the login</u>: When the drawing tool is started (Figure 1) the login of a user to the work group is registered.
– <u>Registering the logout</u>: When the tool is closed with the exit button.

- Movement of the pointer (mouse): When a student moves the mouse pointer, this movement is viewed on the screen of all the students of the group, each pointer shown in a different colour for each student.
- Drawing a figure: With a *click* over a figure icon, the student can draw a line, rectangle or circle; in these two cases it can be empty or filled. In all the figures the *click* over the whiteboard marks the initial point (left-top corner) and the drop marks the final point of the figure (right-bottom corner).
- Selecting a figure: With a *click* in a position (a pair of pixels) in which there was a figure it will be possible to select it, showing a change in colour and form in the figure to reflect this selection; this will be viewed on the screens of all the students.
- Deleting a figure: Once a selection done, the figure will be susceptible of deletion with the delete key.
- Inserting an operator: The operators panel is placed in the left part of the tool. When an operator icon is pressed it is selected, and the corresponding operator will be inserted in the blackboard when a click over it is done. This insertion is automatically viewed in all the screens.
- Selecting an operator: The operator can be selected in the same way as a figure.
- Deleting an operator: The selected operator can be deleted, disappearing from all the student blackboard.
- Linking two operators: When two operators have been selected, they can be linked with the corresponding button; this is shown to the students and stored in the database.
- Selecting a link.
- Deleting the link between two operators.
- Clearing the screen: This option, which clears the work blackboard, will clear the blackboards of all the users. As we think that it is dangerous because it is possible to accidentally delete the work made, it is necessary for each student to confirm this clearing answering a question that appears in a dialog box.

5. IMPLEMENTATION OF THE DRAWING TOOL OF THE ENVIRONMENT

5.1 Sockets

A socket sets a net connection between a client process and a server process. The socket is formed with the host IP address and the port used for carrying out the communication. When the sockets are created they can be used by the server, which waits indefinitely for the establishment of a connection (passive sockets), or by the client, which starts a connection (active sockets). The Java language has, in the java.net package, two classes relative to the socket concept, which are especially useful to the net programming. These classes are Socket and ServerSocket. To get more information about the data members, constructors or methods, you can consult Vanhelsuwé et al. (1997).

The sockets will be the mechanisms that make it possible to set communication channels between the Collaborative Actions Coordinator and the Users (Figure 2), who are the students who make the design. Although the main role of the Coordinator is to be the server, waiting for the occurrence of drawing actions, it plays a client role too when it uses a channel to request a service to the process that has to reflect on the screen the action carried out by another user and that waits in the user machine.

5.2   Architecture

There are two architectural alternatives to build distributed *groupware*: centralized and replicated (Greenberg, 1992; Maher & Simoff, 1999).

In the centralized approach, a program named "central agent" is the mediator of the distributed work performed in all the drawing surfaces. Each user, in his/her machine, runs a "participant process" which takes the user entries and sends them to the central agent. After processing this information, the agent communicates to each participant what he has to draw on the screen. In this way, the agent is a big program that manages the users.

In the replicated approach there is not a central agent. On the contrary, the replicated participants in each machine are responsible of keeping the integrity of the drawing surface. The participants communicate each other directly, in spite of passing information to a central agent.

The advantages and disadvantages of both approaches are shown in Table 2.

Tabla 2. Advantages and disadvantages of the different approximations of implementation.

Approach	Advantages	Disadvantages
Centralized	– The synchronization is easy. – The information of the state is consistent because it is in each place.	– The whole system is vulnerable to fault of the central agent. – A bottleneck can be done in the net.
Replicated	– The net traffic is reduced because the communication does not carry out through a mediator. – The system is stronger if there are faults in the net and in the machines.	– It is more difficult to keep the work surfaces and the user requests synchronized.

A hybrid approach is possible too. For example, the participant processes could use a central agent only for the synchronization and for the mediation in the conflicts between the requests of the users. The rest of activities can be carried out by the participant processes.

The chosen alternative is the centralized approach, which is shown in Figure 2. The managing agent is a Java application that implements a process that waits for the occurrence of actions, with the purpose of communicating to the users processes the effect that has to be produced in their screen. The Users are the Java *applets* that are run in the different machines of the students and that are waiting messages of the agent to reflect actions of other users. For this, both types of processes are clients sometimes and servers other times.

Both the maganing agent and the users recover and store the necessary information in the database. It is done through the use of JDBC to the access to databases (Figure 2).

5.3   Actions Coordinator

The Coordinator stores the object collection that makes up the students design in a private structure (this structure is a vector). This collection is registered in the database to the last recovery in other work session. When a failure is produced (net failure, etc.) any student can ask for the refreshment of the blackboard with a request to the managing agent; it is necessary if the blackboard has not shown certain action and is not synchronized.

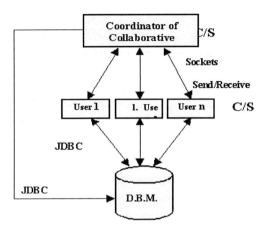

Figure 2. Mediation of the Coordinator as communicator of students' collaborative actions

This managing agent is not only used in the tool of the environment object of study. All the synchronous tools of the environment use the agent's services. For example, the chat tool sends messages to the agent and receives messages from it. These messages are typically the texts that a student wants to communicate to other students.

5.4   Information Sent in the Actions and Packets

Each action of the ones studied represents a packet that will be sent through the socket. The included information in each packet is shown in the Table 3.

Tabla 3. Information sent by the client processes to the Coordinator of Actions.

Basic drawing actions (edition and link tasks)	Information Sent
Registering the login of a user	Host, port and name of the participant
Registering the logout of a user	Participant identifier (id.).
Moving the pointer (mouse)	Participant id., new coordinates
Drawing a figure (line, rectangle, circle)	Participant id., figure type, initial coordinates (x, y), final coordinates (x, y), colour
Selecting a figure	Participant id., coordinates (x, y)
Deleting a figure	Participant id., figure id.
Inserting an operator	Participant id., coordinates (x, y)
Selecting an operator	Participant id., coordinates (x, y)
Deleting an operator	Participant id., operator id.
Linking two operators	Participant id., operator 1 id., operator 2 id.
Selecting a link	Participant id., link id.
Deleting the link between two operators	Participant id., link id.
Clearing the screen	---

The socket is characterized by the host and the port. The participant name is a string of characters. The participant identifier is an internal data that allows us to distinguish it from all the identifiers registered in the system and to access to additional data. The figure type can be 0 (line), 1 (circle) or 2 (rectangle); the types 3 and 4 are related to filled circles and rectangles. The coordinates refers to blackboard coordinates that go from the point (0,0) to the point (354,270). The figure, operator and link identifiers are used to access the related information to these elements that forms part of the design.

To make up a packet a *token* with three characters is used (for example: CNC = registering the user login, DCN = registering the user logout, etc.) for the kind of action and integers are used for the next elements. The *tokens* are separated with spaces. These packets have been used in the first prototype; in future versions *tokens* of a lower length will be used to reduce the time wasted in the sendings and receptions, and the numeric data will be codified in formats that use up less space.

6.   CONCLUSIONS AND FUTURE WORK

This approach of synchronous collaborative work applied to the domotic design is positive to the learners that carry out these tasks, due to the help that means the interaction with other students, because the knowledge is shared, and to the use of a less time in the design of the scenarios

A clear conclusion is that with the existing technology and with the used implementation it is not possible to get an acceptable speed of execution, and that powerful computers are required. In our case, this achieved objective has not been the one we aimed at.

– The current line of work is centred on the following aspects:
– To achieve the object movement in the blackboard and not only their selection and deletion.
– To allow joint actions of drawing in pairs, for example the linking of operators.
– To carry out a quantitative study of the contributions, for example time statistics of the students or to detect the degree of participation.
– To include new figures (free hand drawing, etc.).
– To enlarge the different areas of the tool (chat, drawing blackboard, etc.).

REFERENCES

1. Bravo, C., Redondo, M.A., Bravo, J. & Ortega, M. (1999*) Diseño colaborativo en entornos de simulación para aprendizaje a distancia.* In Actas del I Simposio Ibérico de Informática Educativa. Aveiro (Portugal).
2. Bravo, J., Ortega, M. & Prieto, M. (1997) *Entornos de Simulación en la Educación a Distancia.* In Revista de Enseñanza y Tecnología de la Asociación para el Desarrollo de la Informática Educativa, num. 8.
3. Egido, C. (1988) *Video conferencing as a technology to support group work: A review of its failures.* In Proceedings of the Conference on Computer-Supported Cooperative Work (CSCW'88), Portland. ACM Press.
4. Greenberg, S. & Chang, E. (1989) *Computer support for real time collaborative work.* In Proceedings of the Conference on Numerical Mathematics and Computing, Winnipeg, Manitoba.
Greenberg, S., Roseman, M., Webster, D. & Bohnet, R. (1993) *Issues and Experiences Designing and Implementing Two Group Drawing Tools.* In Readings in Groupware and Computer-Supported Cooperative Work. Baecker, R.M. (Ed.).
Lauwers, J.C., Joseph, T.A., Lantz, K.A. & Romanow, A.L. (1993) *Replicated Architectures for Shared Window Systems: A critique.* In Readings in Groupware and Computer-Supported Cooperative Work. Baecker, R.M. (Ed.).
Maher, M.L. & Rutherford, J.H. (1997) *A Model for Synchronous Collaborative Design Using CAD and Database Management.* Research in Engineering Design, vol. 9, 1997, pp. 85-93.
Maher, M.L. & Simoff, S.J. (1999) *Variations on the Virtual Design Studio.* In Proceedings of Fourth International Workshop on CSCW in Design. Barthès, J.P., Zongkai, L., Ramos, M. (Eds.). Compiègne (France).
Ruiz, J.M., Bravo J., Ortega M. (1995) *Domótica.* Revista de Enseñanza y Tecnología. ADIE. mayo 1995, pp. 46-48.
Vanhelsuwé, L., Phillips, I., Hsu, G., Sankar, K., Ries, E., Rohaly, T., Zukowski, J. (1997) *La biblia de Java.* Madrid: Anaya Multimedia.

Interconnecting Courseware Modules via WWW

J.C. Burguillo[1], L. Anido[1], J.V. Benlloch[2], F. Buendía[2]

[1] *E.T.S.I. de Telecomunicación. Dpto. de Tecnologías de las Comunicaciones. Universidade de Vigo. Lagoas-Marcosende 36200-VIGO (SPAIN). Tel: +34 986813869 Fax: +34 986 812116. E-mail: {jrial, lanido}@ait.uvigo.es*
[2] *E. U. de Informática. Dpto. de Informática de Sistemas y Computadores. Universidad Politécnica de Valencia. P.O. Box 22012, 46071 Valencia (SPAIN). Tel: +34 96 3877575. Fax: +34 96 3877579. E-mail: {jbenlloc,fbuendia}@disca.upv.es*

Key words: Distance Learning, Java, WWW

Abstract: This paper shows some key ideas to interconnect courseware modules by using WWW technologies. This interconnection will allow the user to get a wide view about educational topics that are often scarce. In the frame of the European Thematic Network Ineit-Mucon, this work is encouraging the co-operation between several working groups which are bringing together interactive educational modules about distinct aspects of computers. The paper describes the key design issues in the courseware interconnection. At last, an implementation example is shown and some conclusions are summarized.

1.   INTRODUCTION

Today large-scale deployment of learning technologies is about to take place in all sectors of lifelong learning, from schools and universities to industry, to give access to learning and knowledge to all citizens, regardless of where they study, work or live. There is no doubt that Information Society will have a strong impact on education and training systems in Europe.

With regard to the use of new learning technologies, including elements from the converging multimedia, telecommunications and information technology fields, it is important to point out that a truly new pedagogical approach is required. Many times, the use of new technologies is reduced to access to passive electronic material used previously for oral transmission.

M. Ortega and J. Bravo (eds.), Computers and Education in the 21st Century, 119–126.

Thus, it is necessary to create new powerful learning environments, which force students to be actively engaged in the learning process, improving the rather passive attitudes typically present in our lecture-rooms.

In this framework, the European Thematic Network INEIT MUCON[1] aims at designing, developing and disseminating educational packages, for teaching EIE (Electrical and Information Engineering) in Higher Education. In the Project participate around 40 university institutions, having representatives from each of the European Union country.

The main efforts focus on the design and development of a basic set of didactic resources in the area of Electronics/Informatics which can be disseminated through the Internet to the European university community. A more challenging goal is to get a harmonisation of the curricula in EIE throughout Europe in order to facilitate the exchanges of students (and of teachers also...). This set of developed tools could also act as a virtual library freely usable within LLL (Life Long Learning) /ODL (Open Distance Learning) context enabling the training and knowledge updating of a large number of students and engineering professionals in Europe.

The use of new technologies is one of the milestones of the project as it offers several advantages:

It enables the creation of virtual scenarios where the knowledge transmission can be presented in friendly graphical user interfaces.

It is able to increase the interactivity in the learning process, by using simulators that allow the students to explore and to change system model descriptions focusing and particularizing the scenario around every student.

It eases and unifies the access to disperse information sources (through the Internet) and permit students to adapt the learning process to their own needs and abilities.

In the frame of the Thematic Network, this work is encouraging the co-operation initiated between different working groups which are bringing together interactive educational modules about different aspects of computers, to obtain a more comprehensive material on this topic. The strategy presented here allows the different teams to share efforts and save resources, obtaining better quality products. After three years working in the project, this paper describes the collaboration among two academic groups which have been participating in the elaboration of didactic resources in

---

[1] INEIT MUCON: Innovations for Education in Information Technology through Multimedia and Communication Networks, EU reference: 26173-CP-1-96-1-FR-ERASMUS-ETN. http://lara0.esstin.u-nancy.fr/ineit-mucon/

Informatics and analyses the way to interconnect new materials in order to get more complex educational packages.

The paper is structured as follows: in section 2, the key design issues to attain the courseware interconnection are described; in section 3, the courseware module design and functionality is introduced; in section 4, the implementation issues are presented; in section 5, the future lines are described and finally, in section 6, some conclusions are summarized.

2. INTERCONNECTION DESIGN

Usually, the methods applied to interconnect WWW contents are based on using hypertext links between the different sites that contain the information. This way lets users navigate through HTML documents and access to their contents (text, images, audio, ...). However, when a stronger relationship is required, new interconnection techniques have to be applied. This is the case of courseware modules in which several simulation tools covering different concepts about computers (tackled from certain abstraction levels), have been developed by two working groups in the University of Vigo [7] and Polytechnic University of Valencia [1].

There are several techniques to interchange information between a client and a Web server. The easier way consists in filling forms through CGI (Common Gateway Interface) scripts or similar, that will be transferred from a client site to a server. These forms can contain information (e.g. text) that can be processed at the server site. Nevertheless, this option requires the continuous access to the server to work and therefore, the possibilities of interaction are limited depending on factors as: the server load, its capacity as well as network performance.

Figure 1. Computer architecture simulator[2]

In order to provide a more flexible interconnection between courseware modules, a distributed execution has been proposed so the execution load has been transferred to the client machine. Because of that and for obtaining bigger interactivity and flexibility, we have been using, since the beginning, the Java language [8] which offers platform independence, facilitates the developing of the Internet applications using the object-oriented schema [2] and guaranties a security scheme for the end user. In this way, the access to resources which can be physically located in different servers is enabled. Besides, this communication takes place in the client side minimizing the waiting time and improving application performance.

3.   COURSEWARE MODULE DESCRIPTION

The first module, part of a bigger environment [3][4][7], describes a very simple and pedagogical example of a computer architecture named Simplez [5]. It offers the possibility to be programmed in assembly language which can be automatically converted to machine code and executed in the pedagogical architecture. The simulator [5] makes it possible to display the registers and memory contents, while the program is running. It works as an applet whose appearance can be seen in Figure 1.

---

[2] *Figure structure*:
ALU (Arithmetical and Logical Unit) it has an acumulator (AC). CU (Control Unit).
MM (Main Memory). With 512 memory 12 bits slots. I/O D (Input/Output driver).

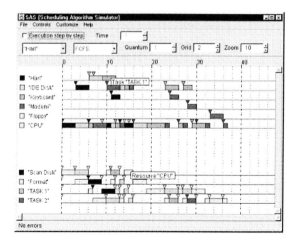

Figure 2. Scheduler simulator

The second module represents a more abstract level in the computer description that focuses on operating system services. It provides, for example, a view about how computer applications can be executed on a generic architecture and how their computational resources are scheduled among the different applications. The execution events are then shown using a timing representation that points out what are the resources used by the application in a given time instant. Figure 2 shows an example of timing representation obtained using the simulator developed in [6].

Both modules can work in a autonomous way but if both are present on the same Web page, then the first module generates timing information which can be displayed by the second one.

4. IMPLEMENTATION ISSUES

In the implementations of these modules, the programming language Java is used both for developing the simulators and the interconnection elements. This language permits to give a high degree of interactivity to the courseware modules and provides extra advantages for communicating them.

One of the main advantages of using Java for interactive Web pages is that a Web page can point to a small program called an applet. When the browser reaches it, the applet is downloaded to the client machine and executed there in a secure way. It is structurally impossible for the applet to access to local resources.

For these reasons, and to achieve portability across machines, applets are compiled to bytecodes after being written and debugged. These bytecode programs are accessed from the Web pages, in a similar way images are accessed too.

Thus, both modules are developed in an independent way and just after their designers agree in a particular interface, they are able to communicate data between them. This communication takes place in the client machine in such a way the server is not overloaded with extra interaction. You can see the elements that collaborate in Figure 3.

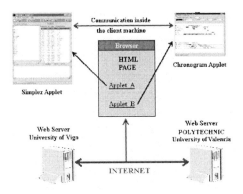

Figure 3. System architecture

The behaviour of the global system is as follows: The "Simplez" applet, that implements the computer architecture simulator (see Figure 1), detects if there is a version of the "Chronogram" applet (see Figure 2). If it does not find the Chronogram applet, then it behaves in a normal way. If the other applet is present then it sends information to a shared memory that acts as an interface between both.

Thus, the Simplez simulator writes information about the execution times of the different instructions while it is working, in a format that can be understood by the Chronogram applet. The Chronogram acts in the same way for getting the information but only reads from the shared memory so it can display the timings at the same time the other simulator is working.

5.   FUTURE WORK: DEVELOPING COMPLEX EDUCATIONAL SYSTEMS USING COOPERATIVE MODULES

The capabilities of the Internet, not only as a vehicle for delivering educational contents but also as a link among applications developed co-operatively, increase even more its educational possibilities.

In the near future, we aim at developing complex systems composed by a set of tools that, according to the user needs, download, from the server, additional Java applets to interact with (to receive or provide information). In fact, the educational server can be seen as an "applet server" that delivers software on-demand, just as required at client side. For instance, an applet could ask for a graphic tool in order to properly present some results just computed.

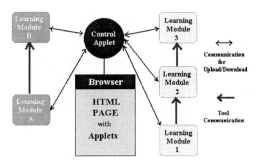

Figure 4. An architecture for dynamic downloading

The proposed approach would make the software development process easier taking into account that all common tasks required from different applications would be performed by the same group of Java applets (e.g., applets to graphically represent the output of other mathematical functions). The necessary set of tools would be developed, debugged and maintained by one of the working groups, while the rest of them would just access the offered services.

This system would be composed by a control applet, common for all the pages in a given environment, that would act as a communication node for the provided tools. Of course, tool interaction would be performed at client side in such a way the server load would be lightened. For example, in Figure 4, when learning module A needs learning module B, it would request the downloading of this applet. Afterwards, module B would register itself in the control applet as a "ready" module. The control applet would notify this fact to module A and then, communication would be carried out directly between those modules. The same behaviour for a three module communication scheme is depicted on the right side of that picture.

Generally, once a module needs the involvement of a different one, it would generate a request to the control applet. The control applet, if feasible, would download the requested module in a different frame. This scheme allows the downloading of new code on request, just as needed.

6. CONCLUSIONS

Key design issues to connect through the Internet educational modules developed by two working groups from different universities have been presented. The outcome of this experience seems very positive, both from a collaborative point of view (our groups had different background) and because it can be considered as the embryo of a framework to develop an educational environment that makes the effective collaboration among different working groups feasible.

ACKNOWLEDGEMENTS

We want to thank the "Escuela Universitaria de Informática" from the "Universidad Politécnica de Valencia" and the "Grupo de Ingeniería de Sistemas Telemáticos" from the "Universidade de Vigo" as well as the European Union for partially funding this work.

REFERENCES

1. F. Buendía, J.V. Benlloch, J.V Saborit. (1998). *"Design and implementation of courseware on computer systems"*. EAEEIE' 98 Annual Conference on Education in Electrical and Information Engineering, Lisboa, Portugal.
2. F. Buendía, M. López, I. Blesa, J.V. Benlloch.(1997). *"Using hypermedia techniques for developing object-oriented courseware about computer systems"*, EAEEIE' 97 Annual Conference on Education in Electrical and Information Engineering, Edinburgh, Scotland, Jun.1997.
3. L. Anido, M. Llamas, M.J. Fernández, J.C. Burguillo. (1998) *"Improving practical training in Internet-based learning environments"*, Szucs, A. y Wagner, A. (Eds.), Universities in a Digital Era. Transformation, Innovation and Tradition, Procs. of the 1998 EDEN (European Distance Education Network) Conference, vol. 2. Bolonia, Italy.
4. M. Llamas, L. Anido, M.J. Fernández, J.C. Burguillo, J.M. Pousada, F.J. Gonzalez. (1998). *"Management, system tracking and maintenance in a teleteaching environment"*, EAEEIE' 98 Annual Conference on Education in Electrical and Information Engineering, Lisboa, Portugal.
5. G. Fernández. (1994) *"Conceptos básicos de arquitectura y sistemas operativos"*, Curso de Ordenadores. Sistemas y Servicios de Comunicación S.L. Madrid.
6. *"Scheduling Algorithm Simulator"*. http://www.eui.upv.es/ineit-mucon/applets/ SAS/demo.htm
7. M. Llamas, L. Anido, M. J. Fernandez. (1997). *"SimulNet: Virtual tele-laboratories over the Internet"*. IFIP Virtual Campus. Trends for Higher Education and Training. Madrid.
8. Jaworski, J. (1997). JAVA Guía de desarrollo. Prentice Hall.
9. "Simplez Simulator". http://www-gist.ait.uvigo.es/~jrial/Proyectos/INEIT-MUCOM/Dagra/Simplez/Simplez

Adaptive Internet-based learning with the TANGOW system

Rosa María Carro, Estrella Pulido, Pilar Rodríguez
Universidad Autónoma de Madrid, Escuela Técnica Superior de Informática

Key words: Distance learning, Multimedia and hypermedia in education

Abstract: In this paper we describe TANGOW, Task-based Adaptive learNer Guidance On the Web, a system for Web-based adaptive learning. Courses developed with TANGOW are adapted to students by taking into account their own features (such as age, language, etc.) along with the actions performed by them during the learning process. There exists a structure per student where the path followed by this student while interacting with the system is stored. This path is restored at the beginning of each session. The courses managed by the system are described in terms of Teaching Tasks and Rules. Teaching Tasks correspond to the conceptual basic units defined by the course designer, while Rules specify the relation among Teaching Tasks. The examples used to illustrate the system features are part of a course about traffic signs.

1.   INTRODUCTION

Over the past few years, the Internet and the World Wide Web have been widely used for information distribution. WWW presents several advantages that make it suitable for educational purposes, since access to information is fast and easy, regardless of location and time. In addition, information updates are immediately available to users, who only need to have standard browsers installed in their computers. Limitations related to net bandwidth, which can give rise to bottlenecks, are expected to be solved with Internet 2.

However, those characteristics on their own do not guarantee the effectiveness of online teaching systems. Other factors, such as the design of contents and the guidance process offered to the student, must be taken into

M. Ortega and J. Bravo (eds.), Computers and Education in the 21st Century, 127–135.
© 2000 *Kluwer Academic Publishers. Printed in the Netherlands.*

account in order to design a learning system qualitatively more useful than a book. From a general point of view, the elements involved in the learning process not only include the students and the subjects to be studied, but also the instructor supervision and, sometimes, the interaction among students [1]. As for the subjects to be studied, it is desirable that the material can be presented in different ways, adapted to each particular student features. This versatility should apply both to contents and to their associated presentation layouts. Furthermore, it is also advisable to provide the system with a clear maintenance procedure that allows the evolution of the subjects offered while keeping the system running. It is important to notice that course designers are not supposed to be expert programmers. These facts make it evident that course designer actions must be included in the whole picture of any Internet based learning system.

On the other hand, if the system is supposed to evolve along time, not only relationships between a user and the system should be taken into account. It would also be useful to provide the learning system with collaboration capabilities so that the students can work together in problem solution, the tutor can give advise to students, and the designers can collaborate in the design of courses [6] [7].

The paper is structured as follows: section 2 discusses the architecture of TANGOW (Task-based Adaptive learNer Guidance On the Web), a system for the creation and teaching of Web adaptive courses accessible through the Web). Section 3 describes the teaching tasks and rules on which the definition of web courses managed by the system is based, while section 4 analyses the most significant aspects of our system compared to other existing systems. Finally, the conclusion section describes the work in progress. More details about TANGOW can be found at [4].

2.   THE ARCHITECTURE OF TANGOW

TANGOW architecture is based on the standard Web paradigm, where the server receives requests from students through their browsers. There is a process for each student connected to the system which takes control of the student learning process during the whole session. If the same student is following more than one course, there will be a process for each of them.

All the above mentioned components of the system are illustrated in figure 1, where dotted arrows represent information flow and solid ones represent inter-process communication. The white arrow represents a function call.

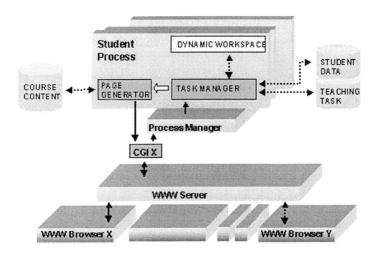

Figure 1: TANGOW system architecture

2.1   The programs

The main modules of the system are the *Process Manager*, the *Task Manager* and the *Page Generator*. All of them are in the server to which the students connect, and are accessible through a *CGI* program. For the system to be operative, the *Process Manager* must be always active, waiting for the students' requests. When the *CGI* receives a request, it sends the received parameters to the *Process Manager* and keeps waiting for an answer from the *Page Generator*.

When the *Process Manager* receives a request, its parameters are analysed and sent to the corresponding *Task Manager*, which is previously launched if it is not already running. The *Task Manager* stores information about the student's actions and sends the relevant information to the *Page Generator* which generates the HTML pages dynamically and sends them back to the student through the *CGI* program. An example of this process corresponds to browser X in figure 1. The requests for static HTML page are not managed by the *CGI* program (see browser Y in the same figure).

The *Task Manager* guides students in their learning process by deciding the next set of achievable tasks that will be offered to them. The elements in this set depend on the active learning strategy, the student's personal data and student's actions previously performed. This information is transferred to the *Task Manager* as parameter values in the submitted requests. Furthermore, the *Task Manager* stores information about the actions performed by the student and their results (the number of pages visited, the number of exercises done, the number of exercises successfully solved, etc) in a dynamic tree. In this tree, the nodes correspond to the tasks achieved by the student while the edges represent the composition relation between those tasks .

Finally, the *Task Manager* provides the *Page Generator* with the parameters that will be needed during dynamic page generation. These parameters are related to the student's profile and the student's actions. Based on this information the *Page Generator* decides which type of media elements (i.e. texts, images, videos, animations, simulations, applets, ...) will appear in the HTML document and how they will be laid out. Information about the student's profile will be used to select specific media elements according to features such as its content difficulty, the language in which they are written, etc. Once the HTML page is generated, it is sent back to the student through the *CGI* program.

2.2   The data

The previous modules use information stored in the *Users DB*, the *Course Content DB* and the *Teaching Tasks Repository*.

The *Users DB* contains data about student's profiles and their actions during the learning process. A student profile includes personal information such as his/her age, selected language and preferences with respect to the learning strategy. At the end of a session the corresponding dynamic tree (part of the Dynamic Workspace) is stored in this database.

In the *Course Content DB*, all media elements that will appear on the HTML pages are stored. They are classified according to student profile features (i.e. language, age, ...).

Finally, the *Teaching Task Repository* contains a general description of all the teaching tasks that have been defined by the course designer, along with the definition of the rules that establish the relationships among tasks.

3.   THE COURSE DESIGN

In order to create a new course, the course designer has to define the tasks and rules corresponding to the course and classify the multimedia elements that will appear on the HTML pages to be generated. In the current version of the system, tasks and rules are written directly in text files which are processed by a compiler that automatically generates the objects that compose the course. This process is illustrated in Figure 2.

Designer **TANGOW System**

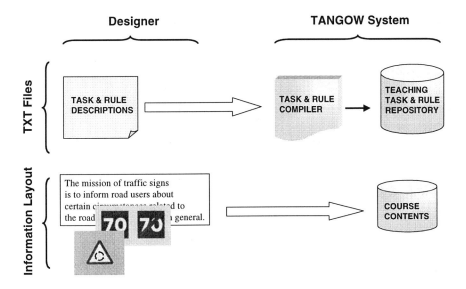

Figure 2: Task & rule description and object generation

3.1   The Teaching Tasks

A *Teaching Task* is the basic unit in the learning process, and it can be atomic or composed. The whole course can be viewed as a main task that has to be achieved which is conceptually divided into subtasks that can be divided into subtasks recursively. Students have to perform all or only some of them so that the main task can be considered as achieved.

With respect to its main goal, each task can be theoretical, practical or contain examples. It may have a method associated that decides, at runtime, whether the task is finished. This method can receive parameters related to the student actions while performing the task (if the task is atomic) or to subtask finalization (if it is composed).

A task may have a list of media element associated, which will be used for page generation. A description language is used to specify the type of media elements that will appear on the pages and their layout.

The multimedia elements are stored and classified depending on their nature (i.e. difficulty level or language). The system selects the most suitable media for each student while generating the HTML pages associated to the task that is being performed by the student at a given moment.

3.2   The relationships among Teaching Tasks

Task decomposition is represented by means of *Rules*. Each rule has a name and it includes information about the composed task, the list of associated subtasks, and a keyword indicating subtask sequencing: it may be necessary for the student to perform all the subtasks in a predefined order (AND), in any order (ANY), or it may be enough to perform some of them (OR or XOR). Moreover, a rule specifies its activation condition, which can depend on parameters related to tasks that have been already performed, the student profile or the strategy that is being used. Finally, the way dynamic parameters (number of visited pages, number of exercises correctly solved, etc.) are propagated from subtasks to composed tasks is indicated.

3.3   Teaching Task and Rule examples

The whole description of the teaching tasks and rules composing a course on driving that has been developed for demonstration purposes can be found at   http://www.ii.uam.es/esp/investigacion/tangow/curso/TaskTree.html.   In this schema, each cell corresponds to a task. Those rules in which the task appear at the LHS of the rule (or the RHS) are written above (or below) the task name. The task and rule definition is independent of the language, except for, in the current version of the system, the "description" field, which is used as the text for the links appearing on the HTML pages presented.

TYPE =	T	
ATOMIC =	Y	
DESCRIPTION =	Description of Circular Signs	
END_METHOD =	F_TEO	
PARAMS =	pags_visited tot_pags	
HTML =	CIRCULAR	M1
	STOP	M1
	C_PROHI	M1
	E_PROHI	M1
	EP_VEHI	M1
	EPV_SIDE	M1

Figure 3: Description of 'Circular_Signs" teaching task

The "Circular signs" task [Figure 3] is an example of a theoretical atomic task. Its finalization method ("f_teo") will receive several input parameters such as the number of pages visited so far by the student ("pag_visited") and the total number of pages related to the task ("tot_pag"). The media elements used to generate the associated HTML pages appear in the HTML field.

With respect to teaching rules, a definition example is shown in Figure 4. It corresponds to the rule "R1", where precondition "c_4" indicates that the rule will be active only if the execution of method "c_4" returns true when it is given the value for the "exer_ok" parameter from "Vertical_Signs" as input.

The parameter propagation is described in "calc_pars" field, where it must be specified, for each parameter whose value must be calculated, its name, the method used for the calculation and a list with parameters which the calculation depends on, along with the tasks where values for these parameters must be found. In our example, the value for "time_in" in "Circumstantial_Signs" task is calculated as a sum of values for the parameters "time_in" in the subtasks "Circ_Signs_Theory" and "Circ_Signs_Exercises".

SEQUENCING =	AND			
LHS =	CIRCUMSTANTIAL_SIGNS			
RHS =	CIRC_SIGNS_THEORY			
	CIRC_SIGNS_EXERCISES			
ACT_COND =	c-4			
PARAMS =	exer_ok	Vertical_Signs		
CALC_PARS =	time_in	msum2	time_in	Circ_Signs_Theory
			time_in	Circ_Signs_Exercises
	tot_pag	mdirect	tot_pag	Circ_Signs_Theory
	exer_ok	mdirect	exer_ok	Circ_Signs_Exercises
	exer_done	mdirect	exer_done	Circ_Signs_Exercises
	tot_exer	mdirect	tot_exer	Circ_Signs_Exercises
	pag_visited	mdirect	pag_visited	Circ_Signs_Theory

Figure 4: A sample rule definition

4.   STATE OF THE ART

Of special interest in the field of intelligent tutoring systems is the work developed by the ELM group in recent years [3]. One of their implementations is ELM-ART II [9], an adaptive Web-based tutoring system on LISP programming which received the European Academic Software Award in 1998. Adaptivity in ELM-ART II is implemented by selecting the next best step in the curriculum on demand. Links in HTML pages are annotated according to a traffic lights metaphor, where different colours are used to indicate, among other things, that a section is ready to be learned and recommended, ready but not recommended or not ready to be learned yet.

This annotation process is performed whenever a learning unit is finished by reviewing all the concepts that are prerequisites to this unit. This differs from TANGOW, where the dynamic tree is used to restrict the set of teaching tasks that need to be reviewed whenever a task is finished.

As for the process of dynamic page generation, the AHA system [2] can be mentioned where filters for content fragments are encoded by means of conditional sentences that are included as comments in HTML pages. In this system the pages are already created and it is decided, at runtime, which portions of them are shown to the student whereas with our approach HTML pages are created at runtime by linking media elements.

In other systems [5], pages related to teaching materials are generated by formalizing the structure of the documents using SGML and by specifying the particular contents for this general structure. In TANGOW there is no need to define different page structures, because each page is composed "on the fly" by choosing from the media elements associated to the active task those that will appear on the HTML pages.

Finally, the approach followed in the DCG system [8] is worth mentioning. Here, course structure is represented as a road-map which is used to generate a course plan for the course. The planner searches for sub-graphs that connect the concepts known by the learner with the goal-concept, and changes the plan if the student is not able to achieve a result higher than a given threshold score. In DCG adaptivity is implemented by modifying the plan to achieve the goal-concept, while TANGOW adapts the course contents to the student's learning progress by changing the set of possible subtasks offered at every learning step.

5.   CONCLUSIONS AND FUTURE WORK

The TANGOW system allows the development of Web-based adaptive courses. These courses are described by means of tasks and rules, which are used at execution time to guide the students during their learning process, so that they will be presented with different HTML pages depending on their profile, their previous actions, and the active learning strategy. Moreover, the HTML pages are dynamically generated from the multimedia information associated to each task and the multimedia elements stored.

TANGOW is written in Java and can be accessed via the Internet by using any standard browser. Thanks to the storage of tasks, rules and multimedia objects in databases, the maintenance cost is low since designers may change, add or remove course components easily. The use of databases also facilitates the reuse of components in different courses. Currently we are working on a designer tool to facilitate course development.

We are also working in the improvement of the adaptation process, including the possibility of changing the teaching strategy at runtime, depending on the results achieved by students. Furthermore, several courses that will be tested by Computer Science students are being developed. This experience will allow us to evaluate the effectiveness of the system.

On the other hand, we think that TANGOW architecture is suitable for supporting collaborative work among system users by establishing communication procedures between student and instructor processes. It is also possible for the designers to collaborate on the development of web-based courses and contents. This will be part of our future work.

ACKNOWLEDGEMENTS

This paper was sponsored by the Spanish Interdepartmental Commission of Science and Technology (CICYT), project number TEL97-0306.

REFERENCES

1. Ausserhofer, A. (1999). Web-Based Teaching and Learning: A Panacea?, *IEEE Communications*, Volume 37, Number 3, pp. 92-96, March 1999.
2. de Bra, P. & Calvi, L. (1998). AHA: A Generic Adaptive Hypermedia System, *Second Workshop on Adaptive Hypertext and Hypermedia,* at the *Ninth ACM Conference on Hypertext and Hypermedia*, pp. 5-11. Pittsburgh, USA, June 20-24, 1998.
3. Brusilovsky, P. & Anderson, J. (1998). ACT-R electronic bookshelf: An adaptive system for learning cognitive psychology on the Web, *WebNet 98 World Conference of the WWW, Internet & Intranet*, pp. 92-97, Orlando, Florida, November 7-12, 1998.
4. Carro, R.M., Pulido, E. & Rodríguez, P. (1999). TANGOW: Task-based Adaptive learNer Guidance On the Web, *2nd Workshop on Adaptive Systems and User Modeling on the Web at the Eight International WWW Conference*. Toronto, Canada, May 11-14, 1999.
5. da Graça, M., Benedito, J., Pontin R. (1998). Tools for Authoring and Presenting Structured Teaching Material in the WWW, *WebNet 98 World Conference of the WWW, Internet & Intranet*, pp. 194-199, Orlando, Florida, November 7-12, 1998.
6. Hmelo, C., Guzdial, M. & Turns, J. (1998). Computer-Support for Collaborative Learning: Learning to Support Student Engagement, *AACE Journal of Interactive Learning Research (JILR)*, Volume 9, Number 2, p. 107, 1998.
7. Nicol, J., Gutfreund, Y., Paschetto, J., Rush, K.& Martin,C. (1999). How the Internet Helps Build Collaborative Multimedia Applications, *Communications of the ACM*, Volume 42, Number 1, pp. 79-85, January 1999.
8. Vassileva, J. (1998). A Task-Centred Approach for User Modeling in a Hypermedia Office Documentation System, in Brusilovsky, P., Kobsa, A. and Vassileva J. (Eds.) *Adaptive Hypertext and Hypermedia*, Kluwer Academic Publ. Dordrecht, pp. 209-247, 1998.
9. Weber, G & Specht, M. (1997). User modeling and adaptive navigation support in WWW-based tutoring systems, *User Modeling '97*, pp. 289-300, Italy, June, 1997.

APRISA: A Tool for Teaching the Interconnection of Open Systems

E. M. De la Calzada Cuesta, B. Curto Diego, A. M. Moreno Montero, V. Moreno Rodilla, F. J. Blanco Rodríguez, F. J. García Peñalvo
University of Salamanca, Dpt of Computer Science and Automation, Facultad de Ciencias; Plaza de la Merced S/N; 37008 Salamanca. Tel. 923 294400 ext. 1303 E-mail:{bcurto,vmoreno, jblanco}@abedul.usal.es;{amoreno,fgarcia}@gugu.usal.es

Key words: learning application, open systems, OSI model, computer networks

Abstract: The purpose of this paper is to present a software learning programme called APRISA (Learning Open System Interconnections). This software focuses on subjects related to computer networks. Our tool provides a way to study and analyse communications under the OSI reference model. Since we have the necessary elements for the configuration and monitoring of each layer, it is possible to learn and implement the reference model. Several applications have been developed which enable us to check the correct performance of each layer. In this way, our tool aims to show the validated and useful set of rules comprising the model. Our tool is being very successfully implemented in different modules of communication areas in Computer Science

1.   INTRODUCTION

In the present information revolution, society as a whole is being highly affected by the impact of the Internet. The already well-known term, *information highways*, is becoming more a reality day by day. Therefore, the teaching of the fundamentals of data communication and computer networks is important if we are to keep up with technology. This is even more so at the university and therefore in the students' general education; computer sciences will be more and more present and, in consequence, so will computer networks.

M. Ortega and J. Bravo (eds.), Computers and Education in the 21st Century, 137–147.

Most networks are organised in a series of layers or levels, in order to reduce the complexity of their design. Each one is built over its predecessor. The number of layers, the name, content, and function of each one varies from one network to another. However, in any network, the purpose of each layer is to offer certain services to the upper layers, thus freeing them from detailed knowledge on how these services are carried out [9].

In the middle of the 1970s, when different types of distributed systems (based on both public and private networks) began to abound, the computer industry recognised the potential advantages of open systems. The result was the introduction of a series of standards, the first of which dealt with the overall structure of the whole subsystem of the internal communication of each computer. This standard was introduced by the International Standards Organization (ISO) and it is known as the ISO Reference Model for OSI: Open Systems Interconnection [4].

The study of these standards is the basis for teaching computer networks. It therefore seems essential that they should be correctly understood by students beginning their studies in this area as well as in other related areas. Abundant literature exists that describes and analyses this model in depth, but always from a basically theoretical point of view [4], [8], [9]. Likewise, the manufacturers of communication equipment claim to comply with the standards promulgated, but the source code is not accessible. Bibliographic endeavours do not seem to be sufficient for the student to be able to understand the model well enough to perform practical implementation. Therefore, why not look for software that would make it possible to explain the concepts and functioning of the model?

The first problem was to decide what our physical layer was going to be. The serial port was chosen because it is the one most used for communication between PCs [1], [2], [10]. The interface selected is also widely used not only in PC communication but also in most network interconnection equipment: bridges, routers, etc. All these have a serial interface for configuring and monitoring their functioning as well as for carrying out remote administration tasks. In industry, most of the equipment that can be connected to a computer, such as robots, programmable automatons, controllers, etc. have a serial port for carrying out tasks for their configuration and control.

There is much software on the market that allows two PCs to communicate through the serial port, but none of it permits total monitoring of all the phases of functioning. Neither does it implement all the modalities of services that, according to the OSI model, can be provided at each layer.

All this led us to propose the making of this application in order to develop our own software, which would meet the necessary requirements for use as supporting material in educational tasks in subjects in the area of communications. Our interest focussed on the pedagogical aspect rather than on efficiency of implementation. Furthermore, the program has been given a graphic user interface which is convenient, easy to use and attractive to students.

The rest of this article is organised as follows. The second section describes the profile of the student to whom the tool is addressed. This, together with the teaching objectives pursued, will allow us to define the requirements that the software should comply with. The third section gives a detailed description of the different modules into which the application is divided from the point of view of its potential user and highlights the aspects that are most important and useful for the student using the program. This section also offers some details on implementation as well as the hardware and software necessary. Finally the main conclusions are given together with possible future studies.

2.   REQUIREMENTS OF THE APPLICATION

Since this is a didactic application, first an analysis will be made of the type of user it is aimed at and the knowledge needed in subjects related to the objective of the application. Thus, the profile of the student is that of a university student with a basic knowledge of electronics and computer architecture. He/she must also have knowledge of data transmission as well as of the theoretical fundamentals of the reference model.

The aim of APRISA is to facilitate the study and analysis of communications through the serial port, following the OSI reference model of the ISO and is intended for use in practical classes as an aid to the teacher. Thus, if the model is to be learned and implemented, it should have the elements necessary for monitoring its layers. Furthermore, it should incorporate a series of applications to validate its functionality.

The tool requires strict compliance with the norms promulgated by the ISO and must show the complete internal functioning at all layers. Thus, it should not only implement the functionality of all layers, but also show at all times the service primitives invoked by each of them, as well as the formation of the protocol data units (N-PDUs) that exchange equal entities on each layer.

Moreover, the application should have an interface that is attractive, useful and comfortable for the student. Another important aspect is that it should be capable of being executed in an operating system that requires low costs in hardware and at the same time gives good performance and speed. Windows thus seemed a suitable choice, since its interface is well known to the students.

3.   DESCRIPTION OF THE APPLICATION

To reach the desired teaching objectives, the physical, data link and network layers were designed covering all the service modalities that they can possibly offer. Thus, it also has an application layer that permits the editing and transferring of files as well as chat. *Figure 1* shows a diagram of the general working blocks of the application.

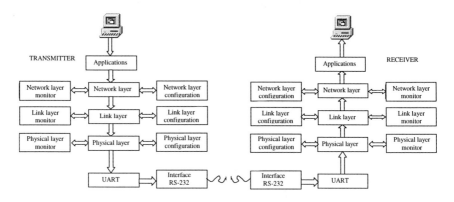

Figure 1. General functioning of the application

As can be seen in the figure, the different modules that make up the application are each of the layers of the OSI tower. In this version of the program, four of the seven layers have been implemented: the physical layer, the data link layer, the network layer and the application layer. In subsequent versions the modules corresponding to the rest of the layers will be approached. In all of them it will be possible to monitor and configure their behaviour.

3.1   The Physical Layer

In order to illustrate the functioning of the physical layer for the student, computers are connected through the serial ports. These are generally used to connect devices such as modems or mouses, or to join two computers in a simple way by means of a null modem cable. The interface used by these devices is the V.24/EIA-232-E (or simply RS-232). This defines the mechanical, electric, functional and procedural characteristics for connecting data terminating equipment (DTE) to data circuit terminating equipment (DCE). Once the interface is defined, the data will come through the hardware. Asynchronous functions carried out by an integrated circuit called UART (Universal Asynchronous Receiver Transmitter) are generally used.

With this type of circuit the reception and transmission of data is simply transformed into readings and writings of bytes (or characters) in the UART, which behaves with respect to the processor as one or more binary memory positions or I/O ports. Our linkage protocols will thus be oriented to character because of the hardware chosen.

To manage the serial port, we used some functions of the Windows API (OpenComm, SetCommState, etc.) which guarantee that data will not be lost when queues for transmission and reception are formed where the data will be stored until the application processes them [5], [6]. When a datum arrives at the serial port, it passes automatically to the queue, and it is from this queue that the application will read the data, ensuring that no datum is lost due to a delay in the processing of other functions.

To begin to use the software and study the functioning of this layer, the student should connect two computers using a null modem cable. Thus, the student must first configure the communications parameters (see *Figure 2*).

Figure 2. Dialogue box for configuring the physical layer

Subsequently, the monitoring of the physical layer will be possible (see *Figure 3*); a window will show the UART state, reception/transmission and control registers. Furthermore, individual characters can be transmitted and variations in the registers can be observed on line.

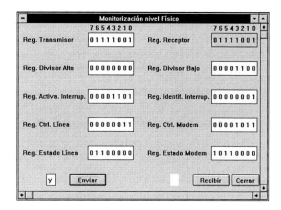

Figure 3. Window for monitoring the physical layer

3.2   The Data Link Layer

The student must be able to understand that, besides sending signals through the transmission link, it is necessary to control and manage the data communication. To do this, it is necessary to have a logical layer on top of the physical interface, which is called the data link layer or data link protocol.

Four different types of protocols have been developed within this layer. In each of them the complexity increases gradually in order to show the student the need for and use of each of the fields that make up the data link layer. The protocol to be used is selected in the configuration box of the data link layer (see *Figure 4*).

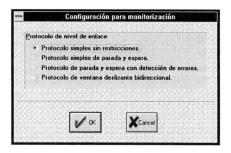

Figure 4. Configuration of the data link level

For monitoring the data link layer, two windows appear, one on each end of the communication, which will take the role of transmitter and receiver. From these windows, one can interact directly with the application as a user of the data link layer. In the transmitter window, a chain of data of up to 64 characters can be entered that will be encapsulated within the frame of the data link layer. The receiver window shows the frame of data received and the data obtained by demultiplexing this frame. At the same time the lower part of the window gives the service primitives of the link layer (see *Figure 5*).

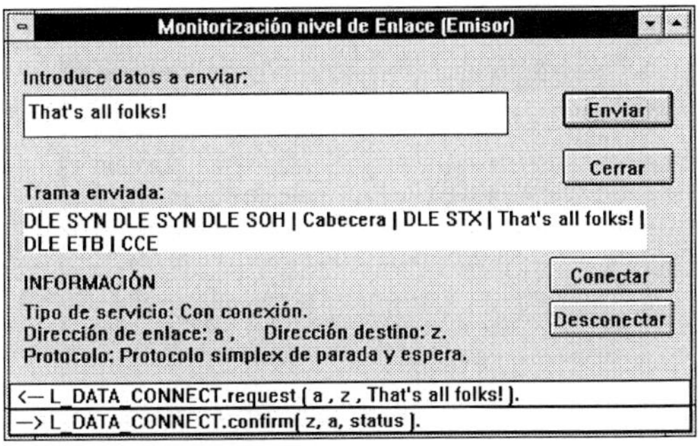

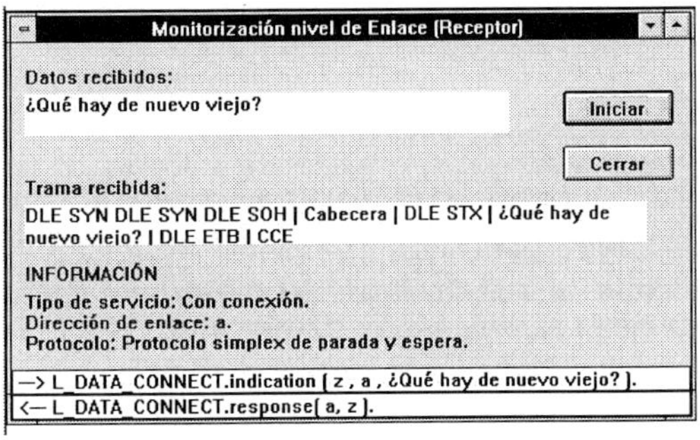

Figure 5. Monitoring of the link level

The exchange of primitives will depend on whether a connection or connectionless service is used. If the connection service is selected, in the transmitter window the connect and disconnect buttons will also appear. These will send the connection and disconnection frames, respectively.

3.3   The Network Layer

Once the student has understood the need for the link layer, its functions and the services that it offers to the higher level, then the network layer functions are presented. The user will see that he/she must send the packets from an origin to a particular destination, passing through several intermediate nodes to get there. Thus, it can be seen how in the network layer, a network layer heading is added to the data from the higher layers (application layer), and the result set (packet) is passed to the link layer, where it will be encapsulated within a frame.

The class of service provided to the higher layers can be selected: a connection or connectionless service. One can also assign the name (or address) of the network of the sending or receiving station. *Figure 6* shows the dialogue box for the configuration of the network layer.

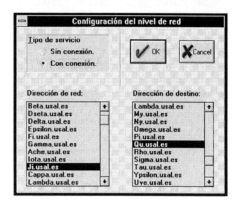

Figure 6. Dialogue box for the configuration of the network layer

Monitoring of the network layer is carried out in the same way as for the link layer, thus making it possible to visualize the service primitives, the packets (or data units of the network protocol) and the encapsulation or demultiplexing of packets. Just as in the link level, the exchange of primitives will depend on whether a connection or connectionless service is used (see *Figure 7*).

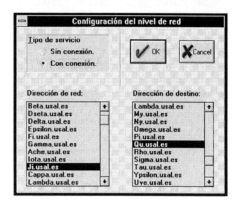

Figure 7. Monitoring of the network layer

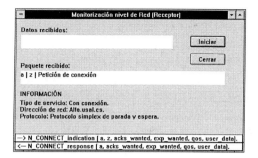

Figure 7. (Cont.) Monitoring of the network layer

3.4   The Application Layer

Applications have also been developed that make it possible to verify the correct functioning of each and every one of the layers. Thus the validity and utility of the set of standards comprising the model can be shown.

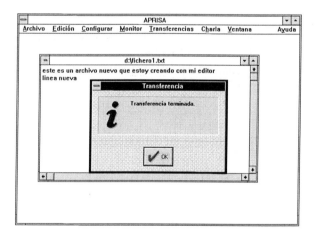

Figure 8. File transfer

The applications are file transfer and chat. File transfer permits the sending and receiving of binary and text files. *Figure 8* shows an example of the sending of a text file carried out with the text editor of the application. Moreover, an application called chat has been designed that allows written communication in real time from users on different computers. *Figure 9* shows the window of this application.

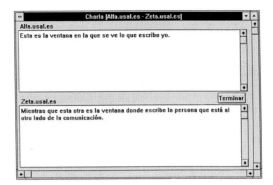

Figure 9. Chat

3.5   Implementation

The software has been developed for Windows type operating systems. The main tool used for its development was Borland C++ & Application FrameWorks, which allows the direct use of the Application Program Interface (API) of Windows and incorporates other high level applications of great utility, such as Resource Workshop. It also allows the use of object libraries for the Windows environment, facilitating the task of programming; among these we can mention the use of ObjectWindows BWCC [3], [5], [6], [7].

3.6   Requirements

In order to run APRISA, 2 PC/AT 486DX or higher (Pentium is recommendable), 1Mb or more of memory, a null modem cable and, optionally, multiplexors are needed. The operating system should be Windows 3.1 or higher.

4.   CONCLUSIONS AND FUTURE WORK

The objective posed, i.e., to develop educational software that would allow any student of the OSI model to configure and monitor each of the first three layers, has largely been fulfilled.

In our case, the physical layer chosen was the serial port, which has traditionally been used for communication between computers. Thus, the experience acquired in handling the serial port in Windows can be used to design software that will interact with any device having this interface.

The layers were developed by strictly following the OSI standard. Each layer provides services to the higher layers through a standardized interface and each layer entity implements the protocols of its own layer for dialogue with its counterpart entity. Each of the layers can be configured and monitored by a student-friendly interface such as Windows.

The programme is being used with highly satisfactory results in applied sessions in the subjects "Data Transmission" and "Computer Networks", which both form part of the curriculum for Technical Engineering in Computer Science.

This is the first version of the APRISA programme, and it will be extended in the future to implement the functionalities of the rest of the OSI layers.

The physical medium used may limit the opportunity of the upper layers of the model in that it may impose restrictions on the network designed over it. Thus, the first task to be tackled is the incorporation to the application of other media (e.g., Ethernet) which will make it possible to design more complete networks where the functionalities of the remaining levels can be shown without the limitations mentioned above.

Another possible line would be the development of the tool in other platforms, such as Windows-NT or Unix/Linux, both very widespread on the market and present in practice laboratories at our universities.

REFERENCES

1. Campbell, J. (1987). Comunicaciones serie. Guía de referencia del programador en C. Anaya Multimedia.
2. Carballar Falcón, J. A. (1996). El libro de las comunicaciones del PC. Ra-ma.
3. Franco García, Á. (1994). Programación de aplicaciones Windows con Borland C++ y ObjectWindows. McGraw-Hill.
4. Halsall, F. (1998). Comunicación de datos, redes de computadores y sistemas abiertos. Addison-Wesley Iberoamericana.
5. Peña Tresancos, J. (1992). Fundamentos y desarrollo de programas en Windows 3.X. Anaya Multimedia.
6. Petzold, C. (1992). Programación en Windows. Guía Microsoft para programar aplicaciones en Windows 3. Anaya Multimedia. Microsoft Press.
7. Shammas, N. C. (1993). Librería ObjectWindows. Guía de programación en Windows. Anaya Multimedia.
8. Stallings, W. (1997). Comunicaciones y redes de computadores. Prentice Hall.
9. Tanenbaum, A. S. (1997). Redes de ordenadores. Prentice Hall.
10. Tischer, M. (1993). PC interno. Marcombo.

Interactive Mathematics Teaching with *Mathedu*

Fernando Díez[1], Roberto Moriyón[2]

Departamento de Ingeniería Informática. Universidad Autónoma de Madrid – Madrid, Spain
[1] Escuela Politécnica Superior de Ingeniería. Universidad Antonio de Nebrija – Madrid, Spain
[2] Instituto de Ingeniería del Conocimiento. Universidad Autónoma de Madrid – Madrid, Spain

Key words: Programming by example, Computer Assisted Learning, Symbolic Computation.

Abstract: Although the end of this century is bringing up a lot of improvements in computer technology, there are no applications for teaching Mathematics with enough level of interactivity with the student. In this paper we are describing how an authoring tool, *MathEdu,* based on the *Programming by demonstration* paradigm and on *Mathematica*®, enables the construction of sets of exercises in Mathematics making use of symbolic calculations in a simple way. *MathEdu* is also designed to solve exercises generated from the teacher's examples interactively with the student.

1.   INTRODUCTION

It is intrinsically complex to apply the most recent and advanced computer based teaching technologies to scientific areas and, specially, Mathematics. The difficulties that arise are of two types: on the one hand, building a suitable user interface is hard; on the other hand, developing a system that is intelligent enough for the underlying task is a challenge that is hard to overcome. The first type of difficulties is closely related to the fact that scientific areas, in general, are expressed in a specific form that combines usually simple written text, formulae, and structured figures, including explicit or implicit references among one another. On the other hand, the main source of problems for the development of a system with the degree of intelligence required to teach scientific subjects is the richness and complexity of the reasoning mechanisms that lay behind them. These

149

M. Ortega and J. Bravo (eds.), Computers and Education in the 21st Century, 149–161.

mechanisms can be formalized at different levels, but it is hard to make them available to the students in a way that is not hard for them to assimilate.

During the last years, several important steps have been taken in an attempt to overcome the difficulties mentioned in the first place by means of programming systems that are especially suitable for their use in scientific contexts, like *Mathematica*® and *Maple*. The most advanced versions of these systems integrate a high capacity of symbolic treatment of all kinds of graphics and expressions with typical aspects of conventional user interfaces that are more and more sophisticated, such as dialogs, selection menus, buttons, animations, etc. All this allows working documents to become active documents under the control of the programs that work behind them. These advancements are giving rise to a new generation of interactive applications for Mathematics and other scientific subjects tutoring. Among them, *Calculus@Mathematica* (www-cm.math.uiuc.edu) is a sample of a complete course, and *Calculus Wiz*, (www.math.uiowa.edu/~stroyan/wiz.html), is one of the systems that makes use of the most advanced technology. It is worth noting here that as more interactive capabilities for the development of generic scientific-technical applications are added to these systems, their programming becomes more complex. This difficulty increases especially when teaching applications are developed, since a high degree of interactivity is required in this case.

There have been important improvements also in the direction of increasing the amount of intelligence available in Mathematics related applications. These improvements are based on new techniques developed in the context of Computational Logic; however, the improvements that have been achieved are limited to the development of systems that participate in competitions for the automatic solution of broad sets of problems, [10]. Applications of these technologies to Computer Assisted Teaching are still to come. From our point of view, using natural deduction mechanisms, similar to the ones used by people when working on Mathematics, [3], might be fundamental in the future in order to make advances in this field available for their use in computer programs that can help in the teaching process.

The development of authoring tools that are designed for expert users (teachers of Mathematics) to build their own interactive programs (courses, sets of problems, etc) is one of the most important goals to be achieved in this field. This is a consequence of the inherent difficulty we have pointed out before for the development of interactive software for the teaching of Mathematics and other scientific subjects. The most powerful techniques that have been developed during the last years trying to simplify the design of generic user interfaces [11], [7] are based on the use of *Programming by Example* [4] in order to allow the designer of the interface to work in the same context the user of the interface will. In this way, the design work is much more intuitive, and the designer can focus his efforts on its most delicate aspects. However, using techniques of *Programming by example* in the context of applications for the interactive teaching of scientific subjects implies the use of highly sophisticated user interfaces for the manipulation of this type of materials, and this increases to their maximum degree the problems that have been commented at the beginning of this introduction. Nevertheless, the main advantages of this approach are: First of all, the work spent on the creation of the authoring tool is accomplished only once, and its output is reused later in all the different applications that are developed by the teachers. Moreover, the development of the interface is done by highly qualified people, who are able to overcome the technical difficulties that are inherent to this kind of problems.

In this paper we describe how the degree of interactivity that is available in the systems previously mentioned can be used in order to allow the development of sets of problems of Mathematics related to different subjects by means of an authoring tool, *MathEdu* [5]. On the one hand, this tool reduces the complexity of the development process of problem sets; on the other hand, the bigger flexibility and power of the application interface that is built, measured in terms of the degree of communication with the student, allows a richer interaction with the student, as well as more intelligent dialogues. Although the programs developed with *MathEdu* actually incorporate a treatment of the mathematical knowledge that is very rudimentary from the point of view of Artificial Intelligence or from that of the most powerful techniques of automatic reasoning, it is remarkable that simply by increasing the interactivity of the system and its capability of symbolic treatment of conceptual structures, together with a very simple set of problem solution rules, allows the achievement of goals that were unaffordable up to now, such as studying systematically common errors among the students and giving interactive explanations of their origins and the way to avoid them. A prototype of the *MathEdu* tool has been implemented, with the capacity to interpret a subset of the set of actions described in this paper, and there is work under way in order to build a complete prototype that will cover the whole functionality. *MathEdu* is developed in the language that lies behind the *Mathematica*® system [13].

The remaining parts of this paper are structured as follows: In the first place, the main features of the applications developed by means of *MathEdu* from the perspective of the student are described. Next, the main advantages that are achieved by its use are shown. Finally, some considerations about the possibilities of the technology used in *MathEdu* are made in the conclusions.

2.   LEARNING WITH *MATHEDU:* THE DIALOG WITH THE STUDENT

Traditionally, tools that help in Mathematics teaching are based on two aspects: contents presentation using hypertext facilities, as in the *MACSYMA Advisor* [6], and *HYPERMAT* [1], and certain degree of interactivity with the student, who can check some aspects of the matters under study by means of the execution of procedures that are associated to the tutor. The most advanced systems include procedures of this type that are sensible to their parametric modification, as in *Calculus@Mathematica*.

During the last years, the main tendency points towards an increase in the student's ability to interact with the system. *MathEdu* is conceived to help the student interactively in the learning process of the solution of problems that require the detection of suitable techniques for their solution and their application. Among these problems the ones related to the computation of limits, derivatives, integrals, solution of Ordinary Differential Equations, etc can be pointed out. Similar problems of one of these types, like computing integrals, are solved in different ways depending on specific conditions, subtle ones at times, that the student must learn how to distinguish. Hence, the first step in the solution of a problem in *MathEdu* is the identification of a *strategy* that is suitable for the problem being solved. Even after choosing a strategy, several slightly different cases can arise, as it happens for example in problems of integration by parts, where the right decomposition of the integrand as a product depends on the kind of integrand. Finally, for each strategy and each corresponding specific case, *MathEdu* starts an interactive session consisting of questions the student has to respond successively. Each question or indication depends on the previous steps taken by the student; this makes the dialogue to be guided in an intelligent way.

For example, if the student has to compute the integral of the function $x^2 \sin x$, first he/she will have to indicate that the appropriate strategy to solve this problem is integration by parts. After this, he/she will indicate the right description of the strategy among a list of alternatives offered by the system. Then he/she will be asked to indicate how the integral should be decomposed as a product, and which of the chosen factors must be integrated and which one must be differentiated. Next, the student must solve two subproblems: computing an integral, in this case that of the function $\sin x$, and computing a derivative, in this case that of the function x^2. Finally, the results of these calculations are used in order to substitute the original problem by a new one that consists in the computation of the integral of the function $x \cos x$. After following the same process once more, the problem to be solved is the computation of the integral of *sin x*, an immediate integral that allows the computation of the integral wanted initially.

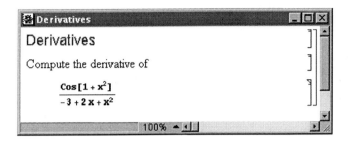

Figure 1.

In order to simplify the interaction of the student with the system, *MathEdu* has been designed in such a way that the working environment is similar to the usual one in a text book or when the student is working with pen and paper. Hence, while working on any *MathEdu* problem, the student will find several elements that allow him to interact with the system. They include the following ones:

a) A SOLUTION WINDOW.
This window shows the statement of the exercise that must be solved to the student, as well as the state of its solving process, including the different messages, actions, strategies, and partial results that have been generated along the solving process and still keep valid information, like the description of the steps that have been given during the solution process. This is, so to say, the working sheet of the student. The sheet includes interleaved texts and formulae that are included by the system, together with some others that reflect data given by the student during the solution process.
Figure 1 shows the statement that is shown to the students corresponding to a derivation exercise as it appears at the beginning of their work.

a) A STRATEGIES PALETTE.
During the solution process of each exercise a specific strategy is involved. For example, within the integration chapter there are strategies for integration by parts, by change of variable, immediate integrals, integration of rational functions, etc. Similarly, in the example of Figure 1, the strategy for the derivation of quotients would be used. Each strategy identifies a specific resolution path for an exercise by means of some specific techniques.
Figure 2 shows a palette of strategies that correspond to different types of Ordinary Differential Equations to be solved by the student. The system is waiting for the student to specify an alternative among the four

possible ones. From a didactic point of view, this identification process helps to structure within the student's mental image of the subject those conditions that make a determined strategy suitable for the resolution of a problem, as well as the actions that have to be performed in order to achieve the solution to the problem.

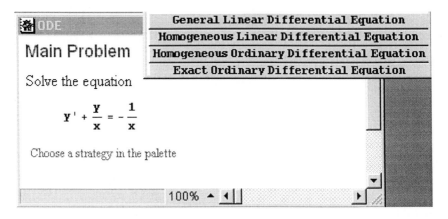

Figure 2.

a) Several DIALOG WINDOWS.

The input windows are used to allow the student to incorporate data to the system. The input can be conditional, in which case it is accepted or not depending on the fulfillment of a given condition, as it is the fact that the value agrees with the derivative of some other data associated to the problem.

Besides the processes associated to the previous components, during its execution the system accomplishes some actions which have some influence on the work flow and the data associated to the resolution process, but which are not associated automatically to the appearance of any specific elements. These actions can be of the following types:

Assign. This action is used to give a value to a variable, equation, etc.

Solve. This action is used in order to ask the student to solve a subproblem within a given exercise that is being solved. Typical examples are calculating a derivative or obtaining the primitive of a function in an exercise of integration by parts, or solving the homogeneous differential equation associated to a first order linear ODE.

Return. This action returns the results of an operation or subproblem solution.

According to these elements and some other auxiliary ones, the students must answer the different questions the system asks them successively, and, in case their answers are correct, they go ahead in the exercise solution. All the palettes of multiple selection are based on exercise types that have been defined *a priori* by the teacher and the students are supposed to know. As we will show in the next section, during the design process the teacher specifies the control of the work flow, including the generation of those dialogues that will interact with the students.

3.   TEACHING WITH *MATHEDU:* THE DESIGN PROCESS

Among the most important features of the structure of problem sets handled by *MathEdu* are the following: on the one hand, the existence of a unique statement for each problem type. For example, if the designer has defined a problem type for *integration* whose strategy is *by parts,* this problem type and its solution method (actions) have to be defined only once. According to this definition, the system is able to generate problems of integration by parts that include, for example, products of either a polynomial and a simple trigonometric function, or two simple trigonometric functions, or a polynomial and an exponential, etc. As a second relevant fact, in all these cases the student is guided during the solution process. *MathEdu* recognises exercises that are based on the same problem type but that use different types of data as similar ones. This is achieved by means of symbolic data patterns. Each resolution strategy for a problem type is based on the verification of a pattern that links the strategy to the type of problem and identifies the best method for the solution of the problem.

In order to clarify these ideas, let us consider the example introduced in the previous section. Let us assume the teacher wants to describe, by means of a pattern, all integrals that are compatible with the structure of the example he/she is introducing into the system. The integral of the corresponding integral must be the product of two expressions; the first one must be a polynomial, like x^2, and the other one must be a simple trigonometric function, like *sin x*. The pattern that generalizes the integral is

    Integrate[Times[u_, v_], x]

where the variable components correspond to the expressions $u\_$ and $v\_$. The values that can be taken by these expressions have to be specified also by the teacher. In our case, he/she must specify that

$u\_$ is a polynomial.
$v\_$ is a simple trigonometric function

These specifications are done by means of the predicates *PolynomialQ* and *trigonometricQ*, respectively. The teacher can also specify other conditions for different cases of the same strategy, such as asking for $v\_$ to be a logarithmic function, *logarithmicQ*. This modifies exclusively these conditions, leaving the same overall structure for the integral.

The use of patterns in order to identify cases for specific solution strategies allows *MathEdu* to admit several different solution methods for the same problem. For example, when computing the integral of the function $x/(x^2-1)$, *MathEdu* will allow the student to propose two different ways to perform the computation: either by means of a change of variable or as the integral of a rational function.

As we had already pointed out previously, this exploitation of the capacities of symbolic manipulation present in *Mathematica*® is one of the most relevant aspects of *MathEdu*. While current commercial systems generate problems that are similar to a given model by means of numerical data that are generated randomly, and then they make the students follow the same steps they had provided for the specific model problem, *MathEdu* generates randomly data with higher complexity, like polynomials and other types of structures, and students are allowed to take any decisions in the solution process that are compatible with the problem that has been generated. Some recent systems for the solution of problems of Mathematics, such as *Wiley Web Test* [12] or *Scientific Notebook* [8] make use also of this power of symbolic manipulation, but they differ from *MathEdu* in a fundamental aspect: patterns that correspond to different data are used only in order to generate problems that are similar to a given one, but they are not used to check the way the student processes those data. For example, if *MathEdu* asks the student within a course on integration to compute the integral of the function *Sen(x) Cos(2x)*, once the student has decided to make the computation by means of integration by parts, he/she has to indicate an appropriate decomposition of the integrand as the product of two functions *u* and *v*. In this case there are two answers that are valid; independently of which factor has played the role of *u* during the problem generation, *Mathedu* is able to recognise both options as being valid when the student makes a selection. All other systems just check that the final result given by the student is identical to the specific solution they have in mind.

In order to achieve an efficient use of the *MathEdu* authoring tool, an important dedication has to be given to the design process. We have to take into account that, for each alternative for the solution of a problem that the teacher wants to be available for the student, he must give an example that includes the corresponding generalizations and conditions, as well as all the specific actions the student must accomplish for its solution. In the next paragraphs we shall describe this process by analysing the design of the problem that has been considered in the previous section, namely the computation of the integral of the function $x^2 \sin x$.

The designer works in the same context the student does, but the system has a specific design mode. Once the formulation of the problem has been introduced in a similar *notebook* to the one that will be used by the student during its solution, the designer indicates the appropriate strategy (integration by parts); in case another case has been already introduced for this strategy, the system already knows that the integrand is decomposed as the product of two *metavariables, u* and *v;* otherwise, the designer has to specify it by selecting consecutively the functions that play these roles in the specific example he/she is working on, and by giving them names as *metavariables.* Afterwards, the system will ask him/her for the conditions that u and v must satisfy so that another problem can be considered as a generalization of the given one. The designer will also have to provide the corresponding generating functions; the specification of these functions can be done at any other time during the design process. The next step is the successive specification of the actions needed in order to solve the problem once the appropriate strategy has been chosen. The actions that lead to this decision are generated automatically by *MathEdu* depending on the strategies and the specific types of problems that have been designed, and those that the student has already studied. First, the designer specifies that two input windows have to be shown to the students so that they can introduce the values of u and v. The teacher gets in the design screen windows that are similar to the ones for the students, and he/she has to fill the corresponding information. He/she also has to indicate the corresponding assignments, as well as the final test of the corresponding pattern to the problem. As the teacher goes on in the design process, the same information as if the students were accomplishing the corresponding actions is shown in the design notebook. In this way, the teacher is constantly in the same context of the students, and hence he/she can detect the difficulties they might have. Afterwards, the teacher indicates the need to accomplish the solution of a subproblem, a *MathEdu* action of the type *solve.* The system asks him/her for the statement, included in a new design *notebook,* as well as the relation between the data from the previous problem and those needed in the statement of the subproblem. In this way the teacher makes a *recording* at the conceptual level of the successive steps that have to be posed to the student. All this *recording* is done by the teacher in the same working context of the student.

This approach to the design, which consists in the accomplishment of the work on a specific example that is generalized after some arbitrary problems of the same type, is the main feature of the *Programming by example* paradigm, which has received a considerable degree of attention by the research community on User Interfaces during the last years. This type of programming can involve very different levels of complexity. Simple versions of this kind of programming are used in very usual programs such as text processors that allow the definition of macros. Besides being used in the specification of simple tasks that are used more or less often, *programming by example* can also be useful for the automation of repetitive tasks, like the automatic resizing of boxes in a graphic. There are several recording mechanisms of tasks that are used by systems based on *programming by example* in order to specify higher level action or actions. Using real specific data as an *example* that allows the system to infer what to do on more general future occasions is essential in the specification of these tasks.

In the case of *MathEdu* the information that corresponds to the generic cases differs from the specific examples in the structure of symbolic expressions, which must match given patterns. Hence, the design work involves a first step where a specific problem is introduced, a second generalization step, and all the remaining steps, consisting of the specification of solution actions, are automatically generalized by the system. For example, the designer indicates that *the subproblem "Compute the integral of the function sin(x)" has to be solved,* but the specification inferred by the system is that *the subproblem "Compute the integral of the function u" has to be solved.*

This mechanism allows the designer to concentrate himself on questions relevant at the purely didactic level, related to the design of the specific actions that are more useful at each step in the solution process, without having to take care of annoying details that concern the problem generalization. We must remark, however, that the use of the *programming by example* paradigm introduces a considerable degree of complexity in the construction of the module of the authoring tool that is in charge of problem generalization.

4.   WORKING WITH *MATHEDU:* ADDED VALUE

The ability of *MathEdu* both to generate different exercises that differ in subtle details, and to follow the process by which the student classifies the type of problem being solved make the students deeply use their deductive ability and their knowledge each time they use the tool. First, they must decide the type of exercise and the adequate strategy and case, and after this they solve the problem step by step by selecting actions to be taken, introducing data and simple symbolic expressions that simplify the statement, and solving simpler subproblems derived from the initial one. This interactive process between *MathEdu* and the students makes them think and use their knowledge. Simultaneously, *MathEdu* must evolve between the different resolution states for the exercise being solved by means of two sources of information: the specifications of the designer and the data and other information introduced by the student.

It is also convenient to analyse the advantages of the use of the authoring tool from another point of view: that of the teacher or designer of the material to be used later by the student. First, it must be pointed out that a tool with the features of *MathEdu* makes teachers reflect with a considerable degree of intensity on the teaching process, by making them assess the usefulness of their explanations, the most important aspects addressed by them, as well as those in which they want the students to practise a posteriori. They also have to think about the usefulness of conceptual and deductive knowledge versus algorithmic knowledge, etc.

During the design process of each problem the teacher has the opportunity to make more emphasis on different aspects of the matter under study by means of the design of specific actions. By using this capacity, it is possible to know in a deep way the degree of the students' knowledge about the subject. It is even possible to keep statistical data that evaluate the behaviour of each student or the global behaviour of a group.

The interactivity between the student and the application allows the students to have an assistant to help him with the troubles they might find. When working with pencil and paper there are no clues and the students are alone between their ideas and knowledge and the problem they are trying to solve, except perhaps for some static information like a book or some notes. *MathEdu* gives a remarkable amount of freedom to this situation by offering alternatives about the different possibilities to solve the exercise. It is worth to remark that the designer can detect through inexact answers from the students some deficiencies in their knowledge. This gives *MathEdu* a specific added value that corresponds more to traditional methods of teaching than to the usual computer applications for teaching Mathematics, while keeping most of the advantages of computer programs over peer tutoring in terms of the costs and efforts needed for each tutoring session.

5.   CONCLUSIONS

In this paper we have shown the main features of a new authoring tool for the development of sets of problems of Mathematics that makes their interactive solution by the student possible. *MathEdu* makes a step forward with respect to traditional Mathematics tutoring systems, since it allows, on the one hand, a richer interaction and on the other hand more intelligent dialogues with the student. The use of the *Programming by example* paradigm for the design of the exercises by the teacher simplifies the design work, so the teacher does not need a deep programming knowledge; moreover, while specifying the problems, the teachers can concentrate their efforts on aspects related to the learning process instead of taking care of tedious and repetitive programming related questions. Teachers can develop their own sets of problems.

At this point the tool is in an advanced phase of development; a prototype is available that is able to interpret a subset of the language of actions that have been described in the paper. The part of the system that corresponds to the design process is already implemented in its final version. A generic inference engine for the control of dialogues with the student and the evolution between the different solution states is under development. When this engine is finished the first complete version of *MathEdu* will be available, and field tests will be conducted. There are plans to include aspects of Intelligent Tutoring Systems, ITS, such as a *Model of the Student* [8], [2], and to make the system adaptive to this model, and a more elaborated interface that allows a more natural communication with the student, in a way much closer to the real dialogue between a student an a teacher. The Model of the Student will determine the abilities and skills of each student in order to determine new exercises to be proposed that are adequate to the abilities the student has shown. In this way *MathEdu* will transmit confidence to the students by correcting their errors and adapting them progressively to their knowledge. In this way, the students will look at the system not as a mere program of symbolic computation, but as a collaborator in their learning task that will motivate its use.

ACKNOWLEDGEMENTS

This work has been funded by the National Research Plan from Spain, projects TEL97-0306 and TEL99-0181.

REFERENCES

1. Bujalance, E., et al. (1994). HYPERMAT, un proyecto multimedia para la enseñanza de las Matemáticas.
2. Carro, R., Pulido, E., and Rodríguez, P. (1999) An adaptive driving course based on HTML dynamic generation, Top Paper Award en la World Conference on the WWW and Internet, WebNet'99. Hawai, USA.

3. Castells, P., Moriyón, R. and Saiz, F. (1995). Solving Mathematical Problems that Involve Reasoning and Calculations. Golden West International Conference on Intelligent Systems. ACM. San Francisco.
4. Cypher, A. (1993). Watch what I do. Programming by Demonstration. Cambridge, MA: The MIT Press.
5. Díez, F., and Moriyón, R. (1999). Doing Mathematics with MathEdu, Proceedings of the IXth Conference of Mathematics/Science Education & Technology. AACE. San Antonio (Texas).
6. Genesereth, M.R. (1982). The role of plans in intelligent teaching systems. Intelligent Tutoring Systems, Academic Press. Londres.
7. Puerta, A.R. (1998). Supporting User-Centered Design of Adaptive User Interfaces Via Interface Models. First Annual Workshop On Real-Time Intelligent User Interfaces For Decision Support And Information Visualization, San Francisco.
8. Scientific Notebook, We page at:
http://www.math.tamu.edu/~webcalc/ictcm_yasskin/ictm_yasskin.html
9. Self, J. (1974). Student models in computer in computer-aided instruction. International Journal of Man Machine Studies.
10. Sutcliffe, G. and Suttner, C.B. (1997). The CADE-13 ATP System Competition. Journal of Automated Reasoning, 18(2), pp. 137-138. Web page at:
http://sunjenssen24.informatik.tu-muenchen.de/~tptp/
11. Szekely, P., Sukaviriya, P., Castells, P., Muthukumarasamy, J. and Salcher, E. (1996). Declarative Interface Models for User Interface Construction Tools: the MASTERMIND Approach. In Engineering for Human-Computer Interaction, L. Bass and C. Unger (eds), pp. 120-150. Chapman & Hall.
12. Wiley Web Test, at: http://www.math.unl.edu/~jorr/webtests/demo/chooser.html
13. Wolfram, S. (1999): The Mathematica Book, 4th Edition. Cambridge University Press.

Teaching Support Units

Ramón Fabregat Gesa, Jose Luis Marzo Lázaro, Clara Inés Peña de Carrillo
Broadband Communications and Distributed Systems Group
Informatics and Applications Institute, Universidad de Girona
Building PII, Avinguda de Lluís Santaló, S/N,
17071 Girona, Spain
E-mail: {ramon, marzo, clarenes}@eia.udg.es

Key words: Open and distance learning, web, adaptability, adaptivity.

Abstract: This paper describes some features of the telematics platform named Teaching
Support Units (TSU), developed by PLAN-G using WWW technology.
PLAN-G was supported by the CICYT TEL98-0408-C02-01 project: Design
and Implementation of a New Generation Telematics Platform to Support
Open and Distance Learning The TSU platform provides a set of tools that
enable teachers to create and edit didactic materials, generate and manage
different types of interactive exercises and create and manage teaching
units. The main goal of these tools is to alleviate the problem of teachers having to
understand various applications and languages in order to make dynamic and
interactive didactic material. The system was set up with structures and
transversal navigation which make learning easier and guide the student during
its use. The student's activities are collected in a personalized database, which
enables teachers to follow his/her navigation and performance. This
information may provide criteria for improving the didactic contents. We
place special emphasis on the personalization of the system so that it can be
adapted to the student's preferences (presentation, languages, etc.), to his/her
way of working and to his/her ability to understand the contents provided.

1.   INTRODUCTION

At the University of Girona an interdisciplinary group of researchers
from the Informatics and Applications Institute and the Pedagogy
Department has developed, by means of the PLAN-G project, the Teaching

163

M. Ortega and J. Bravo (eds.), Computers and Education in the 21st Century, 163–174.
© 2000 *Kluwer Academic Publishers. Printed in the Netherlands.*

Support Units (TSU) platform (see [3] & [4]). In this platform, teachers can create and publish dynamic and interactive didactic materials which make comprehensive use of the new possibilities opened up by the new Information and Communication Technologies and specifically by the Internet. Students can access them in a decentralized way using the WWW as an interface in a closed and controlled environment. The platform also offers tools for communication between students and teachers at various levels.

Access to the platform is personalized by the use of a username and a password, so that any particular user's activity is associated with him/her. The system can be adapted to show different contents and options depending on the users, their privileges, their former activities or any other aspect to be included in the future. At present, there are three distinct types of users: students, teachers and platform managers.

To make it easy for teachers to create and manage the didactic materials, we developed some web-based tools, such as: the Interactive Presentations Generator (JVS) [7], the Interactive Exercises Generator [1], the Documents Organiser [2] and the Teaching Units Editor [6].

Fig. 1 shows the structure of the platform modules and their web tools. While the teacher arranges access to all the modules, the student can only access the Navigation Module.

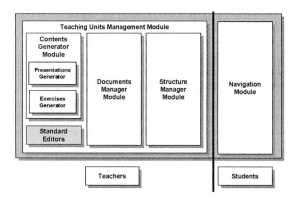

Figure 1. PLANG: Modular Architecture

Each module in the structure is independent and works with the same database. As such, with knowledge of its definition and its way of access, the system can grow as desired and the development of new modules can be divided and ordered by different people.

Figure 2 presents the internal architecture adopted in the system and the general performance, using a standard browser in the client machine and a standard HTTP server and a customized server formed by a set of CGI programs in the server. The customized server acts between the HTTP server and the contents, personalizing the documents requested, including the information stored in the database and enabling all the actions undertaken to be accurately controlled.

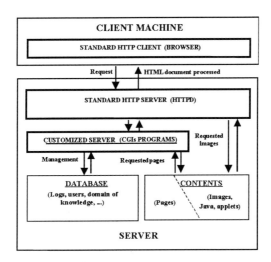

Figure 2. PLANG: Internal Architecture

The centralization of the information in only one database allows the permanent updating of data and access to the correct information module. The possibility of storing the students' platform activities (navigation undertaken, exercise results, communications, etc.) makes it possible to study the students' behaviour and improve their academic performance.

2. PLAN-G PLATFORM GENERAL OPERATION

The teacher can write the didactic material to build teaching units, using standard tools (to create HTML files, images and any other additional files) or the tools included in the PLAN-G Contents Generator Module, such as the Interactive Presentations Generator and the Interactive Exercises Generator (see Figure 1).

The presentations and the exercises created by the Contents Generator Module, are stored directly in the system, while, in order to store the materials created by other tools, the Documents Manager Module has to be used. The Structure Manager Module can create the navigation structure to follow, using the contents previously organised.

Students can access the available teaching unit by means of the Navigation Module, with prior identification and authentication. (Fig. 3) shows the different steps in PLANG platform performance.

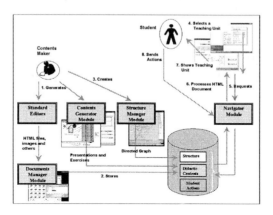

Figure 3. PLANG: General Performance

3.   TEACHING UNITS MANAGER MODULE

The main information entity of the PLAN-G system is the Teaching Unit, which is formed by a closed set of related concepts about a subject or a research field. Each unit is created and managed as a separate element by its owner teacher, who is free to build it. A group of units forms the course contents.

A Teaching Unit is conceptually divided into its didactic contents and the navigation structure. The didactic contents are a set of HTML pages which are shown to the end user; and the navigation structure is the way in which contents are mutually related depending on the way they are consulted.

3.1   Contents Generator Module

The Interactive Presentations Generator (Java Visual Sequence JVS) is a visual environment for developing and publishing interactive presentations (similar to some existing commercial programs) that can be viewed with a standard browser. The screens or photograms in JVS nomenclature are linked and follow a published sequence for access via Internet.

One of the design goals in this application was to create a very easy-to-use graphic environment without loss of any technical potential. To achieve the maximum diffusion and application of this tool, the Java developed language was used.

With JVS, first of all, we can create interactive presentations that include graphic effects and animations, in which case the student moves from being a simple spectator to playing an active part during the learning process (choosing, deciding, evaluating, finding elements, etc.), which stimulates reaction and improves the learning process. Secondly, JVS also allows the presentation of information sequentially and without user mediation; in this case, the presentation maker can include different ways of maintaining user attention, such as graphics in movement, projection time control of each information screen and the graphic effects of changing screens.

The JVS environment was divided into two independent applications of similar importance: the presentations editor (see Fig. 4) that allows the presentations to be made, and the browser that corresponds to the interface for viewing the presentation by means of a standard Internet browser.

Using the JVS editor, the user may create presentations without writing any line of code, just using the mouse and inserting some data through the keyboard. A presentation is a mutually related photogram or screen sequence. In each of those screens the contents maker can include objects like: texts, lines, arrows, squares, circles, images, selection areas, etc.

An important characteristic of the editor is the possibility of defining the desired track to each object or set of objects inside the photogram, which enables dynamism to be added and the user's attention to focus where the sequence maker considers relevant.

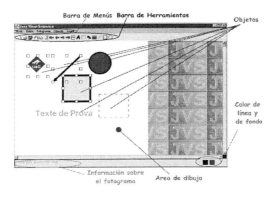

Figure 4. JVS Editor Screen

The Interactive Exercises Generator is an application with access to the Web, designed to help teachers to create and maintain closed-answer interactive exercises that will be resolved by the students on the Internet. We included different types of exercises such as tests, gap-filling, associations, word-search, selecting the correct words, sorting words and paragraphs, etc. The modular design of the application will allow this range to be extended in the future.

The exercises include an important evaluation mechanism for any learning environment. With the exercises mentioned above, we use a closed evaluation that involves comparing the answer given with the correct answer(s), which is/are limited, predetermined and precise. Correction is automatic, which enables the student to know the results at once.

Recently a lot of applications have provided these benefits, but this application has been designed to include the management, creation and general utilisation of the exercises on the Web without the use of any software other than a conventional browser to improve the potential of HTML and Dynamic HTML languages in a transparent way.

The support given by a database enables the student's learning process to be followed by storing the results of the different activities undertaken. By applying statistical methods to those results, such as correlation of the individual answers with the whole set, we can obtain interesting information about the different exercises, such as which questions are more difficult or less significant, and information to improve the exercises.

We also considered the possibility of using self-sufficient and independent HTML pages. These pages have all the codes needed to do the exercises without being linked to the database for their successful performance. This could be useful in places with deficient networks.

Each type of exercise has a module to develop, import, export and modify exercises, to create an HTML page with a selected, independent and self-adaptable exercise, to move parts of an exercise to another exercise, to ask for statistics, to view the exercise and to include multimedia files.

The import option allows an exercise included in an HTML file to be selected with a predetermined format and to be introduced into the database. The export option reverses the import process. The modifying option allows all the exercise properties and their contents to be modified. The following windows show the screens for modifying the properties of the tests and their contents.

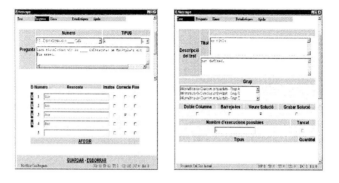

Figure 5. Window Screens to Modify Test Properties and Test Contents

3.2 Contents Manager Module

The teaching unit contents created with HTML pages, images and some additional files must be included in a standard web server. The Contents Organiser tool was developed to simplify the file management. This application allows navigation within the server space files of each owner; its presentation looks similar to the files explorer in windows systems including the folder structure and icons showing the file type. The possible operations with the files are the traditional ones, such as deletion, selection, copying or moving files within the server and transferring files between the server and the client machine. Figure. 6 presents the document explorer environment.

Figure 6. Documents Explorer Environment (Adding a File)

3.3 Structure Manager Module

Once the contents have been stored in the system, the user teacher can utilize the Structure Manager Module to create his/her teaching unit. The teaching units editor allows a logical unit to be created by means of selection of a subset of HTML pages. The same contents of a page can be used to build different teaching units, thus allowing the material to be used on different courses.

One of the main abilities of the system is to permit the building of teaching units using different languages. When a teacher creates the files with the course contents in different languages, he/she can distinguish them in the system using a letter (e, i or c for Spanish, English and Catalan) at the beginning of the filenames; in such a way, the file *unidad.html* could identify the generic name of the files *e.unidad.html* (Spanish contents), *i.unidad.html* (English contents) and *c.unidad.html* (Catalan contents) if they exist.

During the creation of the teaching units, a teacher works with abstract nodes that point to a set of corresponding files; in this way, the structure (nodes relationship) can be created just once per unit because the language selection is solved at the node level. This idea enables the structure to be modified just once, independently of the number of languages in which the unit is available.

When a student uses the system, he/she will be able to select his/her language preference, which will affect the presentation of the contents. For example, the server process for this case could be as follows: if the request is for the node that points to the file *unidad.html*, the system will analize the student's preferences and will proceed to the corresponding file in the selected language marked as the first preference. If the file does not exist, the system will proceed to the selected language marked as the second preference, and so on to the third preference. Finally, if the file does not exist in any of the selected languages, the system will show the teaching unit contents in the language that does exist. All this information stored in the database is used so that the system can adapt to the student's desires in the best possible way.

The pages that the students can see when they navigate through the teaching unit are really nodes or abstract entities that point to files; the units editor enables a directed graph to these nodes to be drawn and different types of relationships between them to be established. These relationships offer the teacher the possibility of establishing a navigation guide through the units.

A teaching unit may have a simple structure or a complex one. The different complexity levels can be summarized as follows:
– The minimum structure of a teaching unit would consist of a set of HTML pages, marking one of them as the initial page and including a title in it. The user could access the contents using the conventional HTML hyperlinks. In this case, the same pages contain the relationship with the others. The system acts as a conventional web server.
– The most simple structure in a navigation traverse is a sequential traverse where the nodes can be sorted; once they have been sorted, the users can utilize the "forward" or "backward" buttons to browse through the unit without having to worry about selecting the page to visit at every moment, because the teacher can establish the best way to pass through it. At any moment, the teacher may change the traverse order, using the units manager module and modifying the nodes' relationships. All teaching unit navigation works by accessing the database which allows the system to decide which page to show next.
– As a more complex traverse than the sequential one, the teacher can create a directed graph as a navigation structure. The directed graph marks the related nodes with some traverse paths suggested by the teacher as paths to follow after visiting the current page. This permits less rigid navigation than the sequential one, because the users may select

the pages desired and get a general vision of the teaching unit contents by means of viewing its data tree structure, when they click on the navigation button. The data tree generates hierarchic indexes, which can, for example, make printing lists.

At any of the options mentioned above, each node may have associated pages to exercises or bibliography that buttons in the navigation environment make available. Figure 7 shows some windows generated by the teacher when he/she builds the teaching unit structure.

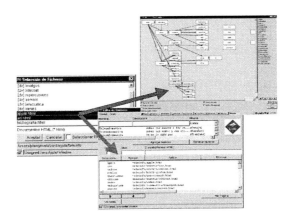

Figure 7. Some Windows of the Structure Manager Module

4.   NAVIGATION MODULE

Once the teaching unit has been built, the students can access it by using the Navigation Module. All the information of the teaching unit used is stored and classified by the users in the database. At any moment the teacher can use the module developed for tracking down the students' activities; in such a way, he/she can see the rate of unit utilisation, when the student has navigated the unit and the pages visited; in addition, actions such as loading a particular page, scrolling a page or following a link are stored in the database. Thus, behaviour models can be determined and the platform can be adapted to the students as well as possible.

Figure 8 shows a windows system with the list of activities undertaken by a student and the list of students connected.

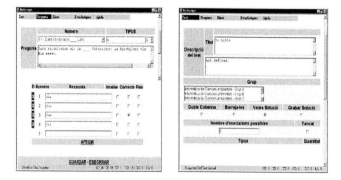

Figure 8. List of the Student Ramon's Activities and the Connected Students at any Moment

4.1   System Adaptability

A student may customize his/her working environment (to determine icon space, icon shape, the status bar, the language, etc.) and undertake the corresponding navigation processes on the teaching units made available by the teacher after a specific traverse.

A navigation window is formed by an icons bar and a contents area. The icons facilitate navigation through the teaching unit at every moment and the results of their actions are observed in the area of contents presentation. Figure 9 shows a window with the result of the action taken when the student clicks on the navigation button (tree of the structure), and the content of any page.

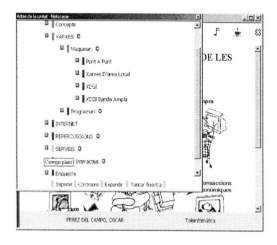

Figure 9. Windows with the Teaching Teaching Unit Contents Tree (front) and a Page of the "Teleinformática" Unit Content (back)

4.2   Navigation Icons

Left button	Right button
Returns to the former node visited.	Opens up a window with links to all the nodes already visited.
Opens up the navigation unit tree if it exists. The visited nodes are marked in red, the nodes not visited in blue and the current page in green. The tree allows its branches to stretch and contract and it can be used to navigate.	Shows a window with the former nodes to the current in the sequential traverse, if the user is a teacher.
Loads, if there is one, the page that the teacher has defined to follow in the sequential traverse.	Shows the permitted destinations from the current node, including the directed graph of the unit.

Shows a printing menu with three options: to print the current page, to print the entire teaching unit or to select the pages to print. With the last option, the system shows the tree of the unit so as to allow the selection of a subset of nodes to be printed. In any case, the contents are processed to build only one HTML page from which irrelevant information such as its URL address, the JavaScript code, the external links, etc., has been deleted.

Allows viewing the exercises associated with the current page and also enables the proposed activities to happen.

Shows the bibliography pages associated with the current page.

Shows the user statistics when using the platform, beginning with his/her personal details, which include photograph and personal data, and ending with the listing of the activities undertaken in different sessions.

Allows access to communication tools like e-mail, chat, etc.

Allows music to work pleasantly to be selected.

Allows for a coffee-break.

Returns to the main menu.

5.   CONCLUSIONS

The use of the Internet as an educational tool will be common practice in the near future. The Teaching Support Units is a young tool which has already been used to good effect. The fact that all the data management is done on the basis of a commercial, stable and tried database guarantees that the simultaneous access of different users from different modules is handled correctly, giving more freedom to programmers and allowing the use of different languages and platforms to develop the application modules.

Massive data collection on students' behaviour helps teachers to run studies to improve and adapt the lessons to different types of individuals. The course of events over the past year seems to suggest that the future of these tools has to include their adaptivity. The information presented and the possible options will be adapted to the students' learning speed and learning technique.

ACKNOWLEDGEMENTS

Thanks to Carles Coll, Jordi Coma, Jordi Ministral, Javier Molina, Lluís Pancorbo, Oscar Pérez and Albert Portugal for their contributions to the development of the different modules of the application. We would also like to thank the members of the BCDS group and of the PLAN-G project for providing a pleasant working environment and unconditional support, and for giving useful feedback on the ideas involved in writing this paper.

REFERENCES

1. Coll-Madrenas, C., & Pérez-del-Campo, O., & Fabregat-Gesa, R., & Marzo-Lázaro, J.L. (1999)."Autogenerador y Asistente de Ejercicios Interactivos Vía Web". *CONIED'99*, Congreso Nacional de Informática Educativa, 17-19 November 1999, Puertollano, Ciudad Real, Spain.
2. Coma-Pol, J., & Fabregat-Gesa, R., & Marzo-Lázaro, J.L. (1999). "Plataforma Multi-Usuario para el Mantenimiento de Buscadores por Palabras en Documentos HTML". *CONIED'99*, Congreso Nacional de Informática Educativa, 17-19 November 1999, Puertollano, Ciudad Real, Spain.
3. Marzo, J.L., & Estebanell, M. & Fabregat-Gesa, R., & Ferrer, J. & Verdú, T. (1998a). Support Units for University Teaching based on WWW. *Proceedings of ED-MEDIA/ED-TELECOM 98*, World Conference on Educational Multimedia and Hypermedia & World Conference on Educational Telecommunications, Freiburg, Germany: June 20-25 1998, CD-Rom.
4. Marzo, J.L, & Verdú, T. & Fabregat, R. (1998b). User Identification and Tracking in an Educational Web Environment. *Proceedings of ED-MEDIA/ED- TELECOM 98*, World Conference on Educational Multimedia and Hypermedia & World Conference on Educational Telecommunications, Freiburg, Germany, June 20-25 1998, CD-Rom.
5. Ministral-Jambert, J., & Fabregat-Gesa, R., & Marzo-Lázaro, J.L. (1999). "Unidades de Soporte a la Docencia". *CONIED'99*, Congreso Nacional de Informática Educativa, 17-19 November 1999, Puertollano, Ciudad Real, Spain.
6. Molina, J. (1999). "Unidades de Soporte a la Docencia". *Users' Manual*, Work Report, http://brakali.udg.es/~plang/estructura.
7. Portugal-Brugada, A., & Fabregat-Gesa, R., & Marzo-Lázaro, J.L. (1999). "Java Visual Sequence: Generador de Presentaciones para Internet". *CONIED'99*, Congreso Nacional de Informática Educativa, 17-19 November 1999, Puertollano, Ciudad Real, Spain.

The Interactive Physics Course on the Internet. Problems and Solutions

Angel Franco García
Dpto. Física Aplicada I. Universidad del País Vasco
Avda. Otaola nº 29. 20600 EIBAR (Guipúzcoa).
E-mail: wupfrgaa@sc.ehu.es

Key words: Physics, problems, interactivity, simulations, Internet, applets, web pages.

Abstract: The Interactive Physics Course on the Internet is an electronic book in which we have enhanced interactivity by means of 124 applets embedded into the HTML documents. These applets are simulations, computer experiments, problems, etc. This article deals with problems because problem-solving is an essential part of the teaching of Physics at undergraduate level. Unlike textbooks in which the information required to solve the problem is provided in the problem statements, some applets of the Interactive Physics Course require the students to observe an animation and sometimes make measurements of relevant parameters. With these applets we intend to help them to develop more expert problem-solving strategies, and to encourage them to solve problems.

1.   INTRODUCTION

The Interactive Physics Course on the Internet [1] is a project that intends to improve the quality of education in Physics, making an effective use of the New Information Technologies. The Course is aimed mainly at first year university students studying engineering and science.

The Course consists of a group of web pages, hierarchically structured. Entering the Course through the index we can move vertically along the hierarchy from the general to the specific, and also horizontally between different sections or topics. The web pages contain text, images, mathematical formulas and applets.

M. Ortega and J. Bravo (eds.), Computers and Education in the 21st Century, 175–184.
© *2000 Kluwer Academic Publishers. Printed in the Netherlands.*

The Course covers almost all topics of an Introductory Physics course: units and measurements, kinematics, dynamics, celestial dynamics, dynamics of rigid bodies, oscillations, waves, transport phenomena, statistical and thermal physics, electromagnetism and quantum mechanics.

At the beginning of each chapter we point out the educational objectives and we provide a broad bibliography, mostly textbooks and articles from magazines and journals.

We insist on the basic concepts inside each topic and specially on those that we consider more difficult for the students. For instance, we have devoted an important part of the course to the study of the basic principles of Quantum Mechanics because we think that the students should be engaged in its learning during this first course.

With the Interactive Physics Course on the Internet [2] we intend to take advantage of one of the most relevant characteristics of computers: interactivity. So, our main task has been to produce a coherent set of 124 applets which are simulations, computer experiments, problems, etc.

With these applets embedded into HTML documents we intend to create a rich group of experiences so that the students can acquire an intuition of the different physical situations programmed in the computer. By means of the interactive dialogue between the student and the program we want the student to be an active participant in the learning process, instead of a passive spectator.

To reach this objective, the web pages have been designed with a structure similar to a laboratory experience:
- The topic is introduced
- The physical principles are stated
- The activities to carry out are described.
- Some hints are provided to tell the student how to use the program

Simulations, in a broad sense, can help the students to approach a wider variety of phenomena that they find very difficult to understand from the analytic point of view.

For instance, several programs have been designed to help the students to understand difficult concepts such as the characteristics of harmonic waves (Figure 1).

Others correspond to prelab exercises, or simulations of laboratory experiments that can be carried out at the school laboratory. Usually, the students work with the simulated experiment before trying the real one. For example, the study of the rectilinear motion, the measurement of fluid viscosity, and so on.

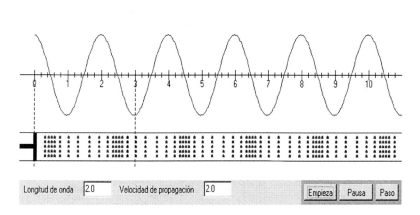

Periodo : 1.0
Frecuencia: 1.0

tiempo: 1.74

Longitud de onda 2.0   Velocidad de propagación 2.0   Empieza   Pausa   Paso

Figure 1. Harmonic waves

The simulation of laboratory experiments is a good didactic resource when these are inaccessible at the school laboratory, because they are expensive, dangerous or difficult to arrange. For example, some applets simulate the mass spectrometer, particle accelerators, etc.

Others recreate relevant experiments from the historical point of view, for instance those that gave place to the discovery of the electron (Thomson and Millikan), the atomic structure (Rutherford), or the existence of discrete energy states (Hertz), etc.,

We have explained those simulated experiments in a previous article [3], so now we will concentrate on another interesting aspect of this Physics Course: the problems and their solutions.

2.   A DATABASE OF PROBLEMS

Problem solving is an essential part of classroom activities and homework assignments. Besides, the student assessment is mainly based on problem solving skills.

A part of the Physics Course is a database [4] of problem statements that we have provided along several years for the first course students at the Technical Engineering School of Eibar to solve in class, at home or in the exams. The students (Figure 2) can select a problem from a certain chapter. Here they have two options by pressing the appropriate button: the result or the complete solution. We also provide some links to the "theory", this is, to the corresponding pages of the Interactive Physics Course.

Two chapters were completed: Statics and Kinematics. However, this initiative did not raise much interest among the students and teachers that visited our website.

There is an additional problem, the mathematical formulas are GIF files, and modifications cannot be made in these image files. This inconvenience will be overcome when the Mathematical Markup Language, an extension of the HTML to publish mathematical formulas on the Web, is available.

Those statements, the solutions and the answers, are static contents similar to those that can be found in a textbook. As we have previously said, the most outstanding characteristic of computers is interactivity, and the efforts of the author of this paper have been put in this direction.

Figure 2. A database of problem statements

3.   VISUALIZATION OF PROBLEMS

In this section, we will see some examples of interactive programs that are made up of the problem statements of an Introductory Physics Course.

A typical problem about the motion of a charged particle in an electromagnetic field is the following one:

The electric field intensity between the plates of the velocity selector of a mass spectrometer is 120000 N/C and the magnetic field in the spectrometer is 8000 gauss (0.8 T). A beam of neon ions with a charge +e describes a circular trajectory of 7.8 centimeters of diameter. What is the mass of the neon isotope in atomic units?

The interactive program allows the student to choose an element (hydrogen, helium, oxygen, neon, carbon, etc.) from a list of elements, and to set the values of the electric and magnetic field intensity so that the radius of semicircular trajectories that the isotopes describe can be measured appropriately on rule scaled in cm. The student is asked to calculate isotope masses in atomic units, and to check his answer with the correct solution provided by the interactive program (Figure 3).

The applet is included in a web page which describes the mass spectrometer. This page has some links to other pages devoted to explain the motion of a charged particle in an electromagnetic field.

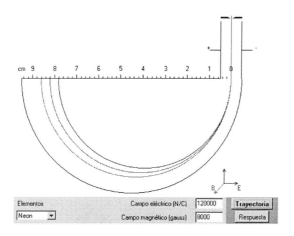

Figure 3. The mass spectrometer

The loop (Figure 4) is a typical problem of an Introductory Physics Course, since it includes the dynamics of the rectilinear motion, the dynamics of the circular motion (in the loop), the concept of work and mechanical energy.

However, many students have difficulty in interpreting not only the statement of the problem but also the figure, since some believe that the loop is a wheel that comes rolling down along the inclined plane.

A. Franco García

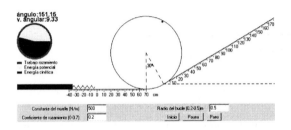

Figure 4. The loop

An applet has been designed to show a situation similar to the real one. The statement provided in this way has the advantage that the students can see the motion of the particle before beginning to solve the problem, and they can analyze the problem from the observation of the different stages of the body motion.

This approach may reduce the tendency of a high proportion of students to memorize the solutions of the problems that the teacher outlines and solves in the blackboard.

The statement is visual and opened up so that the students can build their own physical system changing the spring constant, the friction coefficient of the horizontal and inclined planes, and the loop radius.

The program completes other objectives. The students will be able to realise that the particle has to reach a minimum speed at the lowest point of the circular trajectory to complete the loop. At the upper left of the applet, the student can see how the total energy is distributed, how the energy looses by friction, and perceive the energy transformations along the particle motion.

On the other hand, the applet that describes the problem statement is not isolated but inserted in a web page that explains the different situations that can happen when the spring is compressed and the particle is released.

We have several interactive programs that combine the explanation of the theory with the solution of the problems, for example, the description of the falling bodies or the curvilinear motion under the constant acceleration of gravity. The student can introduce the initial speed of the body and the initial height, and then watch the motion. We can stop the animation when the body reaches the maximum height or impacts on the floor. The students can verify that the results they obtain solving the problem are the same as those that the interactive program provides them. The simulation tackles common misconceptions, for example, a body at its highest point has zero acceleration as well as zero velocity.

4.   PROBLEM-GAMES

   Problem-games can be solved with the help of the intuition and the knowledge that the student gets of the physical system after successive attempts. Later, the students will be asked to solve the problems applying the equations that describe this system, starting from the provided data.
   In general, the purpose of problem-games is to make Physics more amusing and to stimulate the student in the solution of the problems.
   It is necessary to remark that the intuition that the students have of a certain physical situation is not related to their knowledge of the theory or their problem-solving skills. There are students that do not obtain good marks but they capture the physical situation quickly and they work in consequence.
   The intuitive aspects are not very frequent in traditional teaching, but they have been stressed in the Interactive Physics Course.

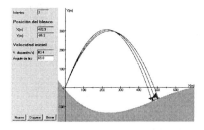

Figure 5. Shooting on a target

   The applet in Figure 5 depicts a typical problem of kinematics: find the shot angles that impact on a target. The program determines a random position of the target on an irregular land and provides the initial bullet speed. The student has to guess the shot angle in the minimum possible number of attempts. Sometimes, the student discovers with surprise that there are two possible solutions to this problem.
   Finally, they are asked to solve the problem and to compare the solution obtained with the simulation.

5.   PROBLEMS CLOSE TO EVERYDAY LIFE

   The purpose of these problems is to connect the classroom of Physics to real-world phenomena.
   We have devoted several web pages and applets to explain some aspects of the basketball game [5].

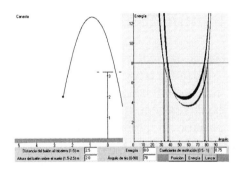

Figure 6. Playing basketball. The effect of the blackboard

As it is explained in the web pages, the effect of the blackboard is like that of a mirror. You can introduce the ball through two baskets: the real one (the grey curve) and the imaginary one (the black curve) located behind the board (Figure 6). The shady regions on the right indicate the possible shot angles to score for each value of the energy (or initial speed). The projections on the horizontal axis indicate the angular intervals that score for an initial kinetic energy of the ball of 8 units. On the left, the trajectory described by a ball introduced in the imaginary basket for an angle of 78 degrees is shown.

The student can understand this physical situation with the only aid of the equations of the parabolic motion, and then he can investigate which ones have the highest probability to score in different situations and all other possible combinations:

- Shots next to the board or far away
- Tall or short player
- High or low trajectories of the ball
- Ball with high or low restitution coefficient.

We have also built an animated model of a bouncing ball which, based on damped oscillations, shows the ball deformation and explains the restitution coefficient. Finally, the collision of the ball against the basket hoop introduces the student to the scattering phenomena.

6.   STUDENT-TEACHER INTERACTION

The publication of educational contents on the Internet has the advantage that the process of teaching-learning extends beyond the environment of the classroom.

The email is the fundamental means of distance interaction between the student and the teacher. Among those received daily asking some questions or giving some opinions on the Interactive Physics Course on the Internet, we have selected one that comes from an Argentinian student that requests help to solve a problem.

```
Date: Sat, 11 Dec 1999 02:37:53 -0300
From: maria alejandra
To: wupfrgaa@sc.ehu.es
Subject: problem


Please
If you can tell me how this problem can be solved: a body of mass m =
1kg compress a spring of elastic constant k=10000N/m
What is the minimum compression of the spring so that the particle,
when released, describes a complete circumference on the loop of R=1 m?
There is no friction in horizontal and inclined planes. Neglect the
particle dimensions in comparison with the loop radius.
I will thank you very much
Maria Alejandra
```

The teacher's answer only provides the address of the page of the Interactive Physics Course that contains the applet that describes the statement of this kind of problems, (see section 3).

```
Date: Mon, 13 Dec 1999 10:32:21 +0100 (MET)
From: Angel Franco Garcia <wupfrgaa@scox01.sc.ehu.es>
To: maria alejandra
Subject: Re: problem
Dear María Alejandra
The answer to the problem can be found at the address
http://www.sc.ehu.es/sbweb/fisica/dinamica/trabajo/bucle/bucle.htm
Kind regards
Angel Franco García - University of the Basque Country (Spain)
```

The student's later answer:

```
Date: Mon, 13 Dec 1999 17:31:59 -0300
From: maria alejandra
To: Angel Franco Garcia < wupfrgaa@sc.ehu.es >
Subject: RE: problem
Dear Franco
Thank you for your help, it was useful for me, thank you!!!!!!
María Alejandra
```

7.   CONCLUSIONS

Finding the appropriate uses of the World Wide Web continues challenging the education community.

Our contribution is an Interactive Physics Course on the Internet that is an attempt to make the computer a tool for teaching Physics, both inside and outside the classroom. So our educational model will comprise two elements: the web resources effectively combined with peer teaching.

The Interactive Physics Course is a complete introductory course with too many aspects to be described in only one article. So, in this paper we have referred to the visualization of problems and their solutions. The necessary information to solve the problem is in the interactive program, not in the text. The students watch the motion and then apply those corresponding physical concepts, making measurements if necessary, or knowing the answer before solving the problem. This approach is totally different to the traditional one

We also intend to increase the student's motivation to solve problems, by means of visualization of problem statements, problem-games and studying situations close to everyday life.

REFERENCES

1. The Interactive Physics Course on the Internet can be accessed at:
    www.sc.ehu.es/sbweb/fisica/default.htm. I appreciate the support provided by Spanish Ministry of Education, CICYT grant DOC96-2537.
2. Franco A. (1999). "Physics with computer" an Interactive Physics Course on the Internet. *Proceedings of CAEE'99* (Computer Aided Engineering Education) Sofia, Bulgaria.
3. Franco A. (1999). La simulación de Fenómenos físicos y experiencias de laboratorio en Internet. *Actas del I Congreso Nacional de Informática Educativa. Conied'99.* Puertollano.
4. A database of Physics problems can be found at: *http://caos.eis.uva.es/db/ problemas/indice.htm*
5. Savirón J. M. (1984). *Problemas de Física General en un año olímpico.* Editorial Reverté.

Task Based Training of Application Users

Federico García Salvador, Roberto Moriyón Salomón
Universidad Autónoma de Madrid, Escuela Técnica de Ingeniería Informática, Madrid, Spain

Key words: Human Computer Interaction, Intelligent Tutoring Systems, User Task
Models, Programming by Demonstration

Abstract: This paper describes an approach to training users of interactive applications.
The technique we propose is based on the use of task user models on interfaces
that include a declarative model. Our approach allows us to offer the students
explanations that are more dynamical than existing tutoring systems. These
explanations follow the activity of the users and act by giving adequate
answers to their actions. Moreover, we describe CACTUS, an interactive
environment for the generation of tutoring courses based on the techniques we
propose, that releases course designers of a significant part of the intense work
implied by their development. CACTUS is based on a metaphor that
represents courses as textbooks. From the point of view of the student,
learning how to use an application is associated to reading a book about a
subject and accomplishing the associated practical tasks.

1.   INTRODUCTION

Graphical user interfaces have a complexity that was hard to imagine a
few years ago. Many of these applications include hundreds of actions that
very often work in a different way depending on the context. In this way,
only very advanced users can benefit from all the possibilities offered by
these systems. However, these applications seldom incorporate an
environment that allow novel users to learn in a systematic way the tasks that
can be accomplished with them. Even today, the most common help systems
are based on hypermedia applications that describe the usefulness of each
option of the application and how to access it. This format is very
inappropriate from several points of view, such as its low level of

M. Ortega and J. Bravo (eds.), Computers and Education in the 21st Century, 185–197.
© 2000 *Kluwer Academic Publishers. Printed in the Netherlands.*

abstraction, the isolation from the interface, the lack of flexibility of the messages, and the lack of feedback with respect to the actions of the user.

Some applications, although not many, incorporate tutoring programs that guide the users during their learning process. But these tutoring systems, which simulate the behaviour of the application, have very high development and maintenance costs, and they do not allow users to practise in their own working context the accomplishment of the tasks that are explained. The users can just practise on predefined examples.

During the last years there has been a large research effort devoted to the generation of help systems for interactive applications, based on different paradigms. We shall point out Cartoonist, (Sukaviriya, 1990), which automatically generates help with animations about the behaviour of an application starting from a model of its interface, as well as the systems by Pangoli and Paternó [8] and TWIW [2], which offer help from models of user tasks. TWIW includes some features that are typical of a tutoring system, since it is able to filter the incorrect actions of the users.

In this paper we introduce a technique for the design of courses for training users of interactive applications. This technique allows automatically tracking the activities accomplished by the students during the execution of the courses and the creation of scenarios that are suitable for practising the tasks that are taught. Our technique is based on the technology of specification of interfaces based on declarative models of them [11, 9], which provides benefits like the possibility to reuse the models, the simplification of system prototyping, and the possibility that other systems can reason and modify the behaviour of the interface during its execution. In this way, the courses based on the technique we propose give their final users, the students, the fundamental advantage of receiving feedback from the tracking of their activities and the evaluation of their knowledge.

Tracking the students' activities is possible thanks to the incorporation to the traditional interface models of a component that represents tasks the user can accomplish, and a universal task management system that parses the events from the user and, depending on the model that corresponds to the application that is being executed, interprets them taking the actions that are appropriate to the situation. In this way, the courses based on our technology make the students practise using the application itself under the control of the tutoring system.

In the paper we also present two systems that are implemented on the basis of the previous ideas: on the one hand, ATOMS+, an extension of the ATOMS management system of user tasks [10, 5]. It incorporates the capacity to make emulation of high level tasks, and on the other hand CACTUS, based on ATOMS+, which tries to alleviate the problems related with current software tutoring systems. CACTUS offers an integrated environment that allows the design of tutoring systems for interactive applications in a simple way by using techniques of programming by demonstration [3].

The CACTUS environment has been tested for the generation of courses for some applications. It has been used with interactive interfaces for teaching systems of continuous digital simulation, like the solar system or the Volterra equations [1]. It has also been used for the generation of tutoring courses for the OOPI-TasKAD system, an object oriented computer assisted design environment that is based on the prototype/instance inheritance paradigm. Moreover, we have made some tests with an electronic organiser, and finally we have generated courses about *Schoodule*, an application that uses a data basis and a constraint solver in order to make schedules for schools.

This paper is structured as follows. First, we present the main ideas on which the technique of user tasks modeling is based in relation with user actions control and tracking. The structure of ATOMS+ is also presented. After this, we introduce the arquitecture of CACTUS, followed by a more detailed description of this system, both for course execution and design. Finally, we shall include some conclusions and future lines of work.

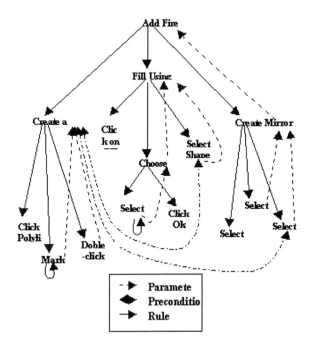

Figure 1. Decomposition of the task *Add Protection to a Beam*

2.   TASK MODELING, TRACKING AND EMULATION

The technique we propose is based on the use of *models of user tasks,* which represent the activities a user of an interactive application can accomplish and the way in which this can be done. A task model for an application defines two types of tasks. *Atomic* tasks model the interactions that can take place with the application in a single step, while *composed* tasks allow the modelization of tasks of a higher level that are composed of other tasks, atomic or not, that are executed succesively according to a determined sequenciation. Atomic tasks, like pushing a button, or selecting a graphical component, correspond to simple user events in the application or to a group of events. Both types of tasks can have associated parameters, which act as contextual information. For example, in an application of architectural design, the task *Add Protection to a Beam* has a parameter that represents the beam that is intended to be protected. In order to protect a beam the user has to C*reate a Shape* that represents the protection of one of the sides of the beam, *Fill the Shape* according to a pattern, and *Create a Symetric copy* of the shape. These three subtasks, which must be performed in the indicated order, have a parameter, the shape that is created; the pattern that is used to fill the shape is also a parameter of the second subtask, while the axis of symetry is a parameter of the last one. Relationships among parameters, like the fact that the shapes that correspond to each subtask are the same, are expressed in the rm of preconditions of the subtasks.

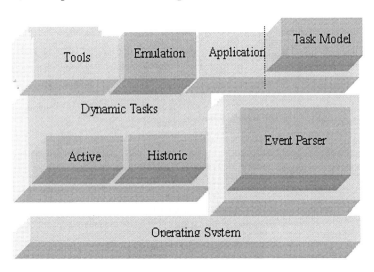

Figure 2. Relation between ATOMS+ and the application

The relation between each composed task and the subtasks that compose it is included in rules. Each rule includes additional information, like the relation that must exist between the execution of the different subtasks, the flow of parameters between them, the tasks that can have an optional or multiple execution and conditions for it, and the pre and post conditions that must be satisfied when a subtask is executed. Figure 1 shows the detailed structure of the task *Add Protection to a Beam*. The task is specified by means of five rules.

ATOMS is a management system for user task models at execution time that implements the task model just described. The extended system ATOMS+ is used in the automatic tutoring of tasks associated to an application. There are two main functionalities associated to it: when in tracking mode, it can follow the actions of the user and translate them in terms of high level tasks. ATOMS uses a parsing mechanism similar to the one used in Natural Language processing. The main conceptual difference with a standard parser comes from the fact that ATOMS allows the user to accomplish tasks in parallel: before a high level task is finished, the user can do actions that correspond to other tasks, like a search. From this point of view, ATOMS behaves as a semantic parser that allows words from several sentences to be interleaved in the text to be parsed. When in emulation mode, ATOMS+ is able to execute a high level task with specific values given for its parameters. In case the execution of the task requires some additional election by the user, the emulation can be executed by indicating default values for the needed low level parameters or by asking the user for their values at the corresponding instant during the emulation. The design system OOPI-TasKAD, which includes in its task model the Beam Protection task, has been implemented in ATOMS+.

Figure 2 shows the architecture of the ATOMS+ system. The modules that form the system are shadowed in dark tone. Each component of the system is connected to the ones next to it, so the *Event Analyser* acts as a filter between the application and the Windows Management System. The functional kernel of ATOMS+ is composed by three blocks: the *Parsing Engine,* the *Dynamic Tasks Module* and the *Emulation Module*. The Analysis Engine uses the second block in order to keep track of the tasks that are being accomplished by the user at each moment.

3. AN ENVIRONMENT FOR THE SPECIFICATION OF COURSES ABOUT APPLICATIONS

In this section we describe how to use the task models that have been described in the previous section in order to specify courses about the use of interactive applications. Starting from the task model of an application, the models of pedagogical units that form the course are defined.

The CACTUS environment for the development of interactive courses about the use of applications includes an implementation of the models that have been explained previously. The general architecture of the environment is shown in *Figure 3*. As it can be seen there, CACTUS makes use of both the HATS system that is described below and the *Module of Execution of Scenarios* in order to offer designers an environment that allows them to create interactive courses for their applications with low costs. The kind of tutoring provided by the system is task oriented, and CACTUS allows designers to specify *scenarios* that are adapted to each teaching session.

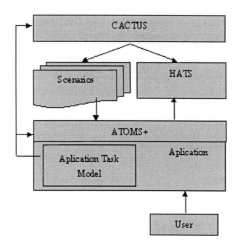

Figure 3. Architecture of the CACTUS environment

CACTUS offers explanations that are more comprehensible and more dynamical than those offered by current tutoring systems. It follows the activities of the user in order to act accordingly. CACTUS also allows designers to skip much of the work involved in the development of the tutoring systems. The CACTUS architecture is based on two modules (Figure 3). The first one, HATS, teaches users how to accomplish specific application tasks, while the second one, the *Module of Scenario Execution,* is in charge of preparing the *scenarios* that are suitable in order to teach the proposed tasks.

HATS [4], is a tutoring system that uses user task models to generate explanations that are given to the users. HATS offers dynamical help to the users, by updating the help messages according to the needs of the users and to what they do at each moment. This system offers contextualized feedback, like messages that are adapted to the work that is being done, or graphical response adapted to the working environment by making appropriate graphical objetcts flash. HATS can act with different degrees of flexibility, by filtering incorrect actions from the users and making them follow one of the correct paths depending on the degree of flexibility that has been established.

The *Module of Execution of Scenarios* makes suitable contexts to teach the tasks included in the courses available to the users. A *scenario* is a procedural description of a process, that includes references to tasks of the application, variables, conditional execution blocks, loops, etc. These descriptions are interpreted by the *Module of Execution of Scenarios*. For example, let us assume that we want to teach in an application for graphic design how to pass from a 2D design to a three dimensional one. In this case, it is reasonable to prepare a *scenario* that teaches students the creation of the design of a kitchen, in such a way that a context is provided that is suitable for the explanation of the procedure that passes the design to 3D. The interpreter of *Scenarios* uses the ATOMS *Emulation* module in order to execute the tasks that are referred by means of animations.

In order to facilitate the designer the maximum possible flexibility, CACTUS allows users to practise the tasks that are being taught to them in their own working environment, without using predefined *scenarios*.

CACTUS integrates different services oriented to the designers, like support for creation, modification, checking and debugging of tutoring courses, and services oriented to the students, like support for the execution of the courses. CACTUS has two working modes: when in *Execution Mode*, it allows course execution, checking and debugging. When in *Edition Mode*, it allows the creation and interactive modification of course contents.

Each pedagogical unit is in charge of teaching a set of tasks. CACTUS courses can be specified using a programming language or by means of the *Edition Mode* of the system, that allows designers to build and modify the contents of the courses in an interactive way. In order to do this, CACTUS uses a metaphore that represents courses as text books. These books can be modified by means of direct manipulation techniques, in particular techniques of visual programming and programming by demonstration [3].

4.   THE BOOK METAPHOR

CACTUS visualizes and allows the modification of the contents of courses by their representation as if they were textbooks. Most part of the contents of those books are generated automatically by CACTUS, which also decides the format in which they are shown. Designers only have to care about including the desired contents of pedagogical units. The main innovation of our courses is that they can follow the activity of the users. This makes it possible to offer them context dependent explanations. In this way the users do not learn by reading the books, but by *executing* them. Another important feature is the automatic generation of hypertext links, that simplify the navigation and liberate designers of their inclusion. In the remaining part of this section we shall describe the structure of a CACTUS tutoring book.

First, CACTUS generates a cover for the Book (Figure 2, left), which includes the title of the course and a general description of its contents. Next, CACTUS automatically generates an index of the pedagogical units that make up the course (Figure 2, center). Each entry is a hyperlink that contains the title of the unit together with a description of its contents.

One of the main features of CACTUS courses is that they can be followed by the students using different itineraries; there is always an itinerary by default. Admissible itineraries respect the precedences among chapters. CACTUS allows users to execute units depending on whether their previous units have been already passed or not. The system also generates a representation, in the form of a directed graph, of the structure of the course (see Figure 2, right). Each node of the graph represents a pedagogical unit, and its colour indicates its state. The state of a unit indicates if it has been executed by the current user, and whether it can be accessed currently. CACTUS updates automatically the states of the different units. An arrow appears in the graph joining a node A to another node B in case the unit A must be executed previously to the execution of unit B. Next, a page with a proposal of a sequencing order for the study of the courses is generated automatically (Figure 3, left). By following this order, CACTUS guarantees that whenever any pedagogical unit is executed, it is not blocked due to the fact that one of its predecessors has not been accomplished previously.

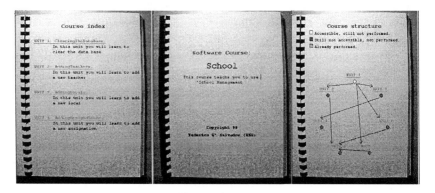

Figure 4. Cover, index and sequencing graph of a CACTUS book

After this, as many chapters as pedagogical units are in the course are presented in the book (Figure 5, center). Each pedagogical unit incorporates a set of task teaching sessions and, probably, some set of *scenarios* that are executed during the course. From the point of view of the presentation, explanations are included about the goals of the different teaching sessions, and about the *scenarios* that will be executed and the images, which are generated automatically by CACTUS.

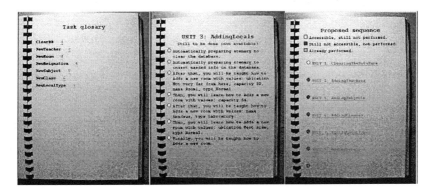

Figure 5. Proposal, pedagogical unit and glossary of a book

Finally, CACTUS automatically generates a glossary of tasks at the end of the books (Figure 5, right). This glossary is formed by hyperlinks to the tasks that are taught along the course.

5. COURSE EXECUTION

When in *execution mode,* CACTUS allows the execution of some of the parts of the books to teach students how to execute some tasks. This mode is used also by the designers in order to test and debug the courses at development time.

CACTUS includes a language that allows the designer of the course to specify the form in which different tasks are going to be performed. In this way, different teaching strategies can be used. The first type of instructions allows CACTUS to take care of teaching how to accomplish a task, how to execute an *scenario* or how to show an emerging message, that is, this set of instructions takes care of activities that have an immediate reflex over the activity of the user.

The second group of instructions controls the way in which the *Scenarios Execution Module* and the HATS teaching module work, including the degree of flexibility of the tutoring module and the amount of information and the type of messages that are shown to the user during the teaching session. A third group includes activities of a lower level, among them typical components of programming languages like loops, etc.

The pages that correspond to the pedagogical units usually contain task learning activities, instructions of *scenario* execution and feedback messages for the users that are related in a suitable way by different control structures. For example, in a course developed for *Schoodule* there is a unit that explains how a new relation of teaching *assignment* can be added. First, by default, a *scenario* is prepared that adds teachers, courses, groups and classes. In this way we can make sure that the users will not have any problem in order to add a new *assignment*. Once the users have added an *assignment*, the course shows them a message about it. They can decide that they prefer to use their own working context instead of practising with the predefined *scenario* provided by the designer.

When the users have satisfactorily accomplished the contents of a pedagogical unit, CACTUS modifies automatically the state of that unit, and it enables the access to the successive units if it is necessary. During the execution of a unit, CACTUS shows at each moment the instruction that is being executed, in such a way that users always know which tasks they have accomplished and what they still have to do.

Finally, the pedagogical units of the course can be executed by the order indicated in the proposal page. In this way, users will never try to execute a unit that is blocked.

6.   COURSE CREATION AND MODIFICATION

The goal of the Edition Mode of CACTUS is to assist designers in the creation and modification of tutoring courses. For the students, CACTUS courses are interactive books that teach them how to accomplish user tasks, and they keep track of their accomplishment. The same is true for course designers who do not have much experience, who only have to interact with the interface of CACTUS in order to create the courses in an interactive way. Advanced designers can have access to the inner representation of the courses and re-programme it directly.

In this section we describe how CACTUS courses are created and modified. The operations for course specification can be reduced to the addition and elimination of instructions. In order to eliminate instructions, the designer selects the elements to suppress, and activates the command *Eliminate*. In order to add new instructions, the process depends on the type of instruction that has to be added, as we shall see in the next paragraphs.

Instructions that represent activities for the user to practise can be inserted in a course in two different ways. The first one uses the command *Insert Teaching Session*. After this, the designer selects the desired task for a list of all the tasks that are specified in the task model of the corresponding application. For example, the designer can select the task *AddTeacher* and force the student to use *Pedro Suárez* as the name of the professor. Another way to add teaching activities is by means of the command *Insert Teaching Components about...*, once the application is being executed. This command makes CACTUS spy and remember all tasks the designer accomplishes next with the application. In this way, CACTUS inserts as many task teaching instructions as tasks are accomplished by the designer until he/she uses the command *Finish teaching insertion*. For example, if the designer adds a new teacher, CACTUS generates automatically a teaching instruction for the task *AddProfessor*. It is worth to mention that the procedures used by the designers in order to accomplish the tasks and those used later by the students when they are practicing are independent. For example, the designer can use menu options to execute some commands that are part of higher level tasks, while users can accomplish the same tasks by pushing on buttons. This independence is achieved thanks to the fact that CACTUS is based on hierarchical task models of the application, and not just on sequences of low level events.

In order to introduce an instruction that executes a *scenario*, the designer can use the command *Insert Defined Scenario...*, which will allow the selection of the *scenario* to execute from any *scenario* library. Alternatively, he/she can use the command *Insert New Scenario* followed by the command *Finish Scenario Insertion* if the application is being executed. The first of these commands makes CACTUS start to keep track of the tasks accomplished by the designer on the application and to record these tasks in a *scenario*. The second command stops the tasks recording. Afterwards, CACTUS inserts a reference to the *scenario* just created in the course. For example, the designer can add some teachers, subjects, groups and classes to the *Schoodule* data base after having selected the *Insert Defined Scenario...* command, and at the end he/she can select the *Finish Scenario Insertion* command, in case the application is being executed. After this, when the course is executed the data basis is initialized with some values by default.

The designer can also add or eliminate pedagogical units, and he/she can interactively modify the sequencing relations among them. These operations force the system to modify some sections of the interactive books, like the index, the precedence graph, the proposal page, or the glossary, in order to maintain the consistency among the different parts of the books.

The remaining constructions of the CACTUS language include a small visual programming environment that also allows the direct modification of the inner representation.

CACTUS reduces the maintenance costs of courses, since most part of these costs come from the modification of tasks models in applications. These modifications are done in ATOMS by means of visual techniques and by programming by demonstration [6]. Moreover, CACTUS manages the tasks in the task model of an application that are taught during the course that is being created. In this way it can tell the designer when a unit has to be modified due to the fact that it is trying to teach a task that is not yet modelled, and about tasks that should be added to the courses.

7.   CONCLUSIONS AND FUTURE WORK

We have described how the technology of user interface development based on models can be used in order to generate tutors for interactive applications. CACTUS courses solve many of the problems associated to courses created with current technologies. CACTUS represents the courses as interactive books that contain hyperlinks, so they are easier and more intuitive to use. Moreover, the courses make use of the capabilities of the HATS tutoring system on which they are based. The resulting courses are completely interactive, and they are able to follow the activity of the students. The development costs of the courses are reduced to a minimum thanks to the intensive use of techniques of programming by demonstration.

CACTUS offers an integrated environment for the creation and execution of courses. This environment offers services oriented toward the creation of courses, like programming techniques by demonstration, and services oriented to the execution of the courses, like preparation of suitable *scenarios* to practise.

As future work, we are interested in the generation of courses that include tasks that involve the execution of several interactive applications and several users. For this, the task engine of ATOMS+ must be generalized for the management of distributed tasks, as if it was a workflow engine. We have already obtained the first results in this direction, [6].

ACKNOWLEDGEMENTS

This work has been funded in part by the National Research Plan from Spain, projects TEL97-0306 and TEL99-0181.

8. REFERENCES

1. Alfonseca, M., García, F., de Lara, J., and Moriyón, R. "Generación automática de entornos de simulación con interfaces inteligentes", Revista de Enseñanza y Tecnología, ADIE, n° 10. Octubre-Diciembre 1998.
2. Contreras, J. and Saiz, F. "A Framework for the Automatic Generation of Software Tutoring". In Proceedings CADUI'96, Computer-Aided Design of User Interfaces, Eurographics, Belgium, June 1996.
3. Cypher, A. "Watch What I do, Programming by Demonstration". MIT press (ed. A. Cypher), Cambridge, Ma., USA, 1993.
4. García, F., Contreras, J., Rodríguez, P. and Moriyón, R. "Help generation for task based applications with HATS". In Proceedings EHCI'98, Creta (Greece), September 1998.
5. García, F., Rodríguez, P., Contreras, J., and Moriyón, R. "Gestión de Tareas de Usuario en ATOMS". IV Jornadas de Tecnología de Objetos, JJOO'98, Bilbao, Octubre 1998.
6. García, F. and Moriyón, R. "A Framework for Distributed Task Management". Third Argentine Symposium on Object Orientation, ASOO'99. Buenos Aires, Argentina, Septiembre 1999.
7. García, F. "Towards the Generation of Tutorial Couses for Applications". Enviado a 5th ERCIM conference on User-Interfaces for All. Alemania, marzo 2000.
8. Pangoli, S. and Paternó, F. "Automatic Generation of Task-oriented Help". In Proceedings UIST'95, Pittsburgh, ACM Press, 1995.
9. Puerta, A.R. "Supporting User-Centered Design of Adaptive User Interfaces Via Interface Models". First Annual Workshop On Real-Time Intelligent User Interfaces For Decision Support And Information Visualization, San Francisco, January 1998.
10. Rodríguez, P., García, F., Contreras, J. and Moriyón, R. "Parsing Techniques for User-Task Recognition". 5th International Workshop on Advances in Functional Modeling of Complex Technical Systems, Paris (France), Julio 1997.
11. Szekely, P., Luo, P. and Neches, R. "Beyond Interface Builders: Model-Based Interface Tools". Proceedings of INTERCHI'93, 1993, pp. 383-390.

SUMA Project (Open Murcia University Services)

Antonio Gómez Skarmeta[1], Pedro García López,[1] Jesús Egea Payá[1], José Jaime Meseguer Navarro[1], Tomás Jiménez García[2]

[1] *Universidad de Murcia, Facultad de Informática; Campus de Espinardo;*
30100 Espinardo (Murcia). Tel. 968 364 640.
E-mail: skarmeta@dif.um.es , pedro@dif.um.es, jegea@dif.um.es, jjaime@dif.um.es ,
[2] *Servicio de Informática; Campus de la Merced; Murcia. Tel. 968 363 328.*
E-mail: tomasji@fcu.um.es

Key words: TeleLearning, Teaching, New Technologies, Internet, Bimodal education

Abstract: The SUMA project, represents the actions taken to develop a whole TIC (Information and Communications Technologies) solution, which allows the pupils in the project to access remotely to the University from their own home. The goals in this virtual access, goes from making the remote control of the administrative and the extra-curricula tasks easy, to making some teaching tasks for a specific course if possible (forums, remote tutorials, e-mail linked to the courses, virtual classrooms, virtual exercises and problems which an Intelligent Card authentifies). These tasks are called TeleLearning. We want to facilitate some tasks, which can be made at the pupil's home, avoiding unnecessary pupil displacements which can be harmful for nature. This kind of teaching is called bimodal. The SUMA project is a long time project, with great teaching and academic interest, really important for the Information Society development in Murcia

1. INTRODUCTION

The main project goal is to allow teachers and pupils at the University of Murcia to use the telematic tools, developed in the information highway context and inside the bimodal learning, to evaluate the possibility of shortening and improving the learning cycles and to blow down the physiological barries, which impede access to the teacher who monitors the pupil.

M. Ortega and J. Bravo (eds.), Computers and Education in the 21st Century, 199–210.
© *2000 Kluwer Academic Publishers. Printed in the Netherlands.*

The project development is based on the university community desire to enhance the telematic communication through Internet. We want to make this desire real within a whole project, which includes the teaching activity and offers the educational sector a solution to extensively use the tools required nowadays.

The project wants to evaluate the use of tools such as the e-mail and the web in the teacher-pupil communication, to introduce security and access control utilities and to evaluate the methodological and organisational changes derived from the introduction of these techniques in a flexible university environment. The SUMA project promotes virtual communication, the use of forums through telematic applications and the possibility of doing self-assessment tests to achieve their own evaluation of the knowledge learnt in every subject.

This project is the University of Murcia contribution to the worries expressed in some community documents like the first annual report of the European Commission from the "Information Society Forum" in June 1996. This report manifests that neither society nor European institutions are ready to use the new technologies and advises that the solution to this situation is essential in order to keep the "Welfare Society" in the European Community countries.

Nowadays we can say that the technological resources to do this already exist. Now we have to introduce them in the improvement process of teaching quality levels, established with the new technologies irruption mainly in the telematic area and in the services related to the Data Highways.

This improvement process is a strategic goal at the University and in other teaching environments. The European Community support every initiative in communication improvement in the telematic area and in multimedia and teaching contents production. The reports of the European institutions speak about a strong social impact with the introduction of the new technologies, which will have unexpected consequences in the near future.

There are a lot of initiatives in Spain using the new technologies in distance learning. University entities covering this teaching level are UNED or UOC. Therefore, the new technologies allow getting a new teaching level, (called bimodal in the OCDE report titled: *"Les technologies de l'informatión et l'avenir de l'enseignement post-secondaire"* edited in 1996, page 49), which takes advantage of the benefits derived from the presential universities, i.e. the usage of research centers and laboratories placed at the university campus.

The structure of this document starts with the goals and module division in SUMA, it continues analysing the security and collaborative systems and it ends with the advantages from a project like SUMA.

2. SUMA PROJECT GOALS

Two main groups of goals have been defined to approach this project:

2.1 Global goals

To shorten and improve the learning cycles, avoiding the problems derived from the physical barriers and reducing unnecessary commuting expenses.

2.2 Concrete goals

- To make the telematic communication level grow using the Internet with a massive implementation of e-mail with database integration, which allows making any simple, fast and direct kind of queries about evaluation and teaching.
- To promote the discussion forums using the existing tools based on telematic applications
- To add new possibilites to teaching such as an self-assessment possibility on some teaching contents, using self-assessment tests.
- To use the new technologies to enhance teaching where people with special needs ared prevented from accesing "peer-to-peer" education.
- To collaborate with enterprises whose activities are in the same technology context, to take the business and transference of products deployed in the SUMA project to the commercial and customer sector.

3. PROJECT MODULES

Eight big modules compound the whole project. The user role (teacher or pupil) determines which customized information every module must show. The role and the user identifier will establish which actions each user can do and which amount of information the user can access.

3.1   Administrative SUMA

This module represents the administrative tasks that will be made through the Internet, i.e. university taxes, courses subscription, report consulting, etc

3.2   Extra-curricula SUMA

This module implements the activities which the University of Murcia offers out of the academic context. Those activities go from reserving computers at special rooms (called virtual classrooms) to publishing announcements and public notices in notice boards interesting for SUMA users.

3.3   Teaching SUMA

The whole teaching aspects related to the user activity compound this module. This module is the most user-type dependant, because a teacher has not the same teaching responsibility than a pupil. This module offers the following activities: Forums, Library, E-mail, Self-assessment, Multimedia Development, Subjects syllabuses, Remote tutoring, and Virtual classrooms

Thanks to this module a user can access to the user lists linked to him/her, i.e. class partners, teacher or teachers in certain subject. Those lists allow the user to contact every user sending an e-mail or opening a chat session if possible.

3.4   Market SUMA

This module allows users to access some services that entities not directly linked to the University of Murcia offer. Those services go from e-commerce to consulting the user data in a database if required.

The user accesses every module, and its particular options, through a browser. After user authentication, the welcome page pops upon the screen. This page shows the last news and allows the user to access the modules. As you can imagine, accessing a module does not avoid accessing another one.

After the user chooses the start module, a 2-framed interface is shown: a control frame to access the modules and options in a module, and a frame to show the selected option results.

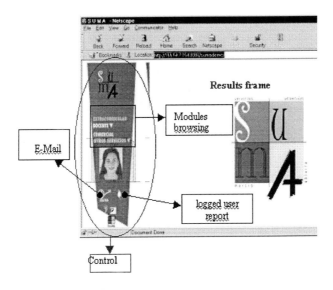

Figure 1. The 2-framed Screen

4. SECURITY: USER AUTHENTICATION

Most information this project manages should be private. We must ensure that no malicious user has free access to the academic file of another user. The user authentication in SUMA is made by using the Intelligent Card; this card keeps the personal data and security information to identify the user in the system. The user will not access without the card, avoiding the danger derived from the typical login-password architecture that other user can steal. This security information (private key) will allow encrypting the information to avoid that some one can intercept the data, steal or alter them.

The Secure Socket Layer (SSL) technology supports this system. SSL has became the most accepted standard and a large amount of browsers and web servers support it.

SSL is an open protocol that Netscape has proposed. This protocol works between the Transport layer and the Application layer. The goal is to get a secure communication between client and server, with the following services: privacy, authentication and message integrity.

SSL uses cryptography techniques based on public key to get this goal plus private key cryptography which client and server negotiates when communication starts, allowing the protocol to add new encrypted algorythms or to keep legal issues related to export and use these algorythms. SSL uses the X.509 certifications for key exchange. These include the public key and the owners' personal data through single X500 names like: their name, e-mail, state, country, etc. making this directory usage easy to spread the certificates.

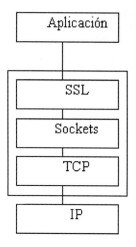

Figure 2. SLL inside OSI

5. COMMUNICATIONS

SUMA wants to get a fast intuitive communication between application users. Connecting with other connected user whenever a user wants, sending a question to a teacher about some topic or consulting the most frequently asked questions, must be as simple as browsing to another page.

We want to support the teacher-pupil and pupil-pupil relationship through the net. A fluent communication allows establishing collaboration lines to improve the teaching quality. If the pupils can ask their doubts to the teacher without leaving their study-room, their performance will improve and they will get better academic results than stopping their studies to go to the teacher office to ask whatever they want. Pupils make groups to solve their own problems because they have now a fast way to communicate. They are learning to work in group and to coordinate their job using the new technologies that they will find when they come to the real life. Every user report (i.e. the pupils or the teachers in a subject) includes an icon to send a mail to the user in the row where the icon appears or to open a chat session if the user is logged in the system.

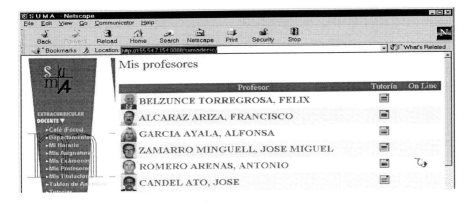

Figure 3. Teachers list

A subject report has more options. Every list entry has an icon to join to the discussion forums created in the subject, another icon to write messages to the notice board (i.e. the date of the exam, time table changes, etc...), another one to access the frequently asked question and its answers, and the last one to get a report with all the pupils in the subject.

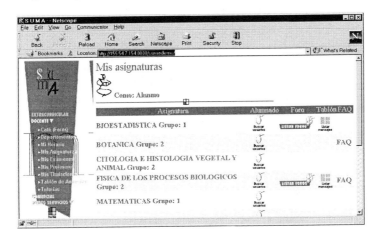

Figure 4. Subject report

5.1 Notice board

Every subject has its own notice board allowing the pupils to get information about the last news in the subject. The teacher manages the notice board, he/she updates the news. The pupils can consult the notice board but they cannot update it.

5.2   Frequently Asked Questions(FAQ)

The teacher manages the FAQ. He or she knows which the most frecuently asked questions are and which the most relevant ones are in the subject. A FAQ includes the question and the answer, it can be printed, and the teacher can include more information in a file that the pupil can download later.

Figure 5. FAQ

5.3   Discussion Forums

Every subject has as many forums as desired. Teachers and pupils can create a discussion forum on any topic. A pupil can access the private forums if he/she is registered in the subject which the forums are linked and he/she can access the public forums in a special zone called: "El café de SUMA" (*"SUMA café"*).

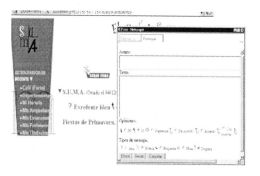

Figure 6. Discussion Forum

5.4   Shared Zone

The development of a Shared Zone is under construction. This zone will offer the following services:

5.4.1   Collaborative browsing

Two kind of roles are defined: the teacher and the pupil. Every event in the teacher browser is caught, sent through the net and re-played in the pupil browsers.

This service starts in the subject init page, which is configured in the SUMA database. The teacher can browse in the normal way from this page, following the links in the page or using the "next", "previous" and "home" buttons given. The teacher can also type a new url address. Every event in the browser is caught, i.e. the scroll bar movement in every frame to allow the pupil to have the same view point as the teacher if the page does not fit in the browser window. Other caught events are mouse clicks on buttons, radio buttons and checkboxes, and the changes in text fields and selection inputs. In this way, every change made in a form by the teacher is re-played in the pupil forms.

5.4.2   Shared pointer

The collaborative browsing service could include the shared pointer, but and its importance, utility and different design are relevant enough to make a separate explanation.

The service catches the events thrown by the teacher mouse, to send them after, and re-play them in the pupil's computers. The Dynamic HTML technology supports this service. We create a dynamic layer that emulates a fictictous mouse pointer in the pupil's browsers. The location of this layer changes dynamically to emulate the mouse movement. To emulate the mouse click the fictitious mouse colour changes from red to yellow.

Joining this tool with the previous one, we can use the shared zone as an online presentation player, where the orator (i.e. the teacher) has the facilities that other programs offer. In this way, pupils will pay their attention in the most interesting zone of the slide (or the web page) which is being explained.

5.4.3   Chat

The chat implemented in the Shared Zone has all the features included in common chat applications and new ones. The teacher controls the chat, so if the teacher is not logged in no one can activate the chat. The main goal of the chat is allowing the teacher to give little explanations or to solve questions. The teacher decides if a pupil can activate the chat or not (this option disables the button in the pupil's chat window). The teacher can make a pupil be quiet in a chat session to keep the chatting in the topic he/she wants.

5.4.4   Audio

The chat is not enough to have real on-line classes, because the amount of information is very low, the feedback that pupils get their questions and the explanations given by the teacher with this system are very poor. A more powerful tool is needed to solve this problem, a tool similar to human communication: voice

With the Java Media Framework support, we have developed a system to allow the teacher to send out the class in the normal way (by speaking). Developing a rotating session system, supervised by the teacher, to let pupils to make questions avoiding the voice overlapping is next step. Moreover, the chat will have voice support soon.

5.4.5   Video

Video conference improves the communication quality, adding the best feedback and the greatest amount of information.

The Shared Zone has this tool in one-way mode, letting pupils to see and listen to the teacher giving a class. Java Media Framework technology avoids the net congestion, using tested video standards to compress the video to transmit it over IP.

5.4.6   Session recording

Every feature mentioned above is an event. Those events can be temporarily stored as they happen if the teacher wants. They are stored in the server later.

In this way the sessions (classes) remain available for teachers and pupils. The teacher will play them every time he/she wants, with pupils broadcast if desired, or delete them from the server. The pupils can attend a class every time they want; this is impossible with traditional classes.

6. CONTENT

The main goal in the project is to find out which subject topics, currently taught at University of Murcia, can be decentralized and can be achieved by this project. All departments at the University should add their efforts to identify those topics. Every case should be studied, with the implied teaching collaboration and guiding, to identify which contents in every discipline can be updated for access in a virtual way.

The teaching offer includes: remote tutoring, program consulting and general information about subjects and exercices, discussion forums with teachers, access to the University of Murcia library and to the colective catalogue, and access to databases of electronic magazines.

In a specific subject we can include for example:

6.1 General Data

The pupil will allow getting subject goals, syllabuses, types of problems and exercices to make. Optionally, evaluation criteria, subject bibliography with access to the University of Murcia library in order to consult books or reserve them, etc. are also allowed.

6.2 Authenticated Access to Class (Infovia and E-Mail)

Only teachers and pupils can access SUMA with a password. Here they will find supplementary material supporting the teaching provided by the provides as notes and interesting texts, virtual communications by e-mail if possible, frequently asked questions, marks publication, etc.

6.3 Debate Forum Accesing Authentication

Only teachers and pupils with a SUMA password for access to several discussion forums will allow access to the discussion forums created by teachers. The teacher will set the username and the password to start the forum. Open forums can be created, too.

7. CONCLUSIONS

Thanks to this project we ensure that the following results soon:

Teaching quality improvement: The possibility of getting the responses to the pupil doubts just looking for them in the frequently asked question section improves the teaching quality. The pupil gets additional knowledge using technology, which will be essential in the near future.

Teaching options increase: This project aims at using the "bimodal" teaching concept. The project making, extends the frame of teaching possibilities and creates technology platforms to achieve a new continued-education based learning.

New teaching contents development: The Data Bank that will be built in the project will be an information repository containing easily accessible contents using different web browser versions. Joining every content generated in every university included in the project with the tools given to easily update those contents will allow improving the data quality and achieving the following principles: *to avoid data duplication, only one user can update the information; everyone who wants to access the information knows where to find it.*

To apply in teaching new technology tools: The new tools defined as "Self-assessment", allow teachers and pupils to access an amount of possibilities to evaluate their knowledge level and to identify their learning needs or teaching needs. The teacher can establish the level suggested to access some course, the pupils can know their real knowledge level every time, and act in response, and avoid losing their time and money.

To open new communication channels between the University and the market world.

REFERENCES

1. TELEREGIONS, (Forms B1 -B3 Proposal Description Part B) (1995) Telematics Applications Programm (1994-1998)
2. CEE (1996)Green Paper Living and working in the information society: People First
3. BIERMAN, D.J., VALK, V.A. (1993) Tele-learning, social and academic consequences (Applica)
4. CCE (1991), Mémorandum sur l'apprentissage ouvert et à distance dans la Communauté européene, Mémorandum COM(91)388 final, Commission des communautés européenes, Bruxelles, 12 Novembre
5. DAVIS, A (1992), Perspectives on distance education. Distance education in single and dual-mode universities, in Ian Mugridge (dir. pub), The Commonwealth of Learning, The Open University of British Columbia, Vancouver, Canada, pp. 63-78.
6. NATIONAL ACADEMY OF SCIENCES AND THE NATIONAL ACADEMY OF ENGINEERING 1995. Reinventing schools: The technology is now!. http://www.nas.edu/nap/online/techgap/welcome.html
7. UNIVERSIDAD AUTÓNOMA DE BARCELONA.Trabajos de Pere-Lluís Barberá. http://blues.uab.es/campus_virtual

Introducing Waves Using Simulations Controlled From Html Files

Mª Adelaida Hernández[1], José M. Zamarro[1], Ernesto Martín[2].
[1]Dpto. de Física, Universidad de Murcia
e-mail: ahernandez@fcu.um.es Tel. 968 3273; (jmz@fcu.um.es) Tel. 968 32 7380
[2]Facultad de Química. Universidad de Murcia. Campus de Espinardo. 30 071 Murcia.
e-mail: ernesto@fcu.um.es Tel. 968 327373

Key words: Teaching Physics, simulations, discovery learning.

Abstract: Teaching Physics has a specific difficulty because of the use of mathematics as
               the language to describe Physics phenomena. Graphic features, animation and
               computing capabilities of computers allow simulating phenomena, then
               computers may hide the mathematical symbols, terms, expressions so that,
               first, concepts are the main concern, and mathematical formalism can be
               introduced later. In this work a didactic unit introducing waves is presented.
               The core of each chapter are simulations that are used by students to perform
               guided experiments. These simulations are Java applets controlled from html
               files that guide the students in their process of discovery learning.

1.   INTRODUCTION.

Teaching science, and particularly Physics, has a specific difficulty because the use of mathematics as the basic formalism to describe natural phenomena. Computers have graphic animation and computing capabilities that allow simulation and visualization of the phenomena, hiding the mathematical expressions. With simulations the user can perform experiments where the main concern are the concepts; then mathematics could be introduced later. There are different ways to use simulations for the students to approach the concepts. We use simulations with interactive animated graphics that show the influence of the different parameters that

M. Ortega and J. Bravo (eds.), Computers and Education in the 21st Century, 211–216.

take part in the phenomena we are studying. Simulations are embedded in text that guide the students in their process of discovery learning.

This work has been performed within the CoLoS group [2,3] whose main goal is to promote the use of modern technologies to get a better and direct approach to the presentation and understanding of the basic concepts of technology and science.

2.   SIMULATIONS CONTROL FROM THE TEXT.

The idea of discovery learning is generally accepted as something very positive in the learning process [1]. Once the student has found out something searching by himself/herself, this knowledge persists in a more stable way than if the process is a passive one. Simulation is a good tool to achieve this kind of learning process, there are students that has enough initiative to get good results with this kind of applications but most of them need remarks and suggestions to take advantage of this kind of environment. To keep a balance between freedom, necessary to discover by oneself, and guidance, not to get lost, is a challenge that will establish the quality of the product. Without any orientation students will just play with the simulation but they will hardly learn anything at all, the same undesirable result will be reached if too much guide is provided.

An easy and multiplatform way to write text to accompany simulations is using HTML files as all Internet navigators can read this kind of files. This format has the advantage to be hypertext, and it is also possible to activate executable applications and control them from the text. The idea of integrating HTML files and simulations was initially used in the INTERACT project [4].

3.   DIDACTIC UNIT TO INTRODUCE WAVES.

The didactic unit that is presented in this paper is intended as an introduction to the study of some basic issues about waves, so it can be used in introductory lectures on Physics. The main objective is to show the basic concepts that are usually hidden by the mathematical formalism in the traditional way of teaching. Simulations are executed from the text; this text is active in the sense that while the student is reading it he/she can click on some words, so that in the simulation they perform the action that is described by the text. On this first walk around the text guides the student very precisely to make him familiar with the simulation; in a second stage some tasks are suggested, so the student is pushed to take direct control on the simulation and to discover performing experiments. Self-assessment informs the student about the level he/she has achieved.

3.1   Set-up.

The main page contains a summary of the goals, a link to general information, an index with links to each chapter and to the experiments, which are the core of them. The general information section provides a detailed description of how the simulations are launched from the text and how they are also controlled from it. A glossary helps the students to remember terms and concepts that they need to get the maximum benefit of the unit.

Each chapter begins with a summary of the issue that will be treated in it and of the objectives to be reached. Some basic theory is also supplied. It will be extended in the Experiments suggested; these Experiments are the most important part of the didactic unit and establish the difference with the traditional teaching process. The challenge is to stimulate the student to learn by searching. The process is divided into three levels: first, a guided experiment launching and controlling the simulation from the text, then some tasks where some experiments are suggested to be performed by the students leaving them the control of the simulation (at this level, the students are expected to develop their creativity by taking the initiative to improve or develop new experiments playing freely with the simulation), and finally a self test where the students must think about what they have learned, it also provides an idea of their learning level.

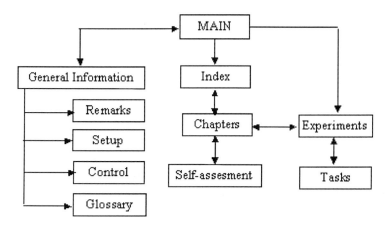

Figure 1. Set-up of the didactic unit

3.2   Content.

The didactic unit has five chapters as we can see in figure 2. The first chapter is devoted to introduce the concept of wave as a perturbation of a physical magnitude that travels. The mechanism for this fact is shown in this particular case as the propagation of the displacement of the elements of a tightened string. The simulation shows how using basic Newton dynamics laws, a perturbation made at one end of the string propagates along it. The perturbation produces a change in the direction of the tension at one end of the element.

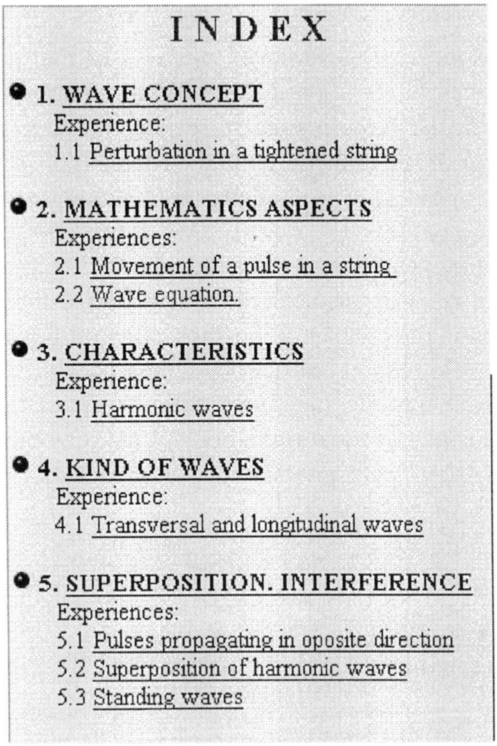

```
                     I N D E X

    ● 1. WAVE CONCEPT
         Experience:
         1.1 Perturbation in a tightened string

    ● 2. MATHEMATICS ASPECTS
         Experiences:
         2.1 Movement of a pulse in a string
         2.2 Wave equation.

    ● 3. CHARACTERISTICS
         Experience:
         3.1 Harmonic waves

    ● 4. KIND OF WAVES
         Experience:
         4.1 Transversal and longitudinal waves

    ● 5. SUPERPOSITION. INTERFERENCE
         Experiences:
         5.1 Pulses propagating in oposite direction
         5.2 Superposition of harmonic waves
         5.3 Standing waves
```

Figure 2. Index of Chapters

Two mathematic aspects of the phenomena are introduced, the first one is a property that every function describing a wave must have and the other one is the wave equation.

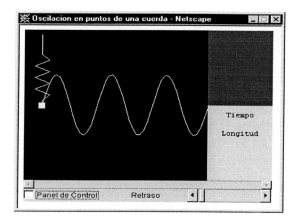

Figure 3. Simulation to study the characteristics of a wave

The third chapter introduces the characteristic parameters using the simulation to facilitate to grasp their meaning and to study their dependence with the magnitudes that take part in the physical phenomena.

A harmonic travelling wave on a string is used to see how the velocity of propagation coincide with the phase velocity.

The tasks are dedicated to investigate dependences between the different characteristics and. between the velocity of propagation and the velocity of any element of the string.

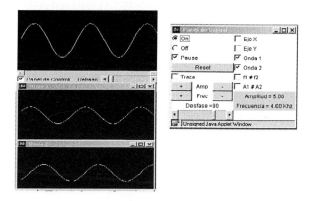

Figure 4. Interference of harmonic waves

The next chapter covers different kinds of waves considered from different points of view. A simulation shows transverse and longitudinal waves. The last chapter deals with a very important property of waves, superposition. To visualize this property three simulations have been developed. The first one shows two pulses of the same look but travelling in opposite directions along a tightened string. Pulses with opposite amplitude are also studied where the reflection coefficient is introduced. The second experiment is about interference. Two harmonic waves travel in the same direction along the tightened string; by changing different parameters you can observe the result.

Figure 4 shows the set-up of the windows and the control panel of the experiment facilitating the observation of the waves involved. Last experiment studies standing waves. Two harmonic waves travel in opposite direction along the string. Traces help to have the envelope of the amplitude, so that you can easily check the nodes and the maximum.

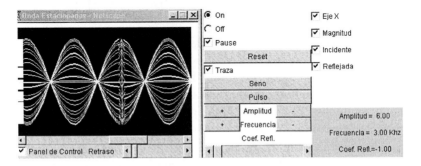

Figure 5. Standing Waves

In this simulation the concept of resonance is also introduced.

ACKNOWLEDGMENT.

J.M. Zamarro, A. Hernandez y E. Martín want to acknowledge the support of the Comunidad Autónoma de la Región de Murcia to make this work possible.

4.   REFERENCES.

1. de Jong, T. "Learning and Instruction with Computer Simulations". Education & Computing, 6, 217-229, (1991).
2. Härtel, H., "CoLoS: Conceptual Learning of Science". de Jong T. Sarti L. (ed): Design and Production of Multimedia and Simulation-based Learning Material. Kluwer Academic Publishers, pp 189-217, (1994).
3. Murcia CoLoS Webpage: http://colos.fcu.um.es.
4. Thomas, R., Neilson, I. "Harnessing Simulations In the Service of Education: The INTERACT Simulation Environment", special Issue of Computers in Education, (1995)

Using Bayesian Networks in Computerized Adaptive Tests

E. Millán, M. Trella, J.L. Pérez-de-la-Cruz and R. Conejo
Departamento de Lenguajes y Ciencias de la Computación
Facultad de Informática, Málaga, Spain.

Key words: Adaptive Test, Bayesian Network, Intelligent Tutoring System

Abstract: In this paper we propose the use of Bayesian Networks as a theoretical framework for Computerized Adaptive Tests. To this end, we develop the Bayesian Network that supports the Adaptive Testing Algorithm, that is, we define what variables should be taken into account, what kind of relationships should be established among them, and what are the required parameters. As parameter specification is one of the most difficult problems when using Bayesian Networks, we suggest the use of several simplifications. By using such simplifications, the required conditional probabilities can be obtained in a relatively simple way.

1.   INTRODUCTION

Computerized Adaptive Tests have come up as an alternative to traditional paper and pencil tests, with the aim of improving both the time required to obtain a precise estimation of the student's level of knowledge yielded by his/her answers to a set of related test items, and the accuracy of such estimations. Thanks to the great capabilities that computers offer for storing and processing data, and to the soundness of probability theory, both goals could be achieved. However, most current Adaptive Tests have been developed to measure the student's knowledge in terms of a single variable and, depending on the purpose of the test, this measure is insufficient. For example, if the Computer Adaptive Test is going to be used to perform diagnosis in an Intelligent Tutoring System (ITS) we need more detailed

M. Ortega and J. Bravo (eds.), Computers and Education in the 21st Century, 217–228.
© 2000 *Kluwer Academic Publishers. Printed in the Netherlands.*

information to know exactly which parts of the subject domain the student is having trouble with. Our approach to solve this problem is based on the use of Bayesian Networks to perform Adaptive Tests.

The paper is structured as follows: in the following section we briefly review the theoretical background of our approach, that is, all the basic related concepts, namely Bayesian Networks, Intelligent Tutoring Systems, and Computer Adaptive Tests. Then we describe the structural model that supports Adaptive Testing based on Bayesian Networks, and propose several approaches to simplify parameter specification. Finally, the most important conclusions and our plans for future work are presented.

2.   THEORETICAL BACKGROUND

This section is devoted to a brief review of the theoretical concepts on which our approach is based, namely Bayesian Networks, Intelligent Tutoring Systems, and Computer Adaptive Tests.

2.1   Bayesian Networks

A *Bayesian Network* is a directed acyclic graph in which nodes are variables and links represent *causal influence* relationships among them. The parameters used to represent uncertainty are the conditional probabilities of each node given its parents, that is, if the variables of the network are $\{X_i, i = 1, ..., n\}$ and $Pa(X_i)$ represents the set of parents of node X_i, the parameters of the network are the conditional distributions $\{P(X_i/Pa(X_i)), i=1, ..., n\}$ (for the nodes without parents, the a priori distributions). Under certain conditional independence assumptions, this set of probability distributions completely describes the joint probability distribution of the variables of the network, as it can be shown that, under these assumptions:

$$P(X_1, ..., X_n) = \prod_{i=1}^{n} P(X_i/Pa(X_i))$$

Thus, to define a Bayesian Network we need to provide:
- The set of variables, $X_1, X_2, ..., X_n$.
- The set of relationships (causal influence) among those variables. The relationships are represented by directed links in the network, and the only condition is that the network should not contain any cycles.
- For each variable, the conditional distribution

$\{ P(X_i/Pa(X_i)), i=1, ..., n \}$.

Once the Bayesian Network has been defined, it can be used to make inferences about the values of the variables in the network. To this end, Bayesian propagation algorithms use probability theory to make such inferences using the information available, that usually is a set of observations or evidences. Such inferences can be *abductive* (which is the cause that better explains the evidence available) or *predictive* (what is the probability of obtaining certain results in the future), that is, every variable of the network can be used either as a source of information or as an object of prediction, depending on the evidence available and on the goal of the diagnostic process. For an easy introduction to Bayesian Networks see [4], and for a more complete and updated presentation, [3].

2.2   Intelligent Tutoring Systems

An *Intelligent Tutoring System* (ITS) is a computer program that is oriented to teaching, organised dynamically, and uses different representations for the knowledge to be transmitted, the tutorial strategies to be employed, and the student's knowledge. The main goal of an ITS is to be able to adapt instructions to each individual student, in a similar way that a human teacher does. In 1995, Shute took an e-mail poll among well-known researchers in the field, in an attempt to elucidate what the word *"intelligent"* means in this context [16]. The almost unanimous conclusion was that the intelligence of a tutor consists in its capability to *adapt* to each individual learner, meaning that, in contrast to traditional Computer Aided Instruction programs, which teach in a static and uniform way, ITSs can create and revise individual instructional plans, guide and assist students in their learning process, and adapt the instruction environment to the student's needs. Therefore, the key component of an ITS is the one that allows these instructions to be adapted to each student: the *student model*. The student model is the component of the ITS where all the information about the student is stored, in particular his/her current state of knowledge. The process of inferring such state of knowledge is called *diagnosis*. So the *student model* is the data structure used to store the information, and *diagnosis* is the process that manipulates such a structure. Both components should be designed together, and this problem, that is central to the design of any ITS, is called the *student modelling problem*. Student modelling is without doubt the most difficult problem in an ITS, not only because of the inherent difficulty of any inference process, but also because it involves dealing with information that usually is uncertain or imprecise.

Unfortunately, this difficult problem has not always been paid the attention it deserves, since developing an ITS represents a big effort. As a consequence, many researchers have preferred to develop their own ad hoc heuristics to perform the diagnostic process. Using such heuristics is an easy way to solve the problem; however, on many occasions their lack of theoretical foundations makes the result unpredictable, especially in situations not sufficiently considered by designers. Only recently have we been able to find works that devote great effort to the use of well-founded theoretical frameworks. Bayesian Networks are used in [5], [6], [11] and [12]. Fuzzy Logic is used in [1], [7] and [8]. In our opinion, the additional effort of using Bayesian Networks is worthwhile, because if the system behaves incorrectly or unexpectedly, we know that this misbehaviour is not due to the inference mechanism. Instead, the assumptions entered in the model should be revised. Numbers obtained by the system might be inaccurate, but never inconsistent.

2.3   Computerized Adaptive Tests

In this section we will briefly review the basic concepts in Computerized Adaptive Tests. An easy tutorial is [15], and more complete descriptions can be found in [18] and [17].

In traditional paper and pencil tests, the storage and analysis of the information were static. The use of computers in evaluation processes based on Tests opened up the possibility of performing both processes in a dynamic way. A *Computer Adaptive Test* (CAT) is a computer-administered test in which the selection of the next question to ask and the decision to finish the test are dynamically adopted based on the current estimation of the student's level of knowledge. Such an estimation is also dynamically obtained from the student's answers to test items.

In more precise terms, a CAT is an iterative algorithm that starts with an initial estimation of the examinee's proficiency level and has the following steps:

– All the questions in the database (that have not been administered yet) are examined to determine which will be the best to ask next according to the current estimation of the examinee's level.
– The question is asked, and the examinee responds.
– According to the answer, a new estimation of the proficiency level is computed.
– Steps 1 to 3 are repeated until the stopping criterion defined is met. This procedure is illustrated in Figure 1:

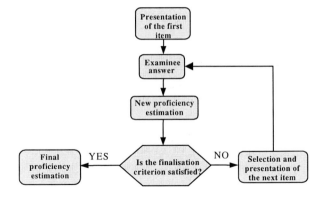

Figure 1. Flow diagram of an adaptive test

The psychometric theory underlying most CATs is *Item Response Theory* (IRT). In IRT, it is assumed that the knowledge level of the student is measured with a single variable θ that is called the *trait*. Using the student's answers as input data, the level of knowledge of the student is estimated (with some statistical method). Then, this estimation $\hat{\theta}$ is used to determine the more informative item to ask next. These steps are repeated until some stopping criterion is met. Different statistical methods to estimate θ and to select the next best question to ask give different IRT models. For example, one of the most commonly used models is the 3-parameter logistic model [2], in which for each test item i three different parameters are considered: a_i, which represents the discrimination index, b_i, which represents the difficulty factor, and c_i, which represents the guessing factor. The *Item Characteristic Curve* (ICC) associated with item i is defined by the expression:

$$P(\theta) = P(\{\text{Correct answer to item } i\}/\theta) = c_i + (1-c_i) / (1 + \exp(-1.7 \cdot a_i \cdot (\theta - b_i))$$

This function is graphically represented in Figure 2, for $a_i = 1.2$, $b_i = 6$, and $c_i = 0.3$.

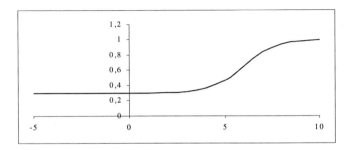

Figure 2. ICC graphical representation

In the figure we can see what is the meaning of each of the associated parameters:

- The guessing factor c_i represents the probability that a student guesses the correct answer when his/her knowledge level is as low as possible,
- The difficulty factor b_i defines the location of the curve's inflection point along the θ scale (lower values of b_i will shift the curve to the left, and higher values to the right), and
- The discrimination index a_i defines the slope of the curve at its inflection point (therefore, a_i denotes how well the item is able to discriminate between students of slightly different ability).

Each time the student answers a question, the ICC is used to obtain an estimation of his/her knowledge level. There are several methods for computing such estimations, but the most commonly used are the *Maximum likelihood method* [9], which consists of finding the value of θ that maximizes the likelihood function, and the *Bayesian method,* which computes the ability level for which the posterior distribution is maximum.

Once the new estimation of the student's level of knowledge has been computed, question selection methods are used to choose the next best question to ask, that is, the more informative item given the current estimation of the student's knowledge. The idea underlying question selection methods is that too easy (difficult) items are not informative, because most probably the student will give the correct (incorrect) answer to them. So, questions should be selected to give the maximum information about the student. Several question selection methods have been proposed. The more popular methods are the maximum information method [19], which selects the item that maximizes the information function, and Owen's method [13], which selects the item that minimizes the a posteriori variance.

Several stopping criteria can be used such as, for example, a maximum time, time length, or error in the estimation of the student's level of knowledge. In order to avoid too long tests, usually a combination of these criteria is used.

A web-based implementation of CATs and IRT is the SIETTE system (http://www.alcor.lcc.uma.es), described in detail in [14]. SIETTE is a web-based tool that allows the online definition of tests. Once the tests are defined, students can take the adaptive tests online.

3.   USING BAYESIAN NETWORKS IN ADAPTIVE TESTS: STRUCTURAL MODEL

In order to use Bayesian Networks as a basis to perform Adaptive Tests, the structural model needs to be defined, that is, nodes and links should be identified. The nodes that will be considered in our approach are:
- *Evidential nodes,* which we will denote by P. In Adaptive Testing, the evidential nodes are test items that can be correctly/incorrectly answered.
- *Knowledge nodes,* which are defined at three different levels of granularity: *concepts (C), topics (T), and subject (A).* The different levels of granularity will allow us to obtain detailed information about the student's level of knowledge, as required by an ITS. This curriculum structure will enable us to know exactly which parts of the domain are mastered/not mastered by the student.

The relationships among those nodes are:
- *Relationships among concepts and test items.* We will consider that mastering/not mastering a concept has causal influence in correctly answering a related test item.
- *Aggregation relationships.* The aggregation relationships are established between a knowledge node and the knowledge nodes in the former level in the granularity hierarchy.

The Bayesian Network defined is depicted in Figure 3.

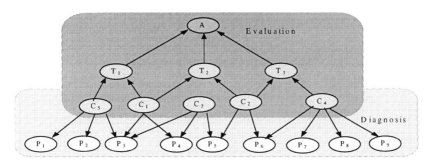

Figure 3. Bayesian Network for Adaptive Testing

Figure 3 shows a Bayesian Network with two parts, which overlap in concept nodes:
- The part that contains the concept nodes and the test items, which will be used to perform the *diagnostic process.* The goal of this stage is to infer from the student's answers the set of concepts that the student masters.

- The part that contains the knowledge nodes, which will be used to get an estimation of how well the student knows each topic and subject from the probabilities of knowing each concept (obtained in the previous stage).

Once that the structural model has been defined, the required parameters need to be specified. It is well known that parameter specification is one of the most difficult problems when using Bayesian Networks. Next, we enumerate the required parameters and propose approaches to simplify their specification:

1. The a priori probabilities of knowing each concept. If there is some information available about the particular student that is going to take the test, this information can be used to specify the a priori probabilities of mastering the concepts. Otherwise, the uniform distribution can be used.
2. The conditional probabilities of each knowledge node given its parents. To specify these probabilities we propose an approach that basically consists in computing the required conditional probabilities from a set of weights that measure the importance of each knowledge node in the aggregated knowledge node. Namely,

- For each topic T_j, let $\{C_{ij}, i = 1, ..., n_j\}$ be the set of related concepts, and w_{ij} represent the importance of concept C_i in topic T_j, $i=1,..., n_j$. Then, for each $S \subseteq \{i = 1, ..., n_j\}$ the required conditional probability distribution is given by:

$$P(T_j/(\{C_{ij}=1\}_{i \in S}, \{C_{ij}=0\}_{i \notin S}) = \frac{\sum\limits_{i \in S} w_{ij}}{\sum\limits_{i=1}^{n_j} w_{ij}}$$

- For each subject A_j, let $\{T_i, i = 1, ..., s\}$ be the set of related topics, and α_j represent the importance of topic T_i in the subject A. Then, for each $S \subseteq \{i = 1, ..., s\}$ the required conditional probability distribution is given by:

$$P(A_j/(\{T_i=1\}_{i \in S}, \{T_i=0\}_{i \notin S}) = \frac{\sum\limits_{i \in S} \alpha_i}{\sum\limits_{i=1}^{s} \alpha_i}$$

In order to illustrate this approach we present a simple example: let us suppose that the subject domain A has three different topics T_1, T_2 and T_3. Each one of these variables is a binary node in the Bayesian Network that is depicted in Figure 4.

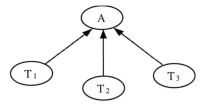

Figure 4. Bayesian Network for a subject and its topics

Let the weights for the topics be $\square_1$=20, $\square_2$ =30, and $\square_3$ =50. Then, the conditional probabilities $P(A/T_1,T_2,T_3)$ are computed using the above expressions, for example:

$$P(A/\ T_1=\text{mastered}, T_2=\text{not mastered}, T_3=\text{mastered}) = \frac{20+50}{20+30+50} = 0.7$$

The behaviour of the Bayesian inference mechanism in this case is as follows:

– If all the topics are instantiated to "*mastered*", we obtain $P(A=\textit{mastered})$ = 1. This means that the student knows 100% of the subject A.

– If, for example, nodes T_1 and T_2 are instantiated to "*mastered*" and node T_3 to "*not mastered*", we obtain $P(A=\textit{mastered})$ = 0.5, meaning that the student masters 50% of the subject.

In this way, we can emulate the method that a human teacher uses to evaluate their students.

Aggregation relationships will be used when it is necessary to obtain a measure of how well the student masters the subject, and/or when a more detailed information relative to each of its topics is needed. We can see that, in contrast to IRT, with Bayesian Networks it is possible to obtain estimations about which parts of the subject the student masters, and this information will allow us to offer him/her individualized instruction if our evaluations system is integrated within a tutoring system.

3. Regarding relationships among concepts and questions, for each test item it would be necessary to specify the probability of correctly answering the question given all possible combinations of mastering/not mastering the related concepts. So if, for example, a question is related to four concepts, the teacher would need to specify 2^4 probabilities. To assist the teacher in this task, we propose the following approach: it is clear that, the more concepts the student masters, the bigger the probability of giving the correct answer (especially in test items, where the student can choose the correct answer simply by discarding the incorrect ones). Moreover, the more important the concept(s) non-mastered, the smaller the probability of choosing the wrong answer. So, we propose the use of a function that

connects in a "smooth" way the probability of guessing the correct
answer when none of the related concepts are mastered (that, of course, is
given by $1/n$, where n is the number of possible answers) with the
probability of giving the correct answer when the student masters all
related concepts (1-s, where s represents the probability of an
unintentional slip and is typically a small number).

So, we would only need to ask the teacher to sort the related concepts by
importance, and then the required parameters can be computed by evaluating
the function in selected points. The function can be chosen to be a logistic
function (such as, for example, the 3-parameter logistic function presented in
Section 2.3), as illustrated in Figure 5.

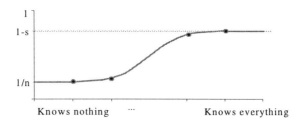

Figure 5. Computing the conditional probabilities by using a 3-parameter logistic function

Moreover, the use of a logistic function also allows us to introduce
parameters associated with each question, that is, the teacher can provide a
difficulty index and a discrimination parameter for the question (recall that
the guessing factor is determined as $1/n$, where n is the number of possible
answers).

4 CONCLUSIONS

In this paper we have defined a structural model that supports the use of
Bayesian Networks to perform Adaptive Testing Algorithms. We have
defined the variables in the model and the type of relationships among them.
We have also proposed approaches to simplify one of the most difficult
problems when using Bayesian Networks: *parameter specification* (other
approaches for the same problem have already been presented in [10]). The
difficulty of obtaining good estimations for the required probabilities is the
most frequently cited reason for discarding the use of Bayesian Networks in
many different applications. We believe that with the approaches presented

here the problem is greatly simplified, and in this way, Bayesian Networks are more accessible to ITS researchers.

The work presented here is only a preliminary study for the application of Bayesian Networks to student modelling. However, there are still many issues to be elucidated which we are working on now, such as, for example, which question selection methods should be used. By contrast, the excellent behaviour of the abductive and predictive inference mechanism leads us think that other questions that traditionally have been difficult to solve in Adaptive Testing are going to be solved within our theoretical framework in a simple way, e.g., propagation algorithms provide an immediate and reliable *scoring method*, that is, a way to process the student's answer to compute an estimation of the student's level of knowledge. Also, the aggregation dimension will allow the automatic generation of *content balanced* tests.

Finally, we would like to emphasize again that the model defined opens up the possibility of performing a more detailed evaluation than the one obtained by using traditional unidimensional IRT models. In this way, Adaptive Testing techniques can be integrated within an ITS in order to improve the accuracy and efficiency of the evaluation process.

REFERENCES

1. Beck J., Stern, M., & Woolf B.P. (1997). Using the Student Model to Control Problem Difficulty. In *Proceedings of the 6th International Conference on User Modelling UM'97* (pp. 277-288). Vienna, New York: Springer-Verlag.
2. Birnbaum, A. (1968). Some latent trait models and their use in infering an examinee's ability. En F.M. Lord & M.R. Novick: *Statistical Theories of Mental Test Scores*. Reading, MA: Addison-Wesley.
3. Castillo, E., Gutiérrez, & J.M. Hadi, A. (1997). *Expert Systems and Probabilistic Network Models*. Springer-Verlag.
4. Charniak, E. (1991). Bayesian Networks without tears. *AI Magazine*, 12(4), 50-63.
5. Conati C., & VanLehn K. (1996). POLA: A student modeling framework for probabilistic on-line assessment of problem solving performance. *Proceedings of UM-96, Fifth International Conference on User Modeling*.
6. Conati, C., Gertner, A., VanLehn, K., & Druzdzel, M. (1997). On-line student modelling for coached problem solving using Bayesian Networks. *Proceedings of UM-97, Sixth International Conference on User Modelling*.
7. González, E., Iida, T., & Watanabe, S. (1994). Measuring the Student Knowledge State in Concept Learning: An Approximate Student Model. *IEEE Transactions on Information and Systems, E77-D* (10), 1170-1178.
8. Herzog, C., & Zierl, H. (1994). Fuzzy techniques for understanding students' solutions in an intelligent tutoring system. *Proceedings of World Conference on Educational Multimedia and Hypermedia*.

9. Lord, F. M. (1980). *Applications of item response theory to practical testing problems.* Hillsdale, NJ: Lawrence Erlbaum Associates.
10. Millán, E. & Agosta, J.M. (1999). Applications of Bayesian Networks to student modeling. *Proceedings of PEG´99, Intelligent Computer and Communications Technology: Teaching and Learning for the 21ˢᵗ Century.* Exeter.
11. Murray, W. (1998). A Practical Approach to Bayesian Student Modeling. *Proceedings of 4th International Conference ITS '98,* LNCS 1452, pp. 425-433, Springer-Verlag.
12. Murray, W. (1999). An Easily Implemented, Linear-time Algorithm for Bayesian Student Modeling in Multi-level Trees. *Proceedings of the 9ᵗʰ International Conference on Artificial Intelligence in Education,* IOS Press.
13. Owen, R. J. (1975). A Bayesian sequential procedures for quantal response in the context of adaptive mental testing. *Journal of the American Statistical Association 70,* 351-356.
14. Ríos, A, Millán, E, Trella, M, Pérez de la Cruz, J.L & Conejo, R. (1999). Internet based evaluation system. *Proceedings of the 9ᵗʰ International Conference on Artificial Intelligence in Education,* IOS Press.
15. Rudner, L. (1998). An On-line, Interactive, Computer Adaptive Testing Mini-Tutorial, (http://ericae.net/scripts/cat).
16. Shute,V. Intelligent Tutoring Systems: Past, Present and Future. (1995). In D. Jonassen (Ed.), *Handbook of Research on Educational Communications and Technology.* Scholastic Publications.
17. Van der Linden, W. & R.K. Hambleton (eds). *(1997). Handbook of Modern Item Response Theory.* New York: Springer-Verlag.
18. Wainer, H., (ed.) (1990). *Computerized adaptive testing: a primer.* Hillsdale, NJ: Lawrence Erlbaum Associates.
19. Weiss, D. J. (1982). Improving measurement quality and efficiency with adaptive testing. *Applied Psychological Measurement, 6,* 473-492..

XML-based Integration of Hypermedia Design and Component-Based Techniques in the Production of Educational Applications

Antonio Navarro, José Luis Sierra, Baltasar Fernández-Manjón, Alfredo Fernández-Valmayor
Dpto. Sistemas Informáticos y Programación. Escuela Superior de Informática,
Universidad Complutense de Madrid. Madrid – Spain
e-mail:{anavarro, jlsierra, balta, alfredo}@sip.ucm.es

Key words: Educational Hypermedia, XML, Document Transformations, Software
Components, Design Methodology

Abstract: This paper describes a XML-based solution for developing educational
hypermedia. This solution is the outcome of the lessons learned in the
development of Galatea application, and integrates a hypermedia design
methodology (ODH) with a generic technique for the construction of XML-
based applications (DTC). Using ODH, designers can describe their
application contents, presentation and interaction as XML documents. DTC
copes with the development of XML based applications by linking XML
documents with component-based software, using document transformations
as needed. The combination of both approaches leads to a solution for
educational hypermedia development that overcomes some of the main
problems that appear in the construction of these applications (communication
between educators and developers, explicit representation of the educational
strategy that underlies the application, development complexity and
maintainability).

1. INTRODUCTION

The integration of new information and communication technologies
enables the provision of a whole range of educational applications
embodying new paradigms for learning [4]. Most of these new applications

M. Ortega and J. Bravo (eds.), Computers and Education in the 21st Century, 229–239.
© 2000 *Kluwer Academic Publishers. Printed in the Netherlands.*

use hypermedia based design because it facilitates learner training through concept linking, providing at the same time the students with compelling interactions and feedback [8].

Despite the advantages provided by this approach, the development of educational hypermedia have specific requirements that are not easy to meet: (1) the need to base the application on solid educational criteria, (2) the need to facilitate the communication between customers (educators) and developers (software experts building the application), (3) the need to lower the development cost when requirements go beyond the scope of authoring environments (e.g. learner evaluation) and (4) the need to maintain an application, where a large amount of highly-structured information sources (e.g. text, exercises, learning plans) coexist and are potentially subject to permanent revision by the educational team. We have identified all these drawbacks during the development of Galatea, a hypermedia educational project for foreign language text comprehension. From lessons learned during this project we are developing a specific hypermedia design methodology called ODH (Over-markup Design of Hypermedia applications), and a generic technique for the development of computer applications called DTC (structured Documents, document Transformations and software Components). Both approaches are based on the application of XML technologies, and although they are independent techniques, they can be combined to solve some of the problems of educational hypermedia development.

The structure of the paper is as follows. Section 2 describes Galatea and its educational strategy. Section 3 briefly describes the ODH methodology, and the solution given to the need of capturing the educational strategy making interaction between educators and developers easier. Section 4 summarizes the DTC approach, and the solution given to the needs for software maintainability and reusability. Section 5 discusses the integration of both techniques and gives an example of this integration. Finally, section 6 shows some conclusions and future work.

2.   THE GALATEA PROJECT

As a result of the SOCRATES/LINGUA EU effort, we have been working for three years in the Galatea project [2] aimed at developing a set of multimedia/hypermedia tutorials for the written and oral comprehension of Romance languages (Figure 1).

The educational strategy in Galatea is centred on the learning processes that arise in text reading comprehension of typologically related languages. This main strategy is implemented in the *Guided Route* module and it is complemented by a free text interaction (*Free Route*) plus a phonetics module to obtain a more natural understanding of the text. In this paper we will focus on the *Free Route* module, conceived as a separate module where the learner can freely interact with the same text considered in the *Guided Route*. In this way the text is presented to the learner who can select any sentence of the text, and any word of these sentences to verify its contextual meaning according to some *contextual dictionary*.

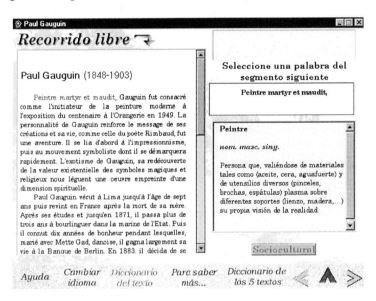

Figure 1. Galatea screenshot

3. THE ODH APPROACH

ODH [7] is a hypermedia design methodology that combines the eXtensible Markup Language XML [13] with object-oriented software development techniques [1,9,10]. ODH uses XML techniques to capture the educational strategy and to alleviate the communication problems between educators and developers. In addition, ODH uses object-oriented techniques to describe those processing activities that need to be included in the final application (e.g. exercise evaluation).

The educational strategy is captured by ODH using an XML DTD (*Document Type Definition*) called the *content DTD*. This construction describes the structure of the application contents and the hyperlinks between these contents. Actual contents are directly provided by educators in a structured *content document* conforming the content DTD. Because content DTD defines a language close to educators' perceptions, the team of educators understand the structure of the document and they are able to write it using a XML editing tool. Besides, these XML documents can be automatically processed by final applications. In this way, use of the content DTD improves the interaction between educators and programmers, and therefore the maintenance of the application, because any change made by educators in the contents can be reflected in the final application without coding. Fig. 2 illustrates a fragment of the Galatea content document corresponding to the contextual dictionary.

```
. . . . . . . . . . . . . . . . .
<text>
 <title>Paul Gauguin 1848-1903</title>
     <paragraph>
          <sentence refToSpliSent="ss1">Peintre martyr et maudit
                                                    </sentence>
          <sentence refToSplitSent="ss2">,Gauguin fut consacre comme
l'initiateur de la peinture moderne a l'exposition du centenaire a
l'Orangerie en 1949.</sentence>
. . . . . . . . . . . . . . . . .
```

Figure 2. A fragment of the Galatea content document

ODH uses another XML DTD, called the *presentation DTD,* to characterize the presentational structure of hypermedia applications. The elements of the presentation DTD describe the application presentational GUI elements (screens, windows, buttons, etc.) and the hyperlinks between them.

```
. . . . . . . . . . . . . . . . .
<!ELEMENT screen (header, links?,(window|button)+)>
<!ATTLIST screen name ID #REQUIRED
                 initial (yes|no) "no "
                 %presAtt1;>
<!ELEMENT header (#PCDATA)>
<!ATTLIST header %presAtt2;>
<!ELEMENT window (header?,element,diagrams?,help?)>
<!ATTLIST window name NMTOKEN #REQUIRED
                  type (frame|picture|virtual) "frame"
                  %presAtt1;>
<!ELEMENT element (content, pres?)>
. . . . . . . . . . . . . . . . .
```

Figure 3. A fragment of the ODH presentation DTD

The instance of the presentation DTD is called *design document*. The separation of content and presentation provides the means to associate different presentations to the same information, allowing educators and programmers to reuse the same content in different views that can change in order to accommodate it to the learner's skills. Fig. 3 illustrates part of the presentation DTD.

The relationship between content DTD and presentation DTD is accomplished through *over-markup*. The basic over-markup idea is that the design document is built in such a way that the contents of the elements of the presentation DTD are chunks of the instance of the content DTD (the content document). That is, during over-markup the contents of the hypermedia application are bound to their presentational layer, to represent the whole hypermedia application.

```
<presentation  >
  <screen  name="contDic" initial=" no" xPos="0" yPos="0" length="640"
wide="480">
  <header  font="garamond" size="18" bold="noB" italic="noI"/>
  <window  name="cdWindow1" type="picture" xPos="0" yPos="0" length="125"
wide="200">
    <element >
     <content >
     <text>
      <title>Paul Gauguin 1848-1903</title>
    <sentence refToSplitSent="ss1">Peintre martyr et maudit,
</sentence>
        <sentence refToSplitSent="ss2">Gauguin fut consacre comme
l'initiateur de la peinture moderne a l'exposition du centenaire a
l'Orangerie en 1949.</sentence>
...............................................
      </content >
      <pres ><presAtt  font="garamond" size="12" bold="noB"
italic="noI"/></pres >
    </element >
...............................................
  </window >

...............................................
  </screen >
</presentation  >
```

Figure 4. Simplified overmarkup example

In addition to presentational aspects, the design document is also involved with other computational activities. These additional complex computational activities (e.g., an exercise that evaluates the learner's knowledge) are represented using object-oriented diagrams (mainly class and state transition diagrams) that are attached to the design document. In this way, this document provides a real representation of the total application for educators and programmers. Educators use the design document to evaluate if it conforms its requirements, and make any necessary change (obviously they ignore the object-oriented diagrams). Developers use part of this document in the coding phase directly, whereas other parts represent the application design that they must translate in real code. The content DTD and the presentation DTD related through over-markup provide a common framework to educators and developers improving their communication. They also help to capture the educational strategy that underlies the application [2]. Fig. 4 illustrates an over-markup example where design document shows the content of the text for the contextual dictionary appearing in a window corresponding to the screen of the contextual dictionary (elements of presentation DTD appear in boldface, and elements of content DTD appear in italic).

4.   THE DTC APPROACH

DTC [11] enables to develop XML-based applications combining XML documents, (reusable) software components [12], and document transformations [6].

In order to build an application according to DTC, first of all, the different kinds of information to be used in the application must be provided as a collection of XML documents. These documents are jointly named as *application documents* and they can be classified into two main categories: (a) *domain documents*, which are those documents containing domain specific information that could be reused across different applications (e.g. a dictionary) and (b) *application dependent documents,* which are documents that only have significance inside a single application (e.g. presentational information for a map, or a GUI layout description).

In parallel to the application document provision, the *application software* is built using software components. Each DTC component is able to process a kind of *componential documents* giving them an operational meaning. In addition, component interfaces are also described in XML terms. DTC components can be classified in several categories. *Primitive components* are the basic building blocks for the application construction. *Containers* allow the aggregation of component conglomerates. Primitive components are subdivided into *markup interpreters* (devoted to giving operational support for abstract markup languages), *primitive facilities* (components that carry out some basic functionality in the final application) and *transformers* (components for adapting information flows between other components). Containers are divided into *GUI containers* (for displaying visual representations of their sub-components) and *controllers* (for describing the behaviour of their sub-components).

The last step is to integrate all the application ingredients (documents and components) in the final application. Frequently, both domain documentation and components are reused, so that multiple disagreements in information structure (between application and componential documents, and between component interfaces in the application software) can arise. Given that all the information accepted by DTC components is XML structured, document transformations can be used as a unified mechanism for solving all these disagreements [5, 6, 14]. Transformations are effectively incorporated into DTC using transformer components. Transformers are used for building *transformations engines* that are executed off-line and make it possible to obtain componential documents from application documents. They also are used on-line as information-flow adapters between other components.

DTC allows developers to reuse pre-existing documents, because with transformations make it possible to integrate them in the executable application. In addition, DTC facilitates reuse of software components, using transformations as a convenient glue. Because domain information can be written in domain terms instead of application software terms, DTC also encourages application maintainability. Domain experts can be engaged in maintaining that information while application builders can make the required tunings in the application-specific documentation in order to incorporate the changes, many times with zero programming effort.

5.   ODH AND DTC INTEGRATION

This section outlines how ODH and DTC can be naturally integrated in a unified solution for the development of educational hypermedia, and illustrates it with a simple example concerning the Galatea application.

5.1   INTEGRATING THE APPROACHES

ODH and DTC are independent approaches, but, because both of them are based on XML technologies, they can be easily integrated in the development of complex educational hypermedia. This integration is schematized in Fig. 5.

In this integrated framework, hypermedia are designed with ODH methodology obtaining the content and design documents given in XML terms. Then DTC approach is used for implementing the final application.

DTC takes as input ODH content and design documents. Because constructs in an ODH presentation DTD have clear intended presentational and/or interaction semantics, initial application software is devised in terms of such semantics. Other behaviours, given in ODH as a collection of object-oriented diagrams, are used to complete the assemblage of the application software. Additional information for deriving the final application is introduced as DTC application dependent documents. Derivation of DTC componential documents is driven by the ODH design document. The DTC off-line transformational process uses this document for indexing the overmarked content fragments. Then it transforms these contents as needed. In addition, presentational metainformation is used for setting presentational features of the GUI components in the application software, using additional application-dependent information as needed.

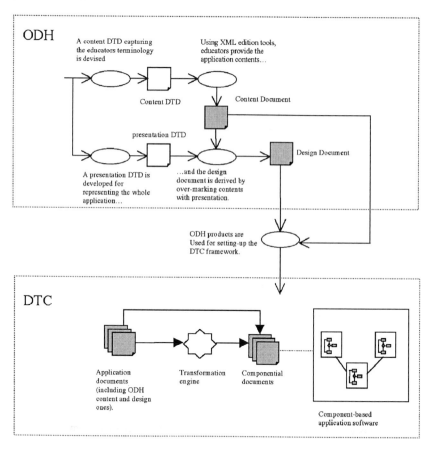

Figure 5. Integration of the ODH and DTC approaches

5.2   AN EXAMPLE

This example uses a simplified version of the Galatea *Free Route* module to illustrate the integration of ODH and DTC. The main content associated with this module is the contextual dictionary. Educators (i.e., the linguistic team) use an XML editor for producing ODH contents such as the one shown in Fig. 2. These contents are over-marked by developers in terms of the presentation DTD (Fig. 3) to configure the final appearance of the module. The resulting design information is encoded in XML terms (as shown in Fig. 4).

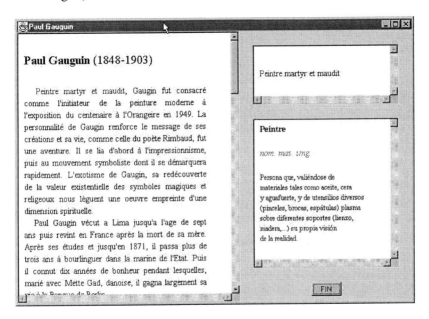

Figure 6. Screenshot of the (simplified) application produced by the integration of ODH and DTC

Once these ODH content and design documents are available, DTC can be applied to build this module. According to the intended semantics attached with the presentation elements, the DTC application software can be built. This software mainly relies on a `SelectableText` markup interpreter that facilitates the selection of text fragments, and a `Navigator` control component facilitating the implementation of the hypermedia relationships for the module. Once the application software has been devised, a transformation engine is configured to produce the necessary componential documents. These documents include, with other minor stuff, text-level   and   sentence-level   contents   for   occurrences   of

`SelectableText` and a description of the navigational control document for the `Navigator` control component. Fig. 6 shows the resulting application. DTC components used in this example has been implemented using Java together with the Oracle XML Parser [3] and its associated XSLT (eXtensible Stylesheet Language Transformations [14]) support.

6.   CONCLUSIONS AND FUTURE WORK

The development of educational hypermedia is a costly task that involves several experts with very different backgrounds. The ODH design methodology improves the communication between educators and developers, and provides the means to capture the educational strategy that underlies the application. On the other hand, the DTC approach to the construction of XML-based applications facilitates application maintainability and different levels of reuse. DTC goals are achieved by a coherent integration componentware and markup technologies in a unified framework.

The integration of ODH and DTC allows a more rational development of (educational) hypermedia. Design document provides a complete guide for educators and developers to build the application. In this way, if a change would be needed (e.g. in the contextual dictionary) educators can edit the content document directly, and automatically the DTC framework rebuilds the new application with zero programming effort.

Next steps in the project are the development of CASE tools for supporting the application of the ODH and DTC processes in a sound and user-friendly way, and the definition of an object-oriented semantics for ODH presentation DTD elements. In addition, we are considering the definition of DTC extensions to facilitate the derivation of domain specific document editors.

ACKNOWLEDGEMENTS

This work has been supported by the EU project Galatea (TM-LD-1995-1-FR89) and the Spanish Committee of Science and Technology (TIC97 2009-CE and TIC98-0733).

REFERENCES

1. Booch G., *Object-oriented analysis and design with applications*, Second Edition, Benjamin Cummings Publishing Company, 1994.
2. Fernandez-Valmayor A., Lopez-Alonso C., Sere A., Fernandez-Manjon B., A hypermedia design for learning foreign language text comprehension, IFIP WG3.2/WG3.6 August 1999 *Working Conference on Building University Electronic Educational Environments*, Proceedings, Co-editors Stephen D. Franklin and Ellen Strenski. Kluwer Academic Publishers, in press.
3. http://technet.oracle.com/
4. Ibrahim, B., Franklin, S.D., 1995. "Advanced Educational Uses of the World Wide Web". *Computer Networks and ISDN Systems*, vol 27, no 6, pp. 871-877.
5. International Standards Organization. "Document Style Semantics and Specification Language (DSSSL)". ISO/IEC 10179. 1996.
6. Kuikka, E. Pentonnen, M. "Transformation of Structured Documents". Tech. Report CS-95-46. University of Waterloo. 1995
7. Navarro, A. Fernández-Manjón, B. Fernández-Valmayor,A. J.L.Sierra. "A Practical Methodology for the Development of Educational Hypermedias". Accepted in *ICEUT2000. IFIP-WCC2000.*
8. Norman D.A., Spohrer J.C., Learner-Centred Education, *CACM* 39 (4) 24-27, 1996.
9. Rumbaugh J., Blaha M., Premerlani W., Eddy F., Lorenzen W., *Object-Oriented Modeling and Design*. Prentice Hall, 1991.
10. Rumbaugh J., Booch G., Jacobson I., *Unified Modeling Language Reference Manual*, Addison-Wesley Object Oriented Series, 1998.
11. Sierra, J.L. Fernández-Manjón, B. Fernández-Valmayor,A.Navarro, A. "Integration of Markup Languages, Document Transformations and Software Components in the Development of Applications: the DTC Approach". Accepted in *ICS2000. IFIP-WCC2000.*
12. Szyperski, C. *Component Software: beyond Object-Oriented Programming*. Adisson Wesley. 1998.
13. W3C, Extensible Markup Language XML Version 1.0, http://www.w3.org/TR/REC-xml, 1998.
14. W3C, XSL Transformations (XSLT) Version 1.0, http://www.w3.org/TR/xslt, 1999.

Approach to Intelligent Adaptive Testing
An optimized fuzzy logic model

Angel Neira, Alfredo Alguero, José A. L. Brugos, Víctor García
Dept. Informática. University of Oviedo. Campus de Viesques, 33201 Gijón, Spain.
E-mail: *neira@correo.uniovi.es*, Tel: 34 985182481 Fax: 34 985 181986

Key words: Intelligent Tutoring System, Fuzzy Logic Application, Adaptive Testing,
                   Bayesian Nets.

Abstract: Considering the evaluation of acquired knowledge as a fundamental element
                   of Computerized Tutoring Systems, the classical Bayesian methods for
                   adaptive testing present several deficiencies, such as arbitrary assignments or
                   prior probabilities, non representativity, the effect of the context and the need
                   to include all the concepts under evaluation. An alternative model of the
                   adaptive test is proposed here based on content-balanced and imprecise
                   interpretations of the information level and prior distribution of each item
                   using Gil's fuzzy relationships instead of Bayesian relationships.

1.   ADAPTIVE TESTING FOUNDATIONS

Adaptation is the keyword for a really effective Intelligent Tutoring System [6]. Starting from this premise, the way to verify knowledge acquisition is to analyse the student's activity [7], the use of the adaptive test being one way to do this. By the word "adaptive" we wish to denote on-line adaptation. An adaptive test might be defined as a test management process where the items that the student executes depend on his/her activity and previous answers. An adaptive test will produce a better measure than a conventional test with a smaller number of items, improving the psychometric characteristics of the test: reliability and validity [7]. Within the standard mechanisms for item selection, the Bayesian method must be highlighted. In this method, each student starts the test with a preset initial level and an associated confidence degree. These are managed as the mean and variance of a prior normal distribution. When an item is answered, the

M. Ortega and J. Bravo (eds.), Computers and Education in the 21st Century, 241–249.
© 2000 *Kluwer Academic Publishers. Printed in the Netherlands.*

levels are recalculated, according to Bayes' formula. At the same time, a Bayesian method is used to select the next item, thus starting again, and so on until the end of the exam.

2.   TOWARDS AN ARCHITECTURE: THREE GENERIC MODELS

A generic architecture for computer system testing, based on three generic models (those of Owen [8], Birnnaum [1] and Huang [3]) will now be presented.

2.1. A network of items

The items are associated with different thematic areas organised hierarchically and defined by the user. The exam is characterized by the tutor by means of included areas, minimum number of questions about each area and a specific weight for each object (fig. 1).

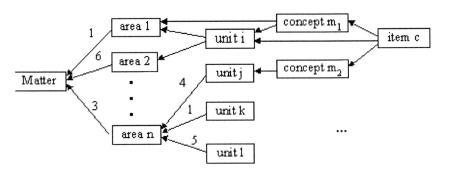

Figure 1: The items inside the network of weights

2.2. The parameters

Each item has three associated parameters:
The level of difficulty evaluates the difficulty of an item. This depends on both the initial value given by the tutor, and the information accumulated by previous uses of the item. Owen's model proposes taking the level of difficulty of the n-th item, d_n, according to the expression: $|d_n-M_{n-1}| < \delta$, where δ is a very small, fixed constant and M_{n-1} is the estimate of average qualification at that time.

The guessing factor describes the probability of a correct answer for an item without knowledge of the matter that it includes. It is useful to penalize a random answer.

The discrimination power of an item value is the ability to verify the student's knowledge about the concrete matter that it embraces. Usually, it is considered to be constant because it is very difficult to determine exactly.

2.3. Test processing.

The algorithm for test processing is divided into three differentiated procedures:

The items selector chooses an item in two steps. In the first step, an area is selected. In the second step, the item linked to that area and which maximized the amount of provided information is chosen [1].

The estimator of temporary qualification qualifies the student each time that an answer is given. Owen's Bayesian estimator [8] is the one most commonly used.

Once the subsequent qualification has been obtained, it must be decided whether the information accumulated is sufficient and, the test is finished, or a new item may be chosen. *The generator of final reports* automatically generates a report where all the information obtained in the examination is collected.

3. SOME CRITICAL ARGUMENTS

The principal argument against the use of Bayesian methods in the evaluation of learning was initially expounded by Samejina [9]. Their principal weakness lies in the use of individual priorities based on past facts or priorities defined for manifold groups, since it may thus occur that two students who respond in exactly the same way to the same items may receive different qualifications. When a person is not representative of a prior distribution, he or she will receive an inappropriate mark. In groups, the results generated by Bayesian methods could have a small error variance, but at an individual level, the qualifications could be quite erroneous. Other aspects to be kept in mind are the effects of the context and their influence on the qualification [4]. Specifically, in classical item selection procedures, it is observed that these could have a short scope in width and content balancing. Items could exist whose information might exert influence on other consecutive items.

Moreover, Birnbaum directly affirms that the established approaches in these methods are considered neither certain nor worthy of confidence, and states that they are considered erroneous by some authors [1]. He indicates that there are no specific methodologies to verify these models; it is only possible to carry out comparisons with their most significant aspects.

In addition, the act of qualifying a student with a mark is, in itself, of a somewhat imprecise nature. We could clearly classify, for instance, a dog in the category of animals, but it not as simple to solely qualify a student according to his or her answers to certain items.

The model proposed here starts from the discussion of two points commonly assumed in statistical models:

Firstly, the preset prior probability of success or failure of an item, required for its presentation to the student, is initialized on the basis of the normal distributions obtained from answers of previous students and subsequently updated with the successive activity of the students. Actually, keeping in mind the fact that for an outstanding student, the items will generally be less difficult than for a student who lags behind, these prior assignments should essentially be based on their previous activity, when this exists, and on the level of difficulty of the item itself.

The consideration of the information level given by an item is not of a statistical nature, but rather, the fact that it should be considered as having an imprecise nature is the second point to be discussed. In fact, it depends on the one hand, on the intrinsic level of difficulty of the item, and on the other, on the actual student who is being examined. The level of difficulty should involve the tutor's evaluation as a function of the student's experience, the structure of the item and the student's evolution in previous executions (which could eventually be statistically considered). The relationship of the item with the student depends on his or her activity in the test up to the moment of the item presentation.

These observations lead to the consideration of fuzzy logic as a suitable and complementary technique alongside the previous architecture. Much has been written [10] about the relationship between probability and fuzzy theory. Statistical theory usually assumes that the information obtained from observations is exact. Thus, researchers are considered capable of clearly perceiving the outputs of their experimental observations. However, in many cases, and especially here, the observer is not capable of discerning with exactness. The usual approach is either to describe each imprecise observation through an exact approximate result (rounding), or to describe the imprecise observation through a class containing it (grouping). The association of each experimental imprecise observation with fuzzy information is a more natural solution.

The main reasons for adopting this solution are, on one hand, the impossibility of finding a pure probabilistic model that characterizes problems with imprecise information, and on the other, the feasible possibility of constructing an effective model through the incorporation of certain concepts of fuzzy sets.

4.   A COMPLEMENTARY FUZZY MODEL

Starting from a probabilistic information system (X, P_q), where X is the set of all the possible observations and P_q the measured probability of q on the space of states Q, it is assumed that the performance of X in order to obtain information about q cannot provide exact observations, but rather each perceived observation in that performance may be assimilated with a fuzzy restriction according to the following premises:

– A fuzzy event -x- in X is characterized by a membership function, μ_X, that associates a real number in the unit interval, [0,1] with each x element in X, this value being represented as $\mu_X(x)$, the grade of membership of -x- in X.
– A fuzzy information system in X is a fuzzy partition of X by means of fuzzy events on X. That is:

$$\sum_{x \in X} \mu_X(x) = 1$$

When Zadeh's probabilistic definition is adopted [11] and the existence of a prior probability measure p on a measurable space is assumed, Gil's definition will be considered [2] for the determination of the posterior probability distribution:

$$h_x(q) = \frac{h(q)\, P_q(X)}{P(X)}, \quad q \in Q$$

h(q) being the density associated with the prior probability distribution p on Q, $P_q(X)$ the conditional probability distribution on X and P(X) the marginal probability distribution on X.

On the basis of this definition, and from the conceptual basis established in paragraph 2, we shall begin to characterize the parameters for the model introduced here that define the i-th item.

4.1. The level of difficulty

This will be determined by combining a value initially given by the tutor based on his or her experience, with a pondering of the results of its use in previous executions, according to the following formula:

$$d_i = \frac{20.\text{dif\_inic} + AC_i}{20 + OK_i + NO_i}$$

dif_inic is a real variable in [0, 1] which indicates the initial difficulty of item i given by the tutor.

AC_i denotes an accumulator of difficulty of item i, which is considered as:

$$AC_i = \sum_{i=1}^{n} k_j \, f(q_j)$$

where k_j acquires the value of 2 if the answer to the item in the previous j question was incorrect and 0 if this answer was correct, $f([qj])$ indicates the student's temporary qualification at the moment of answering the item, adapted to the [0,1] interval, and n is the number of times that this item has previously been executed.

OK_i indicates the number of times that item i was correctly answered,

NO_i indicates, in a complementary way, the times that item i was answered incorrectly, therefore the value of the previous n will be the sum of OK_i and NO_i.

4.2. The guessing factor

In accordance with paragraph 2.2, g_i will be given as the quotient between the number of correct possible answers for item i and the number of possible answers for this.

Once the items are characterized, the process for administrating the test will consist of the following stages:

4.3. Item selection

In order to consider balancing of the content, the item selection will be carried out in two phases, first the election of a conceptual area will take place, followed by the selection of a particular item.

1. As for the area selection, this will be carried out randomly from among a group of candidate conceptual areas. A candidate area is that area of the test for which a confidence degree has not yet been established in the exam.

The probability of an area being selected will depend on its weight:

$$Pos_i = \frac{\text{Weight of area}_i}{\sum \text{Weight of area}_j}$$
$$j : \text{area}_j \text{ is a candidate}$$

2. Inside an area, the selection of an item will depend on the information of this item in relation to its influence in the determination of the student's

final qualification. This information level, Inf, will be related to the level of difficulty established for the item, d_i, and the student's temporary qualification.

With a set of five possible qualification grades: Lacking (L), Fail (F), Pass (P), High Pass (H) and Excellent (E), the d_i relationships will be defined as follows:

$$Inf_L = - d_i + 1 \qquad Inf_E = d_i \qquad Inf_P = \begin{cases} -2\ d_i + 2 & d_i \geq 0,5 \\ 2\ d_i & d_i < 0,5 \end{cases}$$

$$Inf_F = \begin{cases} 4/3\ d_i + 4/3 & d_i \geq 0.25 \\ 4\ d_i & d_i < 0,25 \end{cases} \qquad Inf_H = \begin{cases} -4\ d_i + 4 & d_i \geq 0,75 \\ 4/3\ d_i & d_i < 0,75 \end{cases}$$

The consideration that information increases with the difficulty in proportion with the student's temporary estimated qualification is the essential key to these relationships. This proportionality is upheld until a variable point, since from this level of knowledge onwards, there is no point in raising such difficulty.

When a set of items with the maximum information level has been selected, the items incompatible with those previously answered by the student will be eliminated. Then one will be randomly chosen among the rest.

4.4. Item presentation and processing of the answer

The mechanisms of presentation of the item to the student and the consequent processing of the answer are considered inherent methods of the object itself.

Once the presentation has been made and the answer has been obtained (fig.2), the next phase is the determination of the subsequently estimated qualification according to Gil's formula.

Specifically, for a generic mark of the five possible qualification levels, the certainty of obtaining whatever mark (L, F, P, H, E), on condition that a result has been obtained in the item (Success, Failure) will be:

$$P(Mark/Res) = \frac{P(Previous\_mark)\cdot\ P(Res/Mark)}{\sum_{mark} P(Previous\_mark)\cdot\ P(Res/Mark)}$$

where P(Previous_mark) refers to the student's estimated qualification before the answer to the item, and P(Res/mark) will be considered as the expression:

$$P(Res/Mark) = g_i + (1-gi)P_{Result-mark}$$

where the convergence recommendations of Owen and the prior estimations of success or failure in the item response is contemplated in a related way.

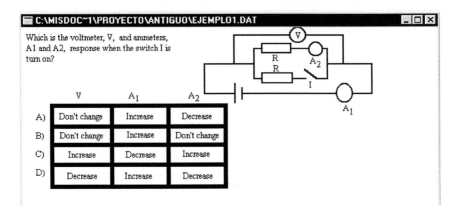

Figure 2. An item

Finally, these prior relationships, $P_{Result-mark}$, are defined by taking into account the fact that the greater the item difficulty, the easier it was for a student with a high qualification to answer it correctly, keeping in mind the fact that easy items will always be answered by a large number of students, thus providing less information. The relationships in the case of error in the answer to the item are supported by the complementary reasoning, i.e. the simplest items will provide less information with respect to the student's level.

Therefore, these prior distributions are, in the cases of a correct and incorrect response to item i:

$$P_{okL} = - d_i + 1 \qquad P_{okE} = 1 \qquad\qquad P_{noL} = \quad d_i \qquad\qquad P_{noE} = 0$$

$$P_{okF} = \begin{cases} -4/3 \ d_i + 4/3 & d_i \geq 0.25 \\ 1 & d_i < 0,25 \end{cases} \qquad P_{noF} = \begin{cases} 4/3 \ d_i + -1/3 & d_i \geq 0.25 \\ 0 & d_i < 0,25 \end{cases}$$

$$P_{okP} = \begin{cases} -2 \ d_i + 2 & d_i \geq 0,5 \\ 1 & d_i < 0,5 \end{cases} \qquad P_{noP} = \begin{cases} -2 \ d_i -1 & d_i \geq 0,5 \\ 0 & d_i < 0,5 \end{cases}$$

$$P_{okH} = \begin{cases} -4 \ d_i + 4 & d_i \geq 0,75 \\ 1 & d_i < 0,75 \end{cases} \qquad P_{noH} = \begin{cases} 4 \ d_i - 3 & d_i \geq 0,75 \\ 0 & d_i < 0,75 \end{cases}$$

4.5. Finishing the test

The test comes to an end when the successive variations of the temporary qualification remain within a fixed threshold and the student has been asked the minimum number of items established by the tutor for each conceptual area.

5.   CONCLUSION AND FUTURE WORK

A large number of comparative studies have been carried out [1], [3]. With the model considered here, due to the definition of fuzzy relationships itself, we can conclude that their results are equal, in the worst of cases, to the probabilistic models. Nevertheless, the definition of the present model was carried out on the basis of empirical criteria and the authors' own educational experience, and consequently, an exhaustive study is needed in order to obtain a more fitting model.

REFERENCES

1. Birnbaum, A. 1968. Some latent trait models and their use in inferring an examinee's ability. In Statistical Theories of Mental Test Scores. Ed. Lord, F.M. et al. Addison-Wesley.
2. Gil, M.A. 1987. Fuzziness and Loss of Information in Statistical Problems. IEEE Transactions on Systems, Man and Cybernetics. Vol.SMC-17, No.11,
3. Huang, S.X. 1996. On Content-Balanced Adaptive Testing. Third Int. Conf. CALISCE'96. Donostia, Spain.
4. Kingsbury, G.; Zara A. R. 1989. Procedures for Selecting Items for Computerised Adaptive Tests. In Applied Measurement in Education 2 (4). Lawrence Erlbaum Assoc.
5. Neira, A.; Alguero, A.; Díaz, J.A.; Brugos, J.A.L.; Garcia, V.; Álvarez, L.; Soler, E. 2000. Sistema Integrado de Procesado de Test. In Aula Abierta 74. ICE, University of Oviedo.
6. Neira, A.; Brugos, J.A.L.; Alvarez, L.; Soler, L.; Liuña A.F. Menéndez, J.R. 1997 Towards total adaptability in the teaching language: Consideration of Tutoring Systems as Adaptive Intelligent Systems. 4 CAEE'97, Cracow.
7. Neira, A; Brugos, J.A.L. 1996. Foundations on an Adaptive Tutoring System based on Systemic Networks. In Lecture Notes in Computer Science 1108. Spinger-Velag
8. Owen, R.J.A 1975. Bayesian Sequential Procedure for Quantal Response in the Context of Adaptive Mental Testing. Journal of the American Statistical Association, June.
9. Samejima, F. 1980. Is Bayesian estimation proper for estimating the individual's ability?. RR 80-3. Univ Tennessee. Dep. Psychology.
10. Special Issue: Fuzziness-Probability. 1994 IEEE Transactions on Fuzzy Systems.
11. Zadeh, L.A. 1968. Probability measures of fuzzy events. J. Math. Anal. Appl. vol.23.

Learning Basque in a Distance-Adaptive way

Tomás A. Pérez, Ricardo López, Julián Gutiérrez, Amaia González
Dept. of Computer Languages and Systems, University of the Basque Country
Aptdo. 649. 20080 San Sebastián, Gipuzkoa. Spain.
Phone (+34) 943 018 000. Fax: (+34) 943 219 306
E-mail:{tomas,gutierrez}@si.ehu.es

Key words: Distance Learning, Intelligent Tutor, Adaptive Hypermedia System, Multimedia, HEZINET, Basque

Abstract: Distance education has experienced a great surge in our society in the past few years. New technological advances have allowed the diffusion of many courses and in a quicker way. Among the scientific advances, we have the creation of the WWW, which has become the information medium with the greatest diffusion, in spite of the fact that it has only been around for a short time. HEZINET is an Adaptive Hypermedia System, which benefits from the advantages of the WWW offering a complete course in Basque for distance learning.

1.   INTRODUCTION

The busy pace of life that our current society demands along with the need for continuous knowledge renewal, the lack of free time and the complex schedules have made distance learning the best alternative to traditional learning. Although it is based on an old idea, the new technologies have produced an enormous *"boom"* as regards the tools and mechanisms which support and implement distance learning, providing a greater offer, better quality and a greater level of acceptance among users. The benefits of distance learning through the Web are clear: geographical and platform independence [2]. An application installed and supported in one place can be used all over the world by thousands of students, who only have to be equipped with a computer connected to the Internet. In some

M. Ortega and J. Bravo (eds.), Computers and Education in the 21st Century, 251–262.
© 2000 *Kluwer Academic Publishers. Printed in the Netherlands.*

cases, simple systems can even get better results than traditional learning [13].

A decade ago nobody could imagine that the WWW would acquire the importance that it has nowadays. In spite of the fact the WWW has only been around for a short time, it is becoming an essential medium for communication and exchange of information. This is due to the quick access and the diffusion of information through the *"network of networks"*. In the same way that the technologies for this diffusion are growing by means of the production of new products of higher quality, capacity, speed and lower cost, the number of WWW users is increasing exponentially.

In the past five years many courses and other educational applications have been created in the Web [2]. However, most of them are no more than static pages of hypertext. Most interactive systems for computer-assisted distance learning are based on a hierarchic structure, like traditional textbooks, thus providing specific tools for the domain concerned [11, 12].

The barrier which impedes greater success is the lack of adaptation to the user shown in the existing products on the market. From the pedagogic point of view, adaptation to the user is fundamental in education systems. Without adaptation to the user, these systems can be ineffective.

Within computer learning systems we can find Intelligent Tutoring Systems (ITS), Hypermedia Systems (HS) and Adaptive Hypermedia Systems (AHS). An ITS is a software program which tutors the student in a given domain. Described in another way, it instructs the student intelligently [4]. On the other hand, we have HS which present static information without taking into account the knowledge acquired by the students. HS do not adapt to the user, they only present information and they do not receive the user's feedback. HS provide flexibility, but they lack adaptability, whilst ITS are very rigid. AHS have emerged as a mixture of ITS and HS. AHS are not as strict as ITS, and these do not give as much freedom to navigate as HS. AHS provide adaptation to the user mainly in two ways. Firstly, the system establishes appropriate performance levels on the student. Secondly, the system selects appropriate didactic material according to the student's characteristics. An online Hypermedia System is considered adapted if it changes, in some way, with regard to its environment and users [7].

1.1   In this article

HEZINET has emerged with the aim of aiding the distance learning of Euskara (the Basque language, one of the official languages in the Basque Country). In this way, the users can study with a method that adapts to their needs, at their pace and without the need to go to an Euskaltegi (a school where Euskara classes are specifically taught). HEZINET is situated within the AHS environment for distance learning. Both teaching through an ITS and educational hypermedia systems are combined taking advantage of the advantages of each one and replacing their inconveniences [6]. Although there are a reduced number of potential speakers, about 3 million people, it can be used to develop new distance courses of other languages with a greater number of speakers on an international scale. It is created in a generic way independent of the language to be taught.

The HEZINET project is described in the following sections, presenting its architecture and the representation of the Pedagogic Domain. Its interface is described in detail. A section is also dedicated to showing the adaptation of the system to the student and the role that the human teacher plays in the system. Finally, we conclude by considering some aspects of the current state and future lines.

2. DESCRIPTION OF THE HEZINET PROJECT

HEZINET is a pioneering commercial system for language learning which replaces the deficiencies that were not taken into account in other systems when they were created [9]. Firstly, most of the tutor systems have been designed for research projects. Some of them have been developed but have not been placed on the market, becoming tools with limited use in schools and universities. Secondly, there is an infinite number of multimedia courses, presented as the best option for flexible learning in any area. In these courses the users only visualize large quantities of information, without taking into account their interaction with the system or the knowledge acquired by them.

The system we are presenting, HEZINET, works on two aspects: the use of intelligent software systems for learning and how to adapt these systems to achieve better results. In the following section, the participants of this ambitious project are named, and the architecture and organisation of the Pedagogic Domain are explained.

2.1 Participants

The HEZINET project has been carried out thanks to financial support from the Basque Government (Eusko Jaularitza) and the association formed by a software company (*Ibermática*), a regional newspaper (*El Diario Vasco*), a cultural foundation *(Aurten Bai)*, a secondary school *(Ekintza ikastola)* and the Group of Hypermedia and Multimedia (*GH&M*) at the Department of Computer Languages and Systems of the University of the Basque Country. *Ibermática* has been responsible for the development of the application interface. On the other hand, the *GH&M* at the San Sebastián Computer Science Faculty has implemented everything concerning the Intelligent Tutor part. The educational material has been prepared by *Aurten Bai*, thanks to the support of illustrious and well-known figures in Basque literature. *Ekintza-ikastola* is established as the fundamental piece of the practical validation of the tool. Finally, *El Diario Vasco* has placed the tools and the human resources needed to achieve its promotion.

The lengthy experience of *GH&M* on Intelligent Tutors in the San Sebastián Computer Science has aided the development of this project a great deal. HEZINET is really a continuation of several years of work and study of these systems. It is the result of the group's work on two prototypes, HyperTutor and WebTutor, HEZINET is created with a particular and complete Pedagogic Domain (which the two previously mentioned prototypes lacked) [5, 6].

2.2   The architecture

HEZINET contains two main modules. One provides the flexibility of hypermedia and the other the adaptation to the user. This symbiosis between these modules makes the system more educational. Each one of the parts benefits from the specific functionality that the other one contributes to the system. In this way, the Tutor or Adaptive part benefits from the hypermedia flexibility (the rigidity that normally characterizes a traditional course does not exist). In addition, it benefits from the use of different audio-visual media, which are used to present the domain information to the user, implemented by the hypermedia part. On the other hand, the hypermedia part benefits from the adaptability to the user performed by the Tutor. The *Hypermedia Component* ponders the hypermedia behaviour and is the only part which comes into contact with the student, whilst the *Tutor Component* adapts the hyperspace to the student and performs an evaluation of the result of the navigation.

As shown in Figure 1, the system is organised in six modules: the Interface, the Auditor, the Course, the Student Model, the Intelligent Module and the Human Teacher Module [9]. Whilst the Interface belongs to the Hypermedia part, the other modules make up the Adaptive part (Figure 1), which is the one that will make the decisions taking into account the student's evolution with the system.

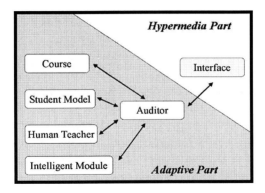

Figure 1. General architecture of HEZINET

The *Interface* interacts directly with the students, it gives them the information that the system's Intelligent Module considers appropriate on the spot and it sends information to this Module via the Auditor. The different screens that are shown to the student are created dynamically and are specially designed for each functionality of the system.

The *Auditor Module* is responsible for negotiating the services of the Intelligent Part and it enables the communication between its components.

The *Course Module* manages all the didactic material, provided by the pedagogic experts, which is stored in a database. It also contains all the information on the Pedagogic Domain described earlier.

The *Student Model Module* manages and stores all the characteristics (login name, password, analytical/multimedia...), the learning (concepts acquired, not acquired...) and the materials used for it.

The *Intelligent Module* consults the Student Model and makes intelligent decisions based on tasks defined heuristically using Artificial Intelligence techniques. In addition, it compiles the tests, evaluates the sessions and changes the Student Model according to the results of the tests or the Hypermedia navigated by the student.

The *Human Teacher Module* provides means to carry out the student's follow-up monitoring and to adapt the system to each student in the best possible way.

2.3 The organisation of the Pedagogic Domain

Several pedagogic experts of the Basque Language made a pedagogic structure of the domain [10] as shown in the following figure (Figure 2). The *contents* are the smaller pedagogic units that will be taught, for example: the verbal forms of the present indicative of the verb *izan* (to be). Some of these units work as a key in relation to others. That is to say, some contents cannot be taught until others, considered to be prerequisites, have been mastered first. For example: before learning the verbal forms of the subjunctive of any verb, the student should learn the verbal forms of the present, past and future. In turn, the contents are grouped in superior units called *work areas*, *groups* and *families*. There are ten work areas, called: verb, declension, syntax, vocabulary, suffix, spelling, connectors, written expressions, oral and written comprehension. A group contains all related contents that belong to the same area. However, a family of contents refers to related contents all over the domain. The human teacher uses these classifications, for example, to gather exercises leading to common mistakes in the language.

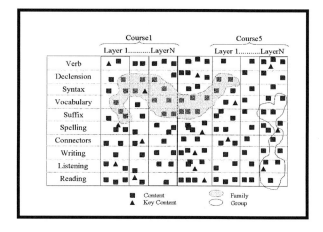

Figure 2. Graphic representation of the Pedagogic Domain structure

Besides having a semantic organisation, the Pedagogic Domain also has a functional organisation. The system manages the learning by dividing it into five *courses*. In turn, the courses are structured in *layers* (Figure3). Inside a course, the layers are placed in order, so that the level of difficulty increases progressively. In a layer, a group of contents is presented structured pedagogically by the experts. The contents that are evaluated in the exercises of this layer are the so-called *key contents*. In the same way, a layer is divided in *sessions* (Figure3). A session is the equivalent of a class that a human teacher usually gives in one hour. Inside a session, there are *activities* that the student has to carry out and it is here where the contents presented within it are evaluated. As you can imagine, within an exercise it is very difficult to consider only the contents presented. Therefore, in some cases, previous knowledge will need to be used when doing the exercises, and it is understood that this knowledge has already been learnt.

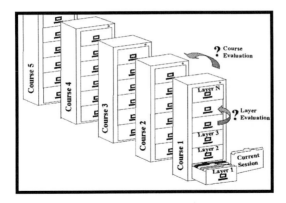

Figure 3. Representation of the organisation of the Pedagogic Domain

3. THE INTERFACE

The hypermedia function is to communicate, making the information accessible in a useful way for the user, aiding access to a great quantity of material in a flexible and interactive way [3]. HEZINET uses hypertext to present the information to the students and allow them to "surf" the material they have to learn. The presentation uses different audio-visual media, thus increasing the system's capacity of expression.

As we pointed out earlier, the multimedia component is very important inside the system. For the task of teaching this language, many different types of multimedia resources have been used: video, text and images. Therefore, within each layer there is a video with sound, around which the activities of the sessions belonging to the layer will rotate. By using the video, we attempt to place the student within a context. In addition, for each activity, it can be said that three differentiated parts exist: introduction, presentation and evaluation. The multimedia possibilities are very wide here depending mainly on the type of activity that is being carried out. Twenty different types of activities are defined inside the system [9], which cover all the abilities that a student can develop, such as reading, writing, and oral and written comprehension.

When choosing and presenting activities, the Tutor takes into account the different profiles of the students to select the materials to use. On the one hand, we have the multimedia students, to whom the system presents activities in a more attractive way, requiring greater interaction from them. In Figure 4 (right) we have an example of this type. The introduction is carried out with a sound file, in this case, to later complete the associated exercise, which in this example consists in ordering several pieces of a puzzle to build a well-formed sentence. The analytical students, on the other hand, are presented with less visual activities; text is normally only used inside them. As we can see in Figure 4 (left), the activity is presented to the user by means of a paragraph of text, in order to later answer a series of questions by filling in the blanks.

Figure 4. Examples of a multimedia student activity (left) and an analytical student activity (right)

4. ADAPTATION TO THE USER

A system is considered adaptive if it is able to make decisions depending on certain information, which changes with time. Adaptive systems are based on two points. Firstly, the student should be able to handle the information available. This is achieved by just presenting the students with the appropriate didactic units, in relation to their characteristics. Secondly, the feedback from the students, with respect to their level of knowledge and assimilation speed, is indispensable to deduce the way to present the new didactic units.

Taking into account the aspects mentioned above, we can say that the HEZINET system adapts to the user. The adaptation can be seen in several places. Firstly, the didactic units are accessed with standard Internet browsers, and can therefore be used at any time from any computer system with a connection to the Internet. Secondly, and as we have already mentioned, users can be classified as multimedia or analytical, and therefore the activities to present are in turn classified in these two types. Thirdly, the system prepares the tests adapted to the concepts seen and acquired by the student. The tests do not generally select items previously used to evaluate that student, and they can require a certain concept already learnt by the student in order to be correctly solved. Of course, in addition, the items can include the already mentioned characteristic of being analytical or multimedia. Fourthly, when the test of a concept is not passed in the evaluation of a session, a new revision session is created so that the student continues working on it. Fifthly, the system also incorporates a grammar book (hyperized) adapted to the student's level of knowledge, which can be accessed by the student as long as he/she is not completing a stratum test, as these are considered exams.

In spite of the adaptation of the system to the students in the previous points, it can be said that these systems are not complete without a minimum amount of interaction from a human teacher. HEZINET enables a human teacher to complete and assure the successful operation of the system. The human teacher can review the students performance, and modify their Student Model. The human teacher has the possibility of generating specific revision sessions for a student and is also responsible for correcting the activities that the Tutor cannot evaluate automatically, such as the correction of an account or résumé. In Figure 5, we can see a part of the interface that the human teacher uses to make the corrections already mentioned. In this case the teacher (*Irakaslea*), code *irakas2*, is correcting the activity of the student, code *ikasle6*, and the current activity to correct is the *1-6 Itsasorantz*. In this example, the student has written a resume of a text. As we can see in the figure, the solving of the exercise by the student, the exercise instructions and the support document to help the student carry out the activity are presented to the teacher. There are different controls which the human teacher can use to correct the text. In the example in figure 5: crossing out a word, underlining and/or highlighting a part of a text written by the student, indicating that something is missing between the words... The human teacher can comment on each of the mistakes corrected and make observations during the correction of the exercise. In this way, a tool has been obtained which is simple to use, complete and quick at evaluating the activities that cannot be corrected automatically.

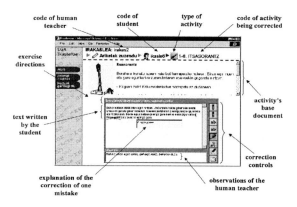

Figure 5: Correction of activities by a human teacher

5.   CONCLUSIONS

HEZINET is a revolutionary AHS; as far as we know, no other system with the same characteristics is on the market. The main differences of this system compared to others are given by the following series of points. Firstly, HEZINET is a commercial system to learn Euskara; it can be easily modified in order to develop the same function with other languages. The tutoring systems we know of are centred on the introductory teaching of other areas, for example: programming [12], algorithms [8], physics [15], chemistry [14], anatomy [1], etc. It was placed on the market in June 1999, when 150 licences had already been purchased, located in town councils and in an important company in the language teaching sector.

Secondly, thanks to the Tutor part and following the theory of ITS and AHS, the system adapts automatically to each student's needs and capacities, to make learning as suitable and pedagogic as possible for the student. Thirdly, the human teacher can intervene in the follow-up monitoring and in the correction of the student's activities. An expert working as an evaluator of the areas that cannot usually be corrected automatically will enable learning in all the areas of language (both oral and written) and better adaptation as well. Fourthly, all the evaluation tests are created dynamically, taking into account the progression and knowledge acquired by each student. Fifthly, the system is easy to handle and can be used from any computer with a connection to the Internet. Using an intuitive and entertaining medium, the student obtains solid learning and avoids the need to go somewhere physically to study with a non-flexible timetable.

In the design and the development of the tools, special care has been taken to achieve a standard, so that it is applicable for learning any language or even any subject. This has provided a series of contacts with important organisations which are dedicated to interactive language teaching. The system may possibly be used for learning English and French shortly, thus confirming the success envisaged in learning Euskara.

As future lines, we intend to create a module that will enable the generation of new didactic material and its inclusion in the system using a visual environment. In addition, we are working to make the "surfing" adapt more and providing the system with new tools has not been rejected. For example, the system has only one dictionary, Spanish-Euskara, which can be supplemented with other dictionaries from Euskara to other languages. With which, the learning of Euskara would be aided in different languages, not only in Spanish as at present. In addition, we could incorporate a Chat area, distribution lists, discussion groups... where the students could exchange knowledge and communicate.

6. REFERENCES

1. Beaumont, I. (1994). User Modelling and Hypertext Adaptation in the Tutoring System Anatom-Tutor. Adaptive hypertext and hypermedia UM'94 (Fourth International Conference on User Modeling), Aug. 17, 1994, Hyannis, Cape Cod, Massachusetts, U.S.A.
2. Brusilovsky, P (1998). Adaptive Educational Systems on the World-Wide-Web: A Review of Available Technologies. In: Proceedings of Workshop "WWW-Based Tutoring" at 4th International Conference on Intelligent Tutoring Systems (STI'98), San Antonio, TX, August 16-19.
3. Dufresne, Aude (1994). Adaptative Hypermedia: Supporting the Comunicaction Process. http://www.education.uts.edu.au/projects/ah/Dufresne.html
4. Frasson C., Gauthier G. and McCalla G.I. (1992) Intelligent Tutoring Systems. Proceedings of the Second International Conference, STI'92. Springer-Verlag, Berlin.
5. Gutiérrez, J.; Pérez, T.A.; Carro, J.A.; Morlán, I; Lopistéguy, P. (1997). WebTutor. Enseñanza Adaptativa a través de WWW. JITEL97, 1997.
6. Gutiérrez, J.; Pérez, T.A.; Usandizaga, I. & Lopistéguy, P. (1996). HyperTutor: Adapting Hypermedia Systems to the User. Proceedings of the fifth International Conference on User Modeling,UM-96. Kailua-Kona, Hawaii, USA. January 1996.
7. Kaplan, G. & Wolff, G. (1990). Adaptive Hypertext, Technical Report, Huinan Factors Center, IBM Santa Teresa Labs, San Jose, CA.
8. López, J.M.; Millán, E.; Pérez-de-la-Cruz; J.L. & Triguero, F (1998). Design and implementation of a web-based tutoring tool for Linear Programming problems. Web-based STI" at STI'98, 4th International Conference in Intelligent Tutoring Systems, 16-19 August, 1998, San Antonio, Texas.
9. Pérez, T.A.; Gabiola, K.; Gutiérrez, J.; López, R.; González, A. & Carro, J. A (1999). Hezinet: Interactive (Adaptive) Education Through Activities. Educational Multimedia and Hypermedia, ED-MEDIA'99. AACE:Seattle, Washington, U.S.A. June 19-24th 1999.

10. Pérez, T.A., Gutiérrez, J.; Lopistéguy, P. & Usandizaga, I. (1995). The Role of Exercices in a User Adaptive Hypermedia. 3rd International Conference on Computer Aided Engineering Education,CAEE'95. Bratislava, Eslovaquia.

11. Pérez, T.A., Lopistéguy, P.; Gutiérrez, J. & Usandizaga, I. (1995b). HyperTutor: From Hypermedia to Intelligent Adaptive Hypermedia. Educational Multimedia and Hypermedia, ED-MEDIA'95. AACE:Charlottesville,EE.UU.

12. Sommaruga, Lorenzo & Catenazzi, Nadia (1998). The Hyper Apuntes Interactive Learning Environment for Computer Programming Teaching. Journal of Interactive Learning Research, Volume 9, Number 1, 1998.

13. Soo, Keng-Soon & Ngeow, Yeok-Hwa (1998). Effective English as a Second Language (ESL) Instruction With Interactive Multimedia: The MCALL Project. Journal of Educational Multimedia and Hypermedia, Volume 7, Number 1, 1998.

14. University of Rhode Island (1993). Chem-Tutor: An Expert System For Teaching Freshman Chemistry. Lessons Learned from FIPSE Projects II - September 1993.http://inet.ed.gov/offices/OPE/FIPSE/LessonsII/urhodeis.html

15. VanLehn, Kurt. Andes: An intelligent tutoring system for physics http://www.pitt.edu/~vanlehn/andes.html

Collaborative planning for problem solution in distance learning

M.A. Redondo, C.Bravo, J.Bravo, M.Ortega
Universidad de Castilla – La Mancha – Spain
{mredondo,cbravo,jbravo,mortega}@inf-cr.uclm.es

Key words: collaborative, planning, distance learning

Abstract: Today, in a great number of situations and teaching experiences aided by a computer (distance or present), such computer is only a passive element. During the teaching session, the work plan is designed by the teacher. The teacher selects the appropriate environment for the concepts to study. This way of work does not envisage the possibility of the learner being alone acting with the computer. With the use of design environments, a fusion of the monitoring of the learner together with the learning by discovery is achieved. We establish a pedagogic organisation of the domain that will be based on the structuring of the domain concepts, the relationships between them, the adaptability of the cognitive abilities of the learner (difficulty levels on learning), abstraction of the knowledge, and so on. This structuring makes planning of the teaching–learning session possible. In this paper we present some tools that facilitate the planning design in a collaborative way in learning communities, where the students provide their partial view of the problem and of the solution. We employ as study domain the design of domotic installations, that is to say, the design of installations for the integral building automation.

1.   INTRODUCTION AND OBJECTIVE

Tom de Jong [1] said that learning by scientific discovery [2] expresses a point of view in the teaching-learning process. In this process much more emphasis is put on the learner as an active agent on the knowledge acquisition process.

M. Ortega and J. Bravo (eds.), Computers and Education in the 21st Century, 263–274.
© *2000 Kluwer Academic Publishers. Printed in the Netherlands.*

The environment SMISLE [3] constitutes an excellent reference to highlight the importance of the concepts related to learning. SMISLE fosters the learning by discovery where the learner is responsible for his learning. In this way the knowledge will be fixed more firmly than in traditional learning communication where the instructions on the domain are provided directly. We must take into account this way of learning can cause failures because it is complex for the learner to discover the concepts and relationships of the domain.

Therefore, a design environment by itself will not offer a mechanical training method due to the fact that the trainer governs the process. Therefore, it is necessary to accomplish guided training sessions to obtain optimal results. In addition to this, the system does not know what the student learns in each moment, so the monitoring of the learning process and the evaluation of the student cannot be controlled.

To attempt to save this obstacle Intelligent Tutoring Systems (ITS) are incorporated. These present the knowledge explicitly instead of being centered on its transmission [4].

The most important aspect in the development of Intelligent Tutoring Systems is Planning [5]. Planning is necessary for the structuring of the domain to study. That is, we must to endow the system with elements to represent knowledge in a clear way, thus avoiding any type of ambiguity that could interfere in the learning process. In the plan a series of instructional activities are collected in order to obtain the expected learning goals.

Instructional Planning is of great importance in this area as it is used in educational environments in order to obtain a greater adaptability to the learner. Instructional Planning can be defined as the process of creating sequences of instructions and actions that provide coherence and soundness during a whole instructional session [6]. With appropriate planning techniques instructional plans are generated containing the didactic goals of the domain to study and the activities to achieve them.

In many domains the application of the planning techniques is extremely hard, due to the complexity associated with them. This problem requires an adequate structuring of the domain, through some type of intermediate language. In this way, Soloway [7] built an improved set of vocabulary terms that serve to build programs. These are decomposed in a set of goals plus a set of previously designed optimum plans. Thus, programming consists of skillfully mixing the set of solution patterns (templates) that an expert uses. The theory underlying these problem solution schemas is based on Cognitive Psychology. It presents these semantic information and organisation units as vital when reading or writing stories. Goals and plans constitute the way in which all the solution processes are approached.

In addition, to reconstruct the learners' reasoning from their traces in the system it is simpler to make it from the tracks that they are leaving in the solution process using an intermediate language [8]. For this reason we consider the structuring of the activities of model design necessary to follow them up and analyse them later.

Nevertheless, the previous solutions can be considered valid, but they lack the organisational and social concept of work, that is, group work.

With the technological advances and research in collaborative learning, a new paradigm emerges: Computer Supported Colaborative Learning (CSCL). It is based on a social-cultural view of cognition. It promotes the substantially social nature of the learning processes, and consequently these are used to study and to experiment methods whose origins are in disciplines such as Anthropology, Sociology, Communication and Pragmatics. From this approach, the technology offers a considerable potential to create, favour or enrich interpersonal learning contexts. Learning is seen as a social process, distributed, in which the dialogue of the participants, the devices involved, the cooperative way the students produce it during the process as well as the perception that the participants have of it are taken into consideration. In this sense, the teacher as well as the technology have a mediating role, as cognitive and social facilitators.

It is necessary to have environments to support the collaborative learning facilitating the students the accomplishment of activities in group, activities that are integrated within the real world, outlined with real objectives, and allowing the evaluation of the benefits that this paradigm provides. Our work follows this line, constituting a design environment where a group of students plan their work in an intermediate solution language, obtaining a solution from group that collects the points of view of each of the members of a group. Furthermore this work is assisted and guided, being based on the expert's knowledge of the domain. Concretely this work presents a solution to the problem of collaborative planning, and some tools that will facilitate the usage of this tool for distance learning.

2.   OUR WORK: A COLLABORATIVE EDITOR OF DESIGN PLANS FOR PEER-TO-PEER AND DISTANCE LEARNING.

This work constitutes a tool that permits to approach the collaborative design of installations for the integral housing automation and buildings, with support for peer-to-peer and distance learning, so we call it Collaborative Plan Editor for Domotic Design. For this, we accomplish to a structuring of the domain that facilitate a first design approximation through an intermediate representation language. This approximation is considered indispensable given its complexity: in the first place inherent to the domain itself, and in the second place, heightened by the side effects of all the activity that is developed in group (planning, cooperation, coordination).

DOMOSIM-TP is presented in [9] It is a system for distance learning of Integral Housing Automation, with a simulation environment and a planner of tasks of design of the model to simulate. In this system secondary students learn the discipline in which the design assisted by the computer is the core of their performance, and it entails the development of a complex project. To limit the freedom that offers the domain itself, the learners are compelled to write, in an explicit way, their development plan of the work session, through a tool for the edition of plans. We call the resulting work "the Student Plan", and it will be monitored by a memory of cases that will contain the "Expert Plans" [10]. In this way we will be able to do a first approximation to the solution of the problem in accordance with the ideas of Bonar [8].

The planning of the domain will allow the student to choose from among a variety of instructional possibilities structured in levels. Each instruction that they compose, according to these levels, will be included in their plan. As it is an open system it also admits the creation and modification of the instructional levels.

Continuing in the line of the previous work, this editor facilitates the learners' planning process of the tasks to perform during the design phase of the model to simulate. It is centered in offering a collaborative work space, where a group of learners works jointly, in an active construction process in group, to design what have been called "the Student Plan".

We have opted for asynchronous collaboration, therefore, as the communication takes place in an asynchronous way, the users (or students) need not be connected simultaneously using the system.

The plan editor is used on the Web, so that the learner can execute it from any place with a browser which supports JAVA. With this editor, the students make their proposal for planning on the design they intend to approach. All the work that the learners develop is registered individually in each learner's own work space, in a database, in the line of Scardamalia [11] and Edelson [12]. It is located in a server that need not be the same as the one which supports the plans editor. It is in charge of registering the contributions of the individuals and showing them to the others so that they can work with updated information. Furthermore the knowledge derived from the interactions between the participants can be employed in subsequent processes of knowledge acquisition, enabling the reflection on the process that carried to the solution, resulting in a recursive and constructive process that Boder [13] named *"Knowledge Reification"*.

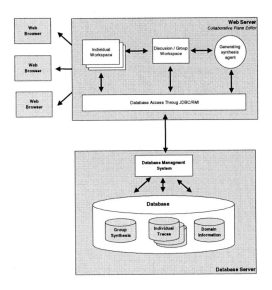

Figure 1. Functional Architecture of the Plans Editor for Groups

The traces of the actions of the learner are collected and carried to the database by using Java Databases Connection (JDBC), leaving the functions of concurrence control, safety, etc. ..., to the database management system choosen. We have used Microsoft Access on Windows NT and Oracle Server on Linux.

In Figure 1 we can observe the functional architecture of the system developed to register all the events that are produced in the interaction of the students and the teachers in our system.

The Web Server shows the user an individual space and a public one. They access the database in the same way. This is, through JDBC and RMI using the structured query language SQL.

In the database, managed by any SGBD compatible with SQL, three clearly differentiated workspaces are established.

The first one constitutes the area where the traces obtained from the interactions accomplished by the learners, their individual workspaces (see Figure 2).

The second workspace is employed to store the synthesis of group, generated from individual work accomplished by the participating students in the work session. Thereinafter they should refine and accept until getting to a group proposal (to see Figure 3), using the collaboration model based on the conversation to collect the contributions of the participants for this [14].

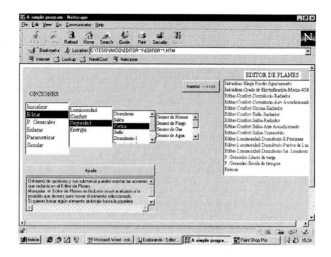

Figure 2. Plans Editor in the individual workspace.

Finally we have a space where there are plans extracted from the knowledge of experts in the domain. They will be used to monitor and to guide the actions of the work meeting, as well as to compare the structure resulting from the work of the learner with the proposal by the experts, extracting conclusions on the accomplished process This enables its usage to evaluate the accomplished work and to make decisions on the aspects to improve and on the way to make it, at individual level as well as at group level, even allowing the employment of scaffolding techniques [15].

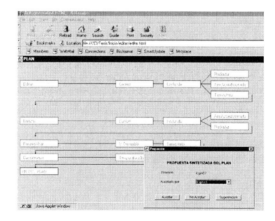

Figure 3. Synthesis of the generated plan and submitted to review by the group

The collection of plans obtained from the knowledge of the experts in the domain, Domotics, was extracted as a result of a formative evaluation process, carried out during the development of the first prototype.

The collaborative design tool for plans is completed with a set of communication and coordination tools intended to constitute what McGreal [16] called a IDLE (*Inegrated Distributed Learning Environment*) and located around the collaborative learning paradigm. It is based on the architectural principles proposed by Barros in her recent research project [17]. The architecture that Barros proposes is organised in four levels: configuration level, experience level, analysis level and organisation level.

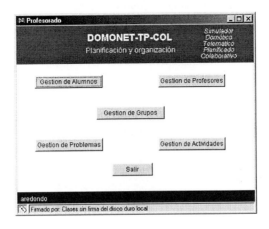

Figure 4. Teacher Workspace

The different subsystems and tools that implement levels are elements that work in an independent way, but they are related through the database of the application. All together they constitute a system that makes it possible to configure, to accomplish and to reuse design and simulation experiences in environments to distance and peer-to-peer education.

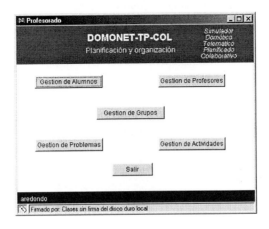

Figure 5. Teachers and learners management

Our system is accessible through the Web and presents three types of access: teacher, learner and coordination. In the teacher space (Figure 4) the configuration and organisation levels are organised, presenting tools for the management of the learners (Figure 5), the management of the teachers, the creation of work groups (Figure 6), the planning of activities and the management of the organisational memory of the problems. The learner space constitutes the experience level (Figure 7), in which the learner, in an identified way, select workgroups and activities associated with proposed problems. They work in this space and transparently for them reflect the traces of their work in the system. This trace will be used thereinafter in the quantitative and qualitative analysis phase.

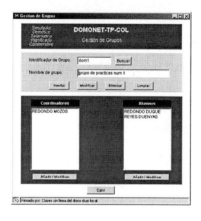

Figure 6. Workgroups configuration

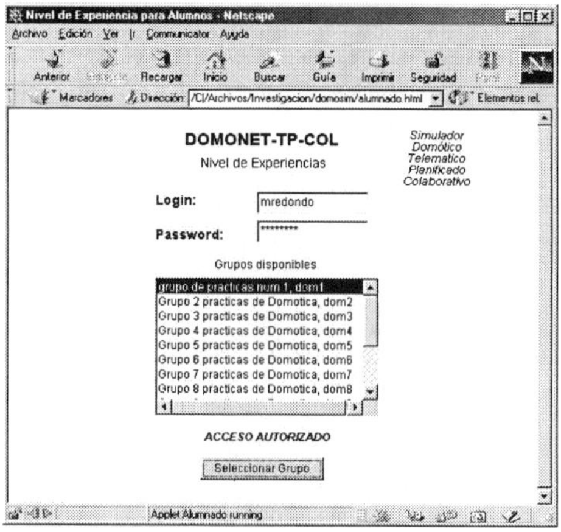

Figure 7. Learner space

We insisted on the need of registering all the accesses of the participants in an experience. This is an inherent need to the cooperative learning concept, to materialize the active process idea of construction in group. In this way, we have a representationof the evolution of the acquisition process of the knowledge and construction of the solution, through argumentation and reflection.

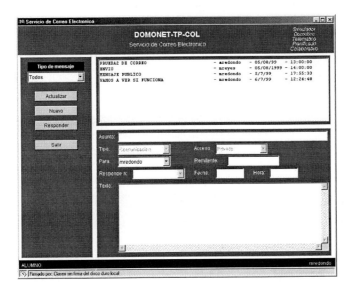

Figure 8. Communication tool based on electronic mail

Once the user has been identified, and the workgroup has been selected, this is authorized to access the system. At this moment we will be able to work directly with the collaborative editor of plans, a tool to accomplish the design of the model to simulate. This tool is described in the following paragraph. Finally, and as a necessary tool in all distance learning systems, the system have a coordination space. In this space we have different subsystems that help and serve as support to the communication, planning and coordination of the members of a group. We have some asynchronous communication tools such as: the electronic mail, which is a absolutely necessary means of communication (Figure 8); the blackboard or news panel (what is new, Figure 9), necessary to maintain the interest of the group, directly accessing the last automatically extracted contributions of the load of information generated; an agenda that serves as a planning element for common activities for the group.

We have the synchronous communication tool by excellence: the CHAT (Figure 10). This tool will permit to know at once the users who are making use of the system and to invite them has maintained a textual conversation in real time.

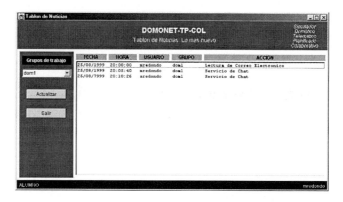

Figure 9. Panel that it shows the last news of the group dom1

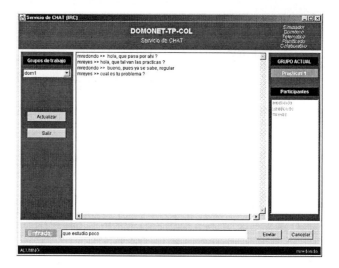

Figure 10. CHAT Service

We emphasize that the whole set of coordination tools are supported in the Web deployment of the technology of databases carrying out an important classification and structuring of all the information generated. Therefore, the tools of the system are totally platform independent. So, to accomplish experiences we only need of the communication technology of the Internet. The system provides the necessary tools.

3.   CONCLUSIONS AND FUTURE WORK.

In this work we have developed a tool which has been used with different techniques and which has already been used separately: intelligent tutors in learning environments, collaboration in the development of a task in group, environments integrated to support distance learning and finally planning of the work. We have facilitated the integration of all these techniques to apply them to the learning of design. The solution that we have adopted has been the collaborative planning assisted or guided as a strategy to support the collaboration in design environments for distance learning.

As a result of the implementation of collaboration in this work, we can extract some conclusions:

- A greater degree of realism in the learning situation, considered from a social point of view,
- Several persons can see a solution better when they work in a complex project,
- There is a clear awareness of the social organisation of the work,
- Computer science and communications constitute the most appropriate means to sustain this new technology.

Our new expectations will be centered on making the system elaborate a synthesis with the different traces obtained from the actions from all the learners that participate in the session. Thus, in a tree form and employing heuristic artificial intelligence, it will constitute the plan deduced from the different proposals of the participants. This synthesis, obtained automatically by the system, will be presented to the learners so that they can refine his design, making different interventions until getting to a thoroughly agreed proposal. In order to get this we will include an intelligent agent, whose presence we consider important, since the dominance in the one we work has a greater complexity that other based on documental synthesis already studied in other projects.

It is planned to use the system in several Professional Trainning Colleges in the province of Ciudad Real (Spain), to evaluate it, that is, it will be submitted to individual work, in group and to distance experiments, to obtain quantitative and qualitative data that will allow us to extract conclusions on this process.

REFERENCES

1.   de Jong, T., van Joolingen, W., Pieters, J. & van der Hulst, Anja, (1993) *"Why is discovery learning so difficult? And what can we do about it?"*. EARLI conference . Aix-en-Provence.

2.   Duffy, T., & Jonassen, D. (1992) *"Constructivism and the Technology of instruction"*. Lawrence Erlbaum Associates, Hillsdale, New Jersey.
3.   de Jong, T., van Joolinger W. & King, S., (1997) *"The authoring environment SIMQUEST and the need for author support"*. In Supporting authors in the design of simulation based learning environments. Ton de Jong (Ed.),Servive Project.
4.   Fernández., B., Vaquero, A., Fernández-Valmayor, A. Hdez. L. (1997), *"Informática educativa: revisión y análisis de los problemas de la utilización de las computadoras en la enseñanza"*. Informática y Automática vol. 30-3.
5.   Verdejo, M.F. (1992) . *"A Framework for Instructional Planning and Discourse Modelling in Intelligent Tutoring Systems"*. In Costa, E. (Eds.), New Directions for Intelligent Tutoring Systems, vol 91, pp 147-170. NATO ASI Series, Springer Verlag, Berlin.
6.   Wasson, B. (1990).*"Determining de Focus if Instruction: Content Planning for Intelligent Tutoring System"* Doctoral Thesis, Department of Computational Science, University of Saskatchewan.
7.   Soloway, E., (1986). *" Learning to Program = Learning to Construct Mechanisms and Explanations"*. Communications of the ACM.
8.   Bonar, J.G. & Cunningham, R. (1988). *"Intelligent Tutoring with Intermediate Representations"* ITS-88 Montreal.
9.   Bravo, J., Ortega, M., & Verdejo, M.F., (1999), *"Planning in Distance Simulation Environments"*. Full Paper in Comunications and Networking in Education COMNED'99. Aulanko, Hämeenlinna, Finlandia. 13-18 de Junio.
10. Bravo, J., (1999) *"Estrategias para la planificación del diseño en entornos de simulación a distancia"*. Tesis Doctoral, Escuela de Ingenieros Industriales, Universidad Nacional de Educación a Distancia. Madrid.
11. Scardamalia, M., & Bereiter, C., (1996) *"Student Communities for the advancement of Knowledge"*. Communications of the ACM, 39(4).
12. Edelson, D.C., & O'Neill, D.K., (1994), *"The CoVis Collaboratory Notebook: Supporting Collaborative Scientific Inquiry"*, NECC'94.
13. Boder, A., (1992), *"The process of knowledge reification in human-human interaction"*, Journal of computer Assited Learning, Vol. 8, No 3, September, pp. 177-185.
14. Bobrow, D., (1991), *"Dimensions of Interaction: AAAI-90 Presidential Address"*, AI Magazine, Vol. 12, No. 3, pp. 64-80.
15. Ortega, M., Bravo, J., Bravo, C., Muñoz, J.J. & Redondo, M.A., (1998), *"Scaffolding and Planning Techniques in Distance Education: A case Study in Statistics"*. Proceeding of 4th International Conference on Technology Supported Learning. Online Educa. Berlin (Alemania).
16. McGreal, R., (1998), *"Integrated Distributed Learning Environtmets (IDLE's) on the Internet: A Survey"*, Educational Technology Review, N°. 9. Spring/Summer, pp. 25-31.
17. Barros, B., (1999), *"Aprendizaje Colaborativo en Enseñanza a Distancia: Entornos Genérico para Configurar, Realizar y Analizar Actividades en Grupo"*, Tesis Doctoral, Departamento de Inteligencia Artificial de la Universidad Politécnica de Madrid.

High Level Design of Web-Based Environments for Distance Education

Miguel Rodríguez-Artacho, Mª Felisa Verdejo
Universidad Nacional de Educación a Distancia, Departamento de Ingeniería Eléctrica,
Electrónica y Control
e-mail: {miguel,felisa@}ieec.uned.es

Key words: Instructional content design, Web-based learning environments, Distance
Learning

Abstract: This paper presents an approach to authoring in a Web-based learning
environment with a high level description and reusable instructional
components. These components have been previously categorized in a set of
knowledge domains according to their instructional, didactic and pedagogical
properties. The design of the learning environment is carried out using a
description written in an SGML-derived language called PALO. PALO allows
describing a variety of instructional scenarios that can be instantiated with a
certain content matter using references to the domain model. This description
is then turned into a Web-Based scenario by means of a compilation process.

1.   INTRODUCTION

Nowadays we can observe a wide development of computer supported learning environments. The growth of telecommunication technologies and an easier and more extensive access to Internet are turning the web into the new mass media. It is a matter of fact that this growth has brought an increasing demand for distance learning, most of the times using Web environments.

The current state of the art has to face problems that affect both users of learning environments and designers of learning contents. On the one hand, learning scenarios do not completely fulfil the users' needs; on the other

M. Ortega and J. Bravo (eds.), Computers and Education in the 21st Century, 275–285.

hand, systems are complex to build and maintain because they are most of the times built from scratch or reduced to an experimental usage.

Other problems are related to the student's budget, whether they can afford high tech environments offered by universities. Not all students have the same bandwidth to access the *Virtual Campus* of their Universities. From this point of view, it is not realistic to offer highly technological environments, because most of the students have only a slow and expensive modem connection to the Internet.

At the same time, facing the problem of the designer of learning content, current approaches do not have an explicit learning content representation, and content is not separated from the system structure. This causes a lack of flexibility and reusability of learning components that does not help to provide an instructional content design process based on incremental authoring and knowledge reusability.

a matter of fact that this growth has brought an increasing demand for distance learning, most of the times using Web environments.

The current state of the art has to face problems that affect both users of learning environments and designers of learning contents. On the one hand, learning scenarios do not completely fulfil the users' needs; on the other hand, systems are complex to build and maintain because they are most of the times built from scratch or reduced to an experimental usage.

Other problems are related to the student's budget, whether they can afford high tech environments offered by universities. Not all students have the same bandwidth to access the *Virtual Campus* of their Universities. From this point of view, it is not realistic to offer highly technological environments, because most of the students have only a slow and expensive modem connection to the Internet.

At the same time, facing the problem of the designer of learning content, current approaches do not have an explicit learning content representation, and content is not separated from the system structure. This causes a lack of flexibility and reusability of learning components that does not help to provide an instructional content design process based on incremental authoring and knowledge reusability.

2.   AN APPROACH TO THE DESIGN OF WEB-BASED LEARNING ENVIRONMENTS

Our goal is to improve the design process of a learning environment, and also to create useful environments for a massive use, considering the increasing number of students in our University.

According to this it would be desirable that our students could be offered:

- To use the remote learning environment any time and anywhere
- To perform interactive tasks (mainly asynchronously)
- To use the material both on-line and off-line without loss of performance
- To access the learning scenario using only a web browser
  Also, content designers, like teachers and tutors, should be able to:
- Build and configure a learning scenario using a straightforward process
- Modelling and managing a knowledge domain separately from the structure of the learning environment
- Have interactive elements to carry out the student's assessment

This kind of scenarios could satisfy most of the remote learning activities in Distance Learning and it is useful to carry out the activities proposed in our University, currently developed over a hardcopy of the didactic material. We propose to use the web to carry out these activities using a web environment, but facilitating the authoring process to the teacher. In this sense, what makes these environments different from other learning scenarios is that the authoring process is carried out at a higher level of abstraction by means of:

- A separate description of the content matter
- Explicit mechanisms to select and refer knowledge components according to its didactic and instructional properties
- An explicit description of the learning environment that can be turned into a variety of different technologies (i.e. for remote and local usage)

In summary, our intentions are that the teacher could in the first place organise and model a given content matter, and then describe, using this knowledge model, interactive working environments where students can carry out the work plan defined by the teacher in the description. Flexibility is provided by using the same knowledge components to describe different scenarios, thus avoiding building them from scratch, and describing them at a higher abstraction level using the mechanisms provided by the description language.

Following sections describe knowledge modelling, environment descriptions and a brief summary of technical and implementation aspects.

2.1 Instructional Objects and Instructional Knowledge

Most commonly known tools like WebCT, Toolbook, etc. are multimedia environments in which building blocks have no pedagogical information. Content and structure are not separated, and instructional content is embedded in web HTML pages and is not reusable. Even if we use the same content in another part of the environment, elements of the content are in physical formats (gif, html, mpeg, ...) and are not treated as elements at an instructional or pedagogical level of abstraction [4] [5].

As we have pointed before, separate content and structure need an instructional knowledge description in knowledge components that could be referred by using instructional properties. This description is called a *conceptualisation,* that identifies the elements of a description of a content matter and creates a conceptual map of the learning content using elements (*example, concept, exercise, ...*) and instructional or didactical relationships (i.e. concept *is prerequisite of* concept, example *explains* concept, etc.)

Needless to say, structuring a content matter into learning components is not a new idea. There are some interesting developments that use an instructional components classification to provide reusability like in [3] and reusability of instructional Web resources using metadata and RDF format as in [6].

However, two main objectives are accomplished using the proposed learning component classification. On the one hand there is an explicit description of the content matter using a domain of elements and instructional relationships. This model allows carrying out a conceptual learning supported by the conceptual relationships of the model [1]. On the other hand an independent knowledge representation is necessary to reuse knowledge components at a certain level of granularity. These components are categorized as suggested in [2] and [4] who pointed out the need of instructional ontologies to structure and scaffold different approaches of instructional knowledge representation.

2.2   Describing a Learning Environment

As pointed above, we have created a SGML based language to describe a learning scenario. The language provides both flexibility and expressiveness to refer to different content; for example, elements of the domain model are selected using expressions at a pedagogical level such as "*include an example to illustrate concept C",* instead of using a low media level description such as an HTML page, etc.

Using properties of SGML, such as its capacity to define a variety of DTDs can lead to the definition of several scenarios, each one to be described using its own DTD. Different scenarios can reuse the same content references and can perform different instructional activities over the same content matter.

For the authoring process, the teacher has, on the one hand, a domain model with a set of classified instructional elements and on the other hand a library of *instructional templates* described with a DTD. Once a given DTD is selected, instructional content can be added by filling the structure with the references to the knowledge domain either by a direct reference "*show concept C*", or using a didactic relationship like "*show prerequisites of* concept C", or a relationship filtered with an attribute like in *"show easy examples to illustrate concept C".*

3.   THE STEED SYSTEM

According to the ideas described in the previous section, we have developed a set of tools to describe and create instructional environments using a high level description.

The STEED[1] System has the following features:

-   It provides an external knowledge representation of the content matter separate from the structure of the learning environment. This representation scaffolds instructional knowledge in a set of domains
-   It describes learning scenarios using an explicit description in a high level language, using references to reusable instructional components
-   It allows including structure and management information into the description.

The authoring process firstly allows us to define models in which content matter is structured, and secondly, using the SGML language, an *instructional template* can be chosen and instantiated with domain content matter. Then, a PALO compiler can build up a fully functional learning scenario using this description.

3.1   Content Matter Modelling

A content matter description can be represented using conceptual models based on an entity-relationship formalism. This kind of representation provides a trade-off between a robust representation and an effective implementation using a relational database.

Knowledge is structured in a set of generic levels using a taxonomy of instructional and conceptual components and a description of its pedagogical relations. Each level describes a particular aspect of the domain based on relationships or on attributes of the learning components.

---

[1] STEED stands for Sistema Telemático para Enseñanza en Educación a Distancia http://sensei.ieec.uned.es/~steed

3.1.1   Knowledge model of a programming subject: An example

A content matter description can be organised using different perspectives, grouping in single domains the entities and relationships that belong to a certain knowledge category. We propose as an example a Course in program verification that can be described using 3 domains:

- A structural approach to describe the taxonomy of entities using relations like *part of* and *type of*
- An instructional approach with a categorisation of instructional components such as *example, problem, exercise, solution* and relationships that link these elements like *illustrate, explains,* etc.
- Finally a pedagogical level combines some properties that could be interesting in order to decide which element to choose from a pedagogical point of view. Examples of these properties are *degree of difficulty* and relationships like *prerequisite*

This generic model can be instantiated with several content matters, especially with those related to a theoretic and practical scientific domain.

3.1.2   Describing Generic Knowledge Models

Using an explicit description of a generic knowledge requires a higher level representation. The model described in the previous section has a generic structure with 3 domain models that is explicitly represented in a *metamodel*, that is, a model that describes a model.

Thanks to this *metamodel*, a tool can manage a set of models according to the knowledge structure explicitly defined in the *metamodel*. This meta level is useful to provide certain interesting operations over the models. In summary, there are two abstraction levels while describing instructional knowledge:

- A metamodel that describes the structure of a model
- A model that has the structure described in its metamodel and that has the appropriate content matter.

Both levels use the same formalism to describe themselves, the entity-relationship model. These abstraction levels provide a way to carry out interesting operations on a model. If a knowledge domain describe a certain content and a new relationship is needed, it could be added just by modifying the metamodel and re-instantiating the model according to the modification.

3.2   Describing *instructional templates*: The PALO language

We propose a way to describe a learning scenario, including content, structure and tasks model, using a mark-up language based on SGML.

SGML interest is based on its capacity to create a set of Document Type Definitions (DTDs) each one describing a certain type of document with its structure and components. If a document claims to be generated from a DTD, a program called *parser* can recognise the document with its content and elements as described in the DTD.

According to this, we have developed a language to describe learning scenarios called PALO. PALO is in fact a library of instructional templates (DTDs) that describe different learning scenarios. PALO templates can be selected, according to the kind of learning scenario that better fits the instructional needs. These templates describe different learning environments to carry out different instructional activities.

Documents written in PALO have a given structure based on the template DTD, but also describe the content matter the instructional activity will be carried out with. This is made using certain tags as in any SGML language.

PALO tags are classified in two different types:
–   Those that describe the document structure. This will become the structure of the learning scenario
–   Those that refer to knowledge components both implicitly (references to the components of the knowledge model) and explicitly (embedded in the document)

The first type of tags is document dependent. Those who describe a practical activity scenario are different from other describing a didactic guide scenario. Different templates have different tags of the first type. Tags of the second type are shared by all the documents. These tags allow inserting a knowledge element from the domain models in any part of the environment. References to these elements have been designed to provide a higher level of abstraction in the authoring process, using the relations between entities described in the models, as shown in the previous section.

Other tags or attributes are related with management aspects such as directories, databases, user tracking of content elements and assessment of tasks.

In order to create the learning scenarios, a PALO compiler has been developed. This tool turns a PALO description into a Web-based interactive environment [8].

4.   EXPERIENCES USING STEED

During the second semester of the 98/99 course STEED tools where evaluated within a programming subject of *algorithms design and verification* corresponding to a first course in Computer Science at UNED[2] University.

This experience served to evaluate the authoring process of the learning environment with PALO and the use of the system with a group of students. The authoring process has consisted in the modelling of the relevant knowledge plus the PALO description of the environments. The final Web environment was used to carry out a practical programming project with the help of a didactic guide to solve conceptual errors.

4.1   Authoring process

Firstly, the authoring process consists in the creation of domain knowledge. This process has the following steps:

- Choice of a content matter and creation of the cognitive structure to represent it (metamodel). Describe in the metamodel the selected conceptualisation.
- Instantiating the metamodel into an empty entity-relationship model.
- Filling the components of the model with the appropriate knowledge components: *concepts, problems, relations,...* according to the content matter.

Using this description, the teacher can now use PALO language to describe a learning scenario using references to this knowledge model.

During the development of these activities, the most time consuming task was the creation of the models and metamodels of the domain content. This took ¾ of the authoring process.

Table 1

Tasks	Time
Conceptualisation	40 Hours (18%)
Creation	10 Hours (4%)
Instantiation	150 Hours (55%)
PALO description	60 Hours (23%)

Table 1 describes the authoring process steps and the total time involved in the development of each of them. Once the knowledge structure is

---

[2] http://www.uned.es

created, the most costly task is the instantiation of the metamodel with the content components. These tasks are carried out using a web-based tool and a relational database.

For this experience we developed three PALO instructional templates:
- A didactic guide of the subject
- A self-evaluation tool
- A small programming project

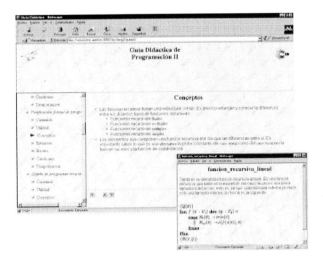

Figure 1.

Figure 1 shows the final result in the creation of the didactic guide environment after the compilation process of the PALO description. The editor used to create the PALO documents was XEmacs, which can edit XML and SGML documents thanks to its ability of parsing DTDs.

4.2 Using the learning material

In June 1999 a group of students at the UNED Associated Centre in Madrid were invited to participate in this experience. The proposed task was a small programming project to be carried out using the environment.

Two groups of 60 students were invited to join the experience. They were offered the possibility of doing it the traditional way (hardcopy) or using the Internet environment. Results are shown in Table 2.

Table 2

Action	Students
Offering	120

Action	Students
Interested	65
Accessed the system	35
Worked over the material (any time)	25
Completely Finished	11

Approximately half of them showed some interest in using the system and asked for a login and password. As shown, the final average of the system use is 20% of the initial population. Students were offered the possibility to quit at anytime and go back to the traditional way (in hardcopy). Thus, taking into account that the use of the system was not mandatory, the final result is acceptable.

At the end of the experience, students were given a questionnaire in order to get their opinion about the reasons to quit. Results showed that the main reason was the cost of the Internet access. Those who continued were mainly motivated because they used free Internet access from their offices or at home.

5.   FUTURE WORK AND CONCLUSIONS

Now we are working in the development of a new PALO compiler that allows creating working scenarios with the possibility of using them *off line*. In this local environment, elements have a Java applet that can save the student response or the user tracking in the local disk. To overcome the rigid security model of the Java VM, applets have been digitally signed. Digital certificates can be retrieved from the University web pages.

Our perspectives in the development of the STEED project also include instructional knowledge modelling. In this aspect, our interest fits in the research of standardisation organisms and the promotion of the use of metadata schemas in order to improve reusability of instructional components.

ACKNOWLEDGEMENTS

STEED Project has been supported by the Comisión Interministerial de Ciencia[3] y Tecnología (CICYT TEL 97-038c0202) and Comunidad de

---

[3] www.cicyt.es

Madrid[4]. The authors wish to thank the participation of J.I.Mayorga and M.Y. Calero in the development of this project.

6. BIBLIOGRAPHY

1. Andriessen, J and Sandberg, J (1999). *Where is education and how about AI?* International Journal of Artificial Intelligence in Education 10
2. Breuker, J. Muntjewerff, A. and Bredewej, B. (1999) . *Ontological modelling for designing educational systems.* In Proceedings of the AI-ED 99 Workshop on Ontologies for Educational Systems
3. Forte, E. Maria, H., Wentland, F. and Duval, E. (1997) *The ARIADNE project: Knowledge pools for computer-based and telematics-supported classical, open and distance education (I/II).* European Journal of Engineering Education, 22(1).
4. Mizoguchi, R. Ikeda, M. and Sinitsa, K. (1997). *Roles of shared ontology in AI-ED research.* In de Boulay, B and Mizogiuchi, R. editors, Artificial Intelligence in Education AI-ED 97, pages 537-544, Kobe, Japan. IOS Press
5. Murray, T. (1996) *From story board to knowledge bases: The first paradigm shift in making CAI "intelligent".* In Proceedings of the ED-MEDIA 96 Conference, pages 509-514, Boston, MA
6. Murray, T. (1999). *A model for distributed curriculum in the WWW.* Journal of Interactive Media in Education (5)
7. Rehak, D. (1999). *Structure guidelines for a distance educational program.* Carnegie-Mellon University Technical Report
8. Rodríguez-Artacho, M and Verdejo, M.F. and Mayorga, J. and M.Y. Calero (1999) *Using a High-Level language to describe and create web-based learning scenarios.* In Proceedings of IEEE Frontiers In Education Conference FIE '99 San Juan de Puerto Rico, Nov 1999 (http://sensei.ieec.uned.es/~steed)
9. Verdejo, M.F., Rodríguez-Artacho, M. Mayorga, J.I., and Calero, M.Y. (1999) *Creating web-based scenarios to support distance learners.* In Proceedings of the Working Group 3.3 and 3.6 IFIP. Chapman & Hall. (http://sensei.ieec.uned.es/~steed)

---

[4] www.comadrid.es

M.A.C. A Hypermedia System for Learning Electronics

A. Salaverría [1, 2]; M.J. Moure[2]; M.D. Valdés[2]; E. Mandado[2];M.Pérez Cota[3]
[1] *Dept. de Electrónica y Telecomunicaciones Universidad del País Vasco (UPV/EHU)*
Avda. Felipe IV 1 B; 20011 San Sebastián (SPAIN)
Phone: +34 943 45 50 22; Fax: +34 943 47 10 97
E-mail: jtpsagaa@sp.ehu.es
[2] *Instituto de Electrónica Aplicada Universidade de Vigo. Campus Universitario Apartado de correos oficial 36200 Vigo (SPAIN)*
[3] *Depto. De Linguaxes y Sistemas Informaticos. Universidade de Vigo. Campus Universitario Apartado de correos oficial 36200 Vigo (SPAIN)*

Key words: Hypermedia, Computer Aided Learning

Abstract: Till now simulation systems were the most common Computer Aided Learning systems. Although they are very powerful tools, using simulation students cannot experiment with real devices. M.A.C. system (from Spanish "Módulo de Análisis de Circuitos") allows students to learn electronics using a friendly interface, hypermedia resources and practical experiences using real circuits connected to the computer by means of an analog to digital converter card. The M.A.C. system requires a computer, an analog to digital converter card connected to the PC, a general interface module containing the power supplies and the experimentation cards. The system is available in two different versions: English and Spanish. The English version contains a basic course on Operational Amplifiers and the Spanish one, contains some other lessons on basic Electronics such as diodes, transistors and digital electronics (they will be translated into English in the near future). The English version needs 32 Mbytes of free hard disk (130 Mbytes remain on the CD) and the Spanish one 40 Mbytes (400 Mbytes remain on the CD). The possibility that M.A.C. offers to experiment with the circuits, while the student learns the theory or solves an exercise, improves her/his knowledge and allows faster learning. At the same time, the student participates in the experiments, changing the components and then the circuit's behaviour.

287

M. Ortega and J. Bravo (eds.), Computers and Education in the 21st Century, 287–296.
© 2000 *Kluwer Academic Publishers. Printed in the Netherlands.*

1.   INTRODUCTION

In Electronics the teaching of Operational Amplifiers has traditionally been carried out combining theoretical education with the practical assembly of circuits using specific measuring instruments such as power supplies, voltmeters, oscilloscopes, and signal generators [1], [2]. But this method is not really useful in the classroom. Oscilloscope screens or voltmeters are very small and it is not possible to use them with a big number of students (only a few ones would be able to see them). The idea is to bring a virtual laboratory to the classroom. Obviously, M.A.C. does not try to replace the laboratory, but it allows the students to experiment while they are learning a new electronic concept or circuit.

The previously mentioned disadvantage can be overcome using Computer Aided Learning (CAL) methods. The potentialities of computer hypermedia resources, and the low cost and widespread diffusion of computers, convert CAL into an essential teaching tool. In the case of Electronics the computer can be used to support both theoretical and practical teaching. In this sense three kinds of applications can be pointed out: Tutoring systems [3] Simulation programs [4] and Virtual Instrumentation systems (VIS) [5].

A hypermedia system oriented to the education of electronics engineers must take into account the following aspects:
1. Consistent theoretical contents allowing progressive and individual learning.
2. Testing capabilities.
3. Possibility of individual (at home) or co-operative learning.

To meet these requirements we developed a CAL system combining theoretical lessons with experiments using adequately chosen electronic cards.

2.   HARDWARE DESCRIPTION

The hardware components are:

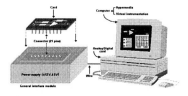

Figure 1. Hardware

1. A set of cards containing the real circuits related to each lesson (Figure - 2) These cards are electronic circuits oriented to the introduction of the applications of simple electronic devices or systems.

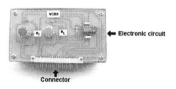

Figure 2. Electronic circuit

The cards have switches, push buttons and potentiometers in order to change some circuit parameters. Acting on these components, students can modify the input voltage, the reference voltage, the power supply, etc, and see the effect of such changes.

Figure 3. An operational amplifier

Many cards are equipped with different types of operational amplifiers (Figure - 3). Students can change them to compare the characteristics of the same operational amplifier produced by different manufacturers. This task is impossible using low cost simulation systems [6].

2. A general interface module to support the cards. It includes power supplies (±12V and ±5V), a 21-pin connector (DIN 41617) and a 50-pin connector, which communicates the cards and the PC.

3. A personal computer, with an analog to digital converter card (ADC) receiving information from selected test points.

3.   SOFTWARE DESCRIPTION

The software system is made up of:
– A hypermedia application oriented to the presentation of theoretical lessons with practical circuits showing the behaviour of the explained circuits or concepts.

- Virtual instrumentation (oscilloscope, logic analyser, voltmeter and functions generator) for data acquisition from different test points.
- A self-evaluation hypertext application containing exercises based on practical circuits.

3.1   Theoretical part of the hypermedia application

The hypermedia application, running under WINDOWS$^{©}$ 95 or WINDOWS$^{©}$ 98, is the core of the system. It is made up of theoretical lessons complemented with exercises and experiments.

When a student runs the program a short presentation including music, appears on the screen. After the presentation the student can read the course general contents. (Figure - 4).

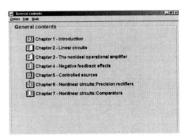

Figure 4. General contents screen

Clicking on the icon the student selects a chapter and its contents appear on a second screen (Figure - 5). The icons on the right indicate if the lesson has a multimedia explanation, exercises or experimentation cards.

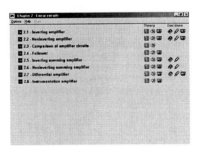

Figure 5. Chapter contents screen

Clicking on the lesson icon, the student selects between theory and exercises (Figure - 6)

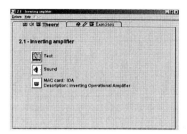

Figure 6. Options in the theory screen

On the theoretical part, it is possible to read the full text (while listening to background music), select the spoken comment or run the virtual instrumentation with the circuit plugged in the basic module (Figure - 4).

If the student selects "Sound", a cassette player-like interface appears on the screen. An audio-visual presentation consisting of a spoken abstract with animated graphics is displayed. It is strongly recommended to begin with this section because in this way the student listens and sees the lesson objectives. (Figure - 7)

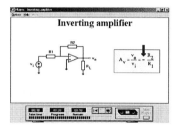

Figure 7. Audiovisual presentation

Clicking on the icon "text", the text appears under html format (Figure - 8). This format is well known by students, since Internet is commonly used. By means of hyperlinks, html texts allow the student to navigate through the book and come back to previous chapters if further reading is necessary.

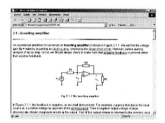

Figure 8. Textual presentation

Moreover, html applications support animated graphics especially useful to compose difficult circuits step by step including explanations for each step.

An interesting part of M.A.C. is a glossary including the most common terms in Electronics. A background music sounds all the time while the text is shown. The music has been carefully selected with the help of Spanish students and psychologists in order to help the student's concentration.

3.2 - Virtual instrumentation

Clicking on the icon "circuit", the student can see how the practical circuit works (Figure - 9).

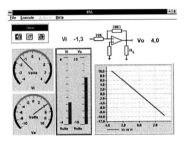

Figure 9. Circuit operation

Virtual instrumentation has been made using Visual Designer© from Intelligent Instrumentation©. Each card uses its own instruments, depending on the circuit under test.

3.3 - Exercises of the hypermedia application

Exercises (Figure - 10) follow the same methodology used on the theoretical part except the spoken comments.

Figure 10. Exercises

Clicking on the icon "exercise", the student reads the text of the exercise (Figure - 11). Then he/she must solve the exercise and has to select between two possibilities: read the solution, or check how the real circuit works.

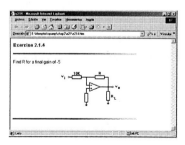

Figure 11. Exercise statement

Clicking on the icon "solution", the student reads the solution including links to the theoretical part of the corresponding lesson (Figure - 12).

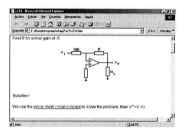

Figure 12. Exercise solution

Clicking on the icon "M.A.C. card" the student see how the circuit works.

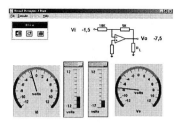

Figure 13. M.A.C. card working

4 - Conclusions

Combining hypermedia with real circuits, we can improve education on Electronics. The M.A.C. system has been experimented during the last four years with Spanish, German and Greek students (University of the Basque Country, Fachhoschule Wilhemshaven and TEI Kavala). All of them admitted that M.A.C. is a useful tool for learning Electronics. At this moment (course 1999-2000), 46 students use the Spanish version of the M.A.C. system at the Escuela Universitaria de Ingeniería Técnica Industrial (University of the Basque Country). The students use the whole M.A.C. system (including ADC and the set of cards) at the Faculty, and a reduced version of the system (without ADC and cards) at home. When students were asked about their experience using the M.A.C. system, they answered the following:

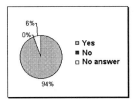

Question: Is it a good idea to have the whole course on multimedia support?

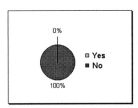

Question: Is there too much text on the screen?

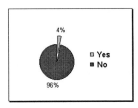

Question: Have you printed the course?

Question: If you have not printed the course yet, would you like to do it in the future?

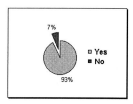

Question: Would you prefer even more multimedia explanations?

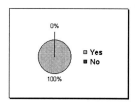

Question: Are spoken explanations good enough?

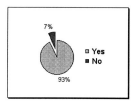

Question: Is the graphic user interface friendly enough?

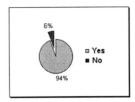

Question: Do you like the music?

REFERENCES

1. Lago A. and Rodríguez F., Manual de Prácticas de Electrónica General y Analógica, (eds.)
   Tórculo Ediciones, 1993.
2. Miri S. Y Fu R., "A Hands-On Practical Approach to Teaching Engineering Design",
   IEEE Transaction on Education, vol. 36, N°1, pp. 131-136, February 1993.
3. Cuetkovic S., Seebold R., Bateson K. and Okretic U.K., "CAL Programs developed in
   advanced programming environments for teaching electrical engineering", IEEE
   Transaction on Education, vol. 37, N°2, May 1994.
4. "MicroSim Applications Notes", MicroSim Corporation, U.S.A. 1996.
5. KEITHLEY, "TestPoint. Keithley Data Acquisition Software", Keithley Instruments
   GmbH, Germany 1997.
6. MicroSim v.8 (Evaluation version)

Computer-Human Learning
Learning through Natural Language on the Internet

Pedro Pablo Sánchez Villalón
The CHICO Team Universidad de Castilla La Mancha.
Escuela Oficial de Idiomas Ciudad Real.
e-mail: ppsanch@fimo-cr.uclm.es

Keywords: Computer-Human Interaction, Natural Language Processing, Internet, IT, Knowledge Management, Computational Linguistics, Learning, Distance Education, Interaction, Interactive Structured Information.

Abstract: Computer-Human Interaction is one of the main fields of research in Computers in Education in the quest for a user interface to facilitate "intelligent" communication between computers and humans. Artificial Intelligence was to "revolutionize" the world of Computer-Human Interaction. However, the Internet is meant to be the true paradigm for communication, and communication is the ultimate goal of language. The huge quantity of information available on the Internet can be considered as the base of global knowledge. Our mind, as well as the Internet, is "hypertextual". This paper suggests an interactive structure of information that will solve the three main obstacles encountered when trying to implement natural language in computers: the problem of coping with the implicit, common sense (by means of inference of textual information), the problem of limited domain (by reference to hypertextual cognitive structures), and the problem of breakdowns in the action plans (by coherence interaction). Hypertextual and textual documents help the Internet and our computer to assimilate natural language. Thus, we will be able to communicate in a truly interactive way, making the computer really capable of understanding. If we implement the natural process of the development of shared knowledge into computers, we will be laying the foundations of collaborative computer-human learning.

M. Ortega and J. Bravo (eds.), Computers and Education in the 21st Century, 297–312.
© 2000 *Kluwer Academic Publishers. Printed in the Netherlands.*

1.   INTRODUCTION

Until recently, the advances in computer science (as regards programming) were carried out with the perspective of the metaphor with human knowledge, since the architecture of the computer and that of knowledge are similar. Considering language as the driving force of knowledge development, programmers tried to elaborate techniques of logical, formal languages centred in programming languages (C languages, LISP, Prolog, etc.) in order to construct a similar architecture in both domains. Natural language was processed and analysed identifying regularities by implementing the digital treatment of information, to finally establish formal models of human knowledge (applying the generative grammar theory of Chomsky, [5]). The aim was to apply them to computers by means of databases (such as in the field of machine translation) and problem-solution techniques (such as the GPS of Newell and Simon [8]. In this way programmers tried to create machines (computers) able to behave intelligently, assuming that computers have the same structure as human knowledge and so they could communicate with us in the same environment, using natural language. But these attempts to create Artificial Intelligence for computer-human interaction have not resulted as successful as expected since the cognitive structure to reproduce is not objective in itself, merely formal or permanent, based on regularities. On the contrary, it is something more dynamic, continually developing, adaptive to the environment, as pragmatic linguistics has proven.

If we channel our efforts into the wider, more flexible trends that the most recent linguistic research is undertaking, we will get a greater mutual understanding and a better computer-human interaction by means of natural language, and so we will be able to develop human-computer shared knowledge, as the basis for collaborative learning.

2.   THEORETICAL FOUNDATIONS

My research as a linguist makes me appreciate the advances developed in the fields of psychology (Piaget and Vygotzky), sociology (Flores), philosophy (Schank, Austin and Searle) and computer science (Winograd), and on their contributions lie the theoretical foundations of this paper. They all consider, whether explicitly or implicitly, language as the basis for knowledge development and communication between people.

Linguistics has language as the object of study. Language is quite complex. The variety of perspectives in the study of language is so wide that, regarding the state of the art in the debate on Artificial Intelligence, we can consider that linguists have already experienced part of the problems in question and can contribute with solutions. Though partial, these solutions can be used as a basis for the development of applied computational components of knowledge. Especially, human language should be the first aspect for us to take into account when developing interfaces that facilitate communication and learning between people and computers.

This should be one of the objectives of the so-called Computational Linguistics. Computational Linguistics has been used in the opposite direction, with the application of computer tools to the analysis of natural language, something successfully achieved mainly with the most formal perspectives of language: grammatical analysis and lexicography. In this direction, the use of computers for linguistics came up to expectations using the calculation of formal elements (words as symbols) as a basis, analysing their structural organisation, carrying out statistics and listings, etc. This suits the formal theory of Chomsky [5], who sees the structure of language as a fixed system of regulations representable with symbols (including mathematical symbols).

Several groups of linguists reacted against this formal perspective. They considered the environment as something that played a central role in the development of knowledge, learning and language. Some followed previous studies by Piaget [9], who, without making explicit reference to language, laid the foundations of the functional component of learning as an activator of the interaction between the person and the environment. Knowledge becomes structured as a result of interaction (in the cognitive development of the child). Other theorists of language such as Searle [13], Rumelhart [11], Schank [14], Van Dijk and Kintsch [6] and Winograd [18] developed principles of natural language structure under the cognitive perspective of language as the driving force of knowledge development. They have studied the components that activate communication such as the environment, the influence of this (the world) in language and vice versa. They consider language as action (Searle and Winograd), as reflection of the world in a structure of shared knowledge (Rumelhart and Schank) and as a combination of both factors influencing the person and the world interactively (Van Dijk and Kintsch).

3.　KNOWLEDGE-LANGUAGE-ENVIRONMENT INTERACTION

It is strange that Schank, having come to the study of language through the function it has influencing the shared environment, is the leader of the attempts to apply language structure from a formal point of view to implement Artificial Intelligence in the research group Fifth Generation (which unfortunately failed, as it was predictable). On the other hand, Searle and Winograd, in spite of the critiques of many colleagues, perceived at once the wrong direction that research in Artificial Intelligence was taking.

Let us see the contributions linguistics can make to cognitive sciences in general and to the field of computer-human interaction in particular.

3.1   Language as knowledge structures

Schank's starting point is that communication is based on language understanding carried out by means of certain mental representations. This author attempts to formalize them in conceptual structures governed by actions ("plans", "scripts" and "goals"), which he tries to make applicable to the architecture of computers. His view grew out of the work of the Schema Theory presented by Rumelhart [10]. A "schema" is a structure of knowledge in which the mind places diverse contents organised by events that can fit in it. He calls them "content arrays". The process of understanding a text consists in finding a "schema" in which it makes sense.

3.2   Language-as-action perspective

Winograd differs with Schank in essence. He says that language is mainly action but not mental representations. These are one of the resources for analysis, reflection and organisation. We use mental representations, but we do not always do it and they are not the basis for communication. When we speak we do not imagine, we do not reflect or think but rather we act. Searle [13], along the same line, had established his theory of "Speech Acts" based on language as a cognitive process. This process was carried out by means of acts of speech with different degrees of intentionality and efficiency as for the interaction with the world and other participants in communication. We assure, we advise, we apply, we give commands through language. Winograd [18] establishes a series of "conversation structures" as actions of the speaker and reactions of the interlocutor. Action plans can be clearly set up, but their implementation is constrained by the problem of deviations or "breakdowns".

On the other hand, not every realisation of language implies intentionality. Anyway, in the event that we could easily transfer that intentionality to the computer by means of user interfaces we would endow the computer with volition, or will, a task that seems impossible at present. Volition could be the necessary element if we were to consider all the complex abilities that a computer can carry out as intelligence.

3.3 Language as communication of information in context

In 1957, Firth [7]views language as a system of signs used to carry out the communicative function with the environment. Through communication we interact with the environment. Here comes pragmatics that complements grammar and lexis as the axes of language study. Pragmatics considers communication with the environment and its manipulation as the essential function of language. Cook [3] points out three functions: communicating information, maintaining social relations and the function that Cook calls the one of cognitive change which influences the receiver in the experience of the world: This function is prominent in both literature and learning. By means of the cognitive function, we process the information received through language (textual function) and through the social relations (interactive function). As we can see the pragmatic perspective conjugates the diverse theories on language, considering the cognitive component as a relational structure of mental shared representations (Schank), the purpose of the speech acts (Searle) as social interaction and the text as the information in itself or message in context (de Beaugrande). These components lead us to present an interactive structure of information for the implementation of natural language in computer-human communication.

It was de Beaugrande [2] who, from the textual point of view, presented all the structuring of the world knowledge and of language knowledge by means of knowledge macrostructures that the participants in the communication have to negotiate to get a mutual understanding. He considers the shared knowledge of the world and of language as the axis in communication where inference of given information through coherence and the relevance of new information play a central role (see "Inference as Coherence" [11]).

4. FROM KNOWLEDGE REPRESENTATION TO THE INTERPRETATION OF INFORMATION

Language is the driving force of knowledge since it helps us interact with the environment internalizing experiences that we record in our internal information system, processing external information. There are other elements such as visuals, sounds, and sensorial perception in general, but their categorization is carried out through language (hence their inclusion in the concept of "text"). Nevertheless, this categorization is not often a conscious activity or it does not always have a permanent effect. It is language itself that dynamically shapes experience, either through communication or through reflection in a process that we call learning. The conceptual relations that build the mental representations are based on the participants" experience of the world and of language. Formalizable conventional elements intervene in their activation through communication or reflection. So do subjective elements, a spontaneous product of intuition and of the subconscious. These elements facilitate learning through matching, assimilation and internalization.

Those mental schemas exist but it is what is not common, what is not obvious that we express when communicating, that is, the new information. What can be implied is not mentioned or expressed unless it is necessary to give way to a new relevant concept. Winograd says that we reinterpret the world, not by matching what we see with our existing mental representations, but adapting them to a new structuring of the environment in our mind.

On the other hand, there are plans already made and objectives already achieved that enrich our experience and our conception of the world, but we do not always act (and communicate) following one of those preconceived plans or patterns; rather, we react to our environment immediately, we interpret situations adapting them to our experience, chaining them by association with other experiences. The nature of that interpretation is due to associations of very diverse nature, sometimes inexplicable, irrational and intuitive. Smoke rising from the chimney of a house can make us think -- according to a standard representation -- that it is inhabited and someone is cooking the food, but it can also make us ponder on an advisable visit to the doctor. The association of ideas is a characteristic mechanism of the human mind; therefore it is free, starting from an individualized perception of the world, from our personal experience.

5.   KNOWLEDGE, ACTION AND INFORMATION

Knowledge is capable of producing and assimilating information. Computers are capable of assimilating (receiving and processing) information. They can also produce it (that is, process and present it) if they are provided with the necessary interfaces such as data-collecting programmes to do it. For their presentation, we need output devices and interfaces, too.

The functions that computers can carry out with the information they receive depend on the interfaces. If they are provided with an interface that can offer, advise, invite, etc. we will have a computer that can behave similarly to humans on particular occasions, that is, it can produce a similar response to certain stimuli. If those actions are organised in a "script" (or sequence of events) based on a specific plan, we will have a "schema" with one or several "conversation structures" derived from knowledge representations as well as from speech acts. This is already implemented in computers (by means of programmes such as ELIZA, or help utilities such as Microsoft Office Assistant). However, these are only mere database applications that follow a procedure based on "if-then" instructions. Their efficiency is limited to a very specific domain, in controlled areas. This is one of the problems that Artificial Intelligence cannot solve.

There are, therefore, certain problems that have hindered the successful implementation of natural language in computers. "Schemas" are much wider (here is the problem of specific domain). Furthermore, it is not always necessary to carry out all the actions of a "schema" or of a "conversation structure". There are also some stages that are perceived as understood (the problem of the implicit), and others that are the points of inflection to other structures or schemas (the problem of breakdowns or deviations to other schemas), marked by relevance. All this is determined by the participants considering the environment, the context of the text and of the situation, and the reaction of the speaker.

That behaviour will be possible if we can provide the computer with these three components or functions: the necessary information about the world, the ability to structure that information in knowledge schemas and the techniques of interaction between person and computer; that is, *information, structure* and *interaction*.

If we applied this to the computer, we should consider knowledge as the base of information available ("knowledge base"). This can be structured in schemas or "macrostructures", comprised of "content arrays", organised in "plans" governed by events. The macrostructures are accessible and modifiable by means of certain activation devices ("activators") for the user to receive and present them and to adapt the knowledge base on their way back. These devices are sensitive to the user's reaction.

The effectiveness of that activation would rely on the capacity of overcoming the obstacles derived from the implementation of those three components of natural language to the computer. The quantity of knowledge shared between the computer and the user is very limited if we only consider the recorded textual information entered by the user. On the other hand, the current structuring of information by means of directories and names of files makes it hard to search for, relate and transfer information in the computer. Specific software should be developed to structure that information. Upon introducing new contents, by entering text, images, sounds and other functionally informative applications, the programme would analyse them and would mark them establishing relations with the previously recorded information, providing feedback to the whole system. Finally, it would be necessary to tell the computer what to do automatically by means of scripts (sequences of events) that might be left aside in order to activate other scripts as a response to the user's reactions in the process of information exchange.

6.   INTERNET, THE SOLUTION TO THE PROBLEMS OF NATURAL LANGUAGE IMPLEMENTATION

The information that a single user can communicate to his/her personal computer will be very limited considering the quantity of information necessary to represent the environment. Winograd warns about this limit of domain as an additional difficulty when trying to create Artificial Intelligence. As a result, they only get expert systems and partial applications. One of these, the SHRDLU, created by Winograd himself, first succeeded in communicating with the user learning from their conversation and from the analysis of the world in a basic way. SHRDLU gave birth to one of the most productive branches of AI, the neuronal networks. Nevertheless, they have the constraint that when generating multiple nodes of relations for each new action and for each group of data they create such an enormous quantity of data that they exceed the storage capacity of personal computers in a short time.

The quantity of information necessary to describe and represent the world would be so vast that no single computer could store it. However, we have that base of information and it is already digitized. Internet is the computer. Linking the access to information in servers connected through the Internet would enable us to make use of such amount of information that it would even exceed the amount a person can acquire in his/her life. All information, a great part of the global experience, the shared knowledge, is somehow on the Web partly formalized, represented by means of natural language (in writing and by audiovisual means). Improving the techniques of reference, analysing, identifying and marking the contents of information on the Internet automatically would enable us to record only the references (the location of the contents, their structure and their relations) in our computer. That information would be available on the fly at the first access and it would be getting modified with the experience of subsequent access. This would shape the "cognitive schemas" that we would share with our computer.

Considering that one of the participants is the computer, which tends to act automatically, would it not create such explicit schemas where everything would interrelate that the direct copy of the information to our computer would be better? How can the computer perceive the environment, distinguishing the relevant from the common or implicit? It is the digitization of the implicit what is causing so many problems to AI. Currently, there is a project called CYC [4] whose objective is to define daily routines, common sense, to make the implicit explained, a huge task which is unnecessary when almost everything is already digitized on the Internet. They are trying to make the implicit explicit, which will distort the essence of the implied, resulting in an output functionally different from the one expected. It would be better to create mechanisms to infer information through the Internet, which would be similar to the natural mechanism of inferring the implicit. A new type of search engines is being implemented using natural language to find the references necessary to identify concepts through keywords. These are being included in the head of HTML documents as "metatags". Inference can be implemented in the computer by designing server-side programmes to process the search, identifying and interrelating, analysing and selecting the concepts requested by the user at the background, without presenting the process to the user. The programme will select the new, truly relevant information in order to activate the schemas necessary to communicate and develop the shared knowledge of that information.

The relevant elements would operate as nodes in the schemas where these can break down or deviate to other schemas in the process of computer-human communication. These would be the "action plans" governed by relational coherence established by previous information and experience.

7.   HYPERTEXT FOR CONCEPTUAL RELATIONS

Once the problems have been analysed, we will study the possibilities of applying natural language to communicate with the computer. The computer has the possibility to access shared knowledge; then, interaction with people relies on people themselves. In order to be understood we will have to design an intermediate communication tool: an interface to interpret the input and output information in both directions, person-computer and computer-person. This can be really achieved neither through simulation (analogy) nor through similarity (metaphor). There is only one way: assimilation. In communicating knowledge to the computer (or network of computers) and its internalization, information must be assembled for easy reference through adaptation or coupling of that knowledge to the computer's structure.

Not only has the information already been communicated to the computer, but the relational mechanism has also been transferred. There is a conceptual relation on the Internet that has been transferred from the human mind. It is the hypertextual relation that mirrors the possible associations of ideas that the mind carries out. As [16] already pointed out in 1939, mind and speech do not coincide, we access the mind instantly, but speech is realised in a successive way. Language can be sequential in their production in time, lineal in its written representation, but the mind is "hypertextual", and so is understanding. We express the concepts we understand by relating them to others previously mentioned, by means of deictic reference and pronouns, for example, and by means of inference to something implied, as seen above. Sometimes, a thought can take us to another, possibly without any logical relationship (cause-effect, location, temporal relationship, condition, generalization or concretion), but through the relevance of an attribute or event. On some occasions, for certain people, the concept "smoke" can have connotations (attributes) with contamination, dirt, etc. in the relation smoke-illness, instead of the standard connotations with home, food, etc. Internet has all those concepts available.

The task now is to design programs that will enable the computer to track and trace (and so learn) the itinerary of the navigating user, perceiving the information received as experience. In this way the computer can see the probable tendency of the user's intentions, showing options or asking for breakdowns; that is, if we navigate with an objective, the computer can give us the option of guiding us along a plan with a script generated according to our behaviour in previous visits or if we are accustomed to getting lost in hyperspace, and that is what interests us, it can offer us options according to previous experience (spontaneously, by means of conceptual, sensorial or attributive relations, rather than by identification and narrative).

The fact that the Internet is so vast, so difficult to regularize and control does not mean that everything is chaos. The same happens to our minds. Establishing a categorization based on systematic domains and recurrent environments will help to design common user interfaces. Starting from these interfaces, an individualized adaptation will be possible in order to match the Internet's cognitive contents to the user's personal experience. We can create "profiles" and "personal portals" in our browser. There are interfaces that, by means of hypertext and hypermedia, enable the computer to present the information requested by the user, independently of the medium or the platform. HTML and its implementation in Java, Javascript and Perl, allows to design multiplatform (and, say, multi-user) interfaces. Moreover, these languages, so much because some are object-oriented, others object-driven, follow the axis of natural language based on the load of meaning, mainly supported by nominalization and structured in thematic aspects.

8.   SCOPE OF PRACTICAL APPLICATION

If we follow the textual perspective, it will be easier to find those user interfaces that the computer science is looking for in order to establish a reciprocal communication between the user and the computer. The global tendency after half a century reinforces our idea, since, although the computer started to be programmed by means of binary operations, it has evolved to the point that the most common effective components in computer programming are symbols and information. This is still being used for computing and carrying out mathematical calculations. However, in programming, most mathematical symbols have taken a structural meaning, being considered as the syntax of sentences. In fact, in search engines on the Internet, AND can be used instead of +, and NOT instead of -. We can find more programme keywords like IF, WHILE, etc., which takes programming languages in general closer to natural language.

Natural language is composed of structural categories and lexical categories. The range of structural or grammatical categories is fixed, closed and susceptible of formalization. They rely on primary conceptual relationships. They are, for example, the expression of number (by means of determiners, articles, inflection, etc.), of time (in their verbal and circumstantial expression), of reference (with pronouns and deixis) and other diverse relations (prepositions and conjunctions), etc.

Lexical categories, on the other hand, (even from the perspective of traditional grammar) are nouns, adjectives, verbs and adverbs. They are open categories that provide meaning, the conceptual entities. They are susceptible of amplification and change.

There are other superior levels of textual organization, macrostructures relying on the type of information: "written texts" such as books, newspaper articles, letters, reports, advertisements, etc., "oral texts" such as songs, readings, radio broadcasts with interviews, commentaries, news, etc., and "visual texts" such as images (photographs and drawings), sequences of images, videos and films. These also have their structural organisation (which is typical of the genre) and lexical organisation (which is thematic) where the topic of the text is divided in aspects (paragraphs as to the written level) that we can divide into ideas (sentences) developing structured concepts (words).

Formal programming languages already deal with objects, attributes, events and methods. Computational linguistics has succeeded in applying grammatical analysers (parsers)[1] and lexico-grammatical analysers to sentences in written language. If we relate them in databases such as electronic dictionaries, it will not be difficult to establish a structural and relational categorization of language. If we succeed in programming those analysers with hypertext mark-up languages and scripting languages so that they can identify names as objects, adjectives and equivalent expressions as attributes, verbs as events and adverbs or equivalent expressions as functions or event handlers, we will establish the architecture of natural language as hypertextual. That will help us identify the grammatical structural words as operators and keywords.

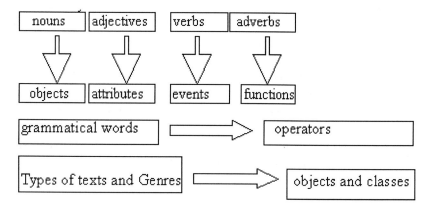

Figure 1. Natural Language-Programming Languages Correspondence

The perception of those objects through their attributes and functions can guide us on the possible associations in them. Relating one with another is something partly subjective, originated from our personal experience, but if we succeed in indicating to the computer the great quantity of objects, events and possible attributes and functions that we can manage, we will provide it with the necessary information to interact. The computer and the user will learn one from each other establishing a tendency of individualized interpretation that will facilitate our communication with the machine.

---

[1] See Tagger, by Pedro P. Sanchez Villalón, 1995 in http://chico.inf-cr.uclm.es/ppsv/macrotagger.htm

9. INTERFACES

Although we will need to investigate what possibilities we have when programming at certain intermediate level accessible to the user in order to fit the possible interaction of cognitive coupling with more specialized fields of information, it is not at the programming level but in intercommunication that we are interested in text. Text is necessary in order to present information (introduced by the user and presented by the computer). In order to interact the computer presents buttons, scrollbars, menus, etc. that usually have mixed text. Iconography is another aspect that helps to a more direct user response if it is standardized, that is, if it is part of the common knowledge schemas in certain environment (the three icons of the top right corner of onscreen application windows are already part of the global shared knowledge). Currently, oral interfaces (with voice recognition software) for command reception are being developed within the Windows environment. We can also consider this a textual element.

The design of user interfaces is advancing fast in this field. Once they are designed, time and practice will make the user aware of those devices for communication with the machine and, at a global level, these will be standardized; that is, they will configure those shared knowledge schemas that allow the greater quantity of possible users to use them and the greater quantity of computers to implement them. This process will be subject not only to the evolution of interface design, but also to commercial, corporate interests and others of diverse nature.

The design of this interface should consider several aspects. Among others, we should consider the following components:
- User profile (PROFILE)
- Selection of the domain (DOMAIN)
- Intentionality of the textual activity (GOAL)
- Selection of the level of conceptual assimilation (LEVEL)
- Relational or marked categorization (MARKING)
- Possible schemas of cognitive coupling (MATCHING)

On the other hand, after the analysis of the user's actions and of the information acquired from the Internet after presenting options for a possible intervention in order to modify them, this interface would automatically establish the following factors:
- Origin of the information (data input, the Internet, copied file): SOURCE
- Situation, register, media (written text, oral or visual) and type of information: GENRE
- Schema of contents: SCHEME
- Keywords or activators: NODE
- Plans of practice and problem solution: PLAN

These elements can form part of the thematic scheme of each information entity on the Internet and be used as a mechanism for marking the textual experience of a user through the computer. Their evolution would remain recorded in the "knowledge base" of the user profile.

10.   IMPLEMENTATION TO LEARNING

All this interactive mechanism would carry out feedback functions, receiving information, analysing its structure and content and matching it to the knowledge base the personal computer and the user share, developing a process of common learning. In this process, the computer would learn from the actions carried out by the user and the user would learn from the information received from the Internet, contrasted and filtered by the personal computer structural mechanisms. The process of information reception, selection and assimilation is a mechanism that develops the knowledge base. This is a natural learning system based on the exposition to textual experiences. A series of mechanisms for reinforcement and practice would complete the system, assuring the assimilation and internalisation of the information at different levels, relying on the information entity according to certain objectives established by the user, and offered to the computer through an interface created for that purpose.

The result of that internalization would be based on the modification of existent shared knowledge structures, with the extension or concretion of the schemas, marking the new relations based on the perceived objects and their location. This would be added to a history trace. This trace would record the textual experience of those objects shared by the user and the computer. The computer would place those relations available for later retrieval whenever activated by a function or a similar attribute (an activator).

The implementation to education would imply the creation of a user profile assigned to each student that would register the cognitive evolution concerning a domain, a subject or a group of subjects, in computerized form. At first, the computer would react to the students' actions directing them and presenting them with the requested information, marking the experienced textually, reinforcing it with practical exercises for revision, with summaries of contents and key data such as names, dates, etc. The processes of deduction and discovery would be implemented with problem solution exercises in simulated and virtual environments on the Internet (with practice in the world of business, advertising, etc.). Internet would also be used for the great availability of resources as a real environment for consulting, practice of conversations, reading, realisation of works in collaborative environments, etc. User profile domains would be implemented with guides designed by experts (teachers or instructors). These experts would check the acquisition and the level of internalization of the domain knowledge, and would guide the student to a superior level and to the improvement in the domain skills. The tasks for their attainment can be implemented in the domain programme or be indicated by the expert teacher or instructor.

All this student activity would be recorded in their user profile. The knowledge base and the relational mechanisms would be developing with the textual experience perceived by the student through the computer. This would be compounded with the data of the textual experienced relations and would be recorded in the student's personal computer, in physical portable storage hardware. Otherwise, it could be recorded in a server on the Internet to which the student would always access when using computerized media for their learning.

11.   CONCLUSION

The fourth generation of computers is foreseen as the possibility of using computers through the implementation of natural language and artificial intelligence. This seems to run slow and it is robotics the turning point.

I am not going to contradict that arrangement but we can then consider a fifth generation to be the outgrowth of the Internet and its global access. This can help to match the computer's prospective meeting point with natural language. The Internet is the "killer application" that puts an end to the necessity of specific programs in platform-dependent languages, opening the possibility of programming in Java and ActiveX in HTML as programming languages based on commands and instructions expressed by means of lexical terms in natural language, and based on operators as functional elements. The Internet is the Computer, which has the knowledge of the world available for users. It will be the task of programmers to structure the available information into databases of schemas and macrostructures, to develop macroactions in the sense of de Beaugrande [2] or conversation structures according to Winograd. These will help to create user interfaces to activate communication. So we will make the Internet assimilate natural language and we will both communicate really interactively. The computer will truly understand us. Whether intelligence takes part in this process or not is another question. We should consider whether will is essential to intelligence. Yet there is one-year time to come before HAL-9000, according to Arthur C. Clarke's prediction in *2001: A Space Odyssey*.

REFERENCES

1. AUSTIN, J. L., (1962) *How to Do Things with Words*, Cambridge, MA: Harvard U.P.
2. BEAUGRANDE, R. DE, (1991) *Linguistic Theory,* New York: Longman.
3. COOK, G., (1994) *Discourse and Literature*, Oxford: Oxford University Press.
4. CYCorp, (1997) at <URL=http://www.cyc.com>
5. CHOMSKY, N. (1965) *Aspects of the theory of syntax*, Cambridge, Mass., MIT Press.
6. DIJK, T. VAN, & KINTSCH, W. (1983) *Strategies of Discourse Comprehension*, N.Y: Academic P.
7. FIRTH, J. R. (1957) *Papers in Linguistics.* Oxford: Oxford University Press.
8. NEWELL, A y SIMON, H., (1972), *Human Problem Solving*, Englewood Cliffs: Prentice-Hall.
9. PIAGET, J. (1952), *The origins of intelligence in children*, New York: Norton.
10. RUMELHART, D. E. (1976) " Understanding and summarizing brief stories". in D. LaBerge and S.L. Samuels (eds.) *Basic Processes in Reading.* Hillsdale: Lawrence Erlbaum Associates.
11. SÁNCHEZ VILLALÓN, P. P., (1999) "Inference as Coherence: Function as Determinant of Text-type Organization" in *Estudios Funcionales sobre Léxico, Sintaxis y Traducción: Un homenaje a Leocadio Martín Mingorance*, Feu, M.J.& Molina,S. (eds.) Cuenca:Ed.UCLM
12. SCHANK, R., ABELSON, R., (1977) *Scripts Plans Goals and Understanding*, LEA, Hillsdale.
13. SEARLE, J.R.(1969) *Speech acts: an essay in the philosophy of language,* Cambridge: Cambridge U. P.
14. SEARLE, J.R. (1992) *The Rediscovery of the Mind.* Cambridge, MA, MIT Press
15. SEARLE, J.R. (1997) *The Mystery of Consciousness.* New York: New York Review Press
16. VYGOTZKY, L. S., (1939) "Thought and speech", *Psychiatry 2.*
17. WINOGRAD, T. (1972) *Understanding Natural Language,* New York, Academic Press.
18. WINOGRAD, T. & FLORES, F. (1986) *Understanding Computers and Cognition.* Addison-Wesley.
19. WINOGRAD, T. (1996) *Bringing Design to Software*, Addison-Wesley

Index

Keywords Index

Adaptability 29, 163, 249, 252, 254, 263-264
    Adaptive Hypermedia System 135, 251-252
    Adaptive Test 217-228, 241, 249
Agent 37-45, 90, 114-116, 263, 273
Authoring Tools 65-66
Automatic generation of courses 47

Basque 183, 251-255, 294
Bimodal education 199

CAL
    CBT 54, 65-67
    Computer Aided Learning 287-288
    Computer Assisted Learning 149
    Instructional content design 275
Collaboration 3-7, 263-274
Components 195, 229, 230, 239
Computational Linguistics 297, 299
Courseware 21, 65-77, 119-126

Design 6, 15, 107-109, 118, 126, 161, 163, 197, 216, 229-230, 238-239, 261, 265, 275, 296, 312
discovery learning 16, 107, 211-212, 273
Distance learning 93, 127
    Active and personalized distance learning 93
    Open and distance learning 163
    Open systems 137-138
Document Transformations 229, 239

Evaluation of educational environments 55

Fuzzy Logic Application 241

HEZINET 251-260
Human Computer Interaction 185
Human-Computer Interface 17

Intelligent Tutoring System 160-161, 185, 217-219, 228, 241, 252, 261, 264, 274

Interaction 7-8, 12-13, 23, 41, 43, 70, 102-103, 108, 110, 117, 121, 124, 125, 128, 151, 153, 160, 182, 229-235, 253, 257, 259, 267, 274, 297, 298, 299-305, 309
Interactive exercise 37, 42-43, 163, 167
Interactive learning-apprentice systems 93
Interactive Structured Information 297
Interactivity 31, 38, 43, 70, 120-123, 149-152, 159, 175-178
Internet ix, x, 3-9, 24, 32, 40-55, 69-70, 77-78, 93-110, 120--124, 126-128, 134-137, 160, 164, 166, 167, 173-176, 182-184, 199-202, 212, 228, 251, 258, 260, 272-276, 283, 284, 291, 297, 304-311
    virtual learning environment 28-29, 37-41, 45
    Virtual University 93
    Web 8, 10, 21, 22, 24, 27, 41, 48, 54, 66, 101-104, 128, 163, 164, 169, 170, 175-184, 200, 203, 207, 210, 275, 277, 284
    WWW 40, 69, 119, 121, 127, 135, 160, 163, 164, 174, 251-252, 261, 285
IT 65-66, 297
    Information Technologies 5, 65, 175
    ITT 37-40, 46
    New Technologies 199

Java 37-50, 54, 70, 74, 110, 114-125, 134, 166, 174, 208, 211, 238, 267, 284, 306, 311
    applets 43, 45, 70, 115, 123, 125, 126, 130, 175, 176, 177, 181, 211, 284

Knowledge Management 297

labware 65, 66, 70
learning application 137
Lexical Database 17

Multimedia and hypermedia
    Graphics 55

315